PARTNER TO PARTITION

The Jewish Agency's Partition Plan in the Mandate Era

YOSSI KATZ

Department of Geography
Bar-Ilan University

FRANK CASS
LONDON • PORTLAND, OR.

First Published in 1998 in Great Britain by
FRANK CASS PUBLISHERS
Newbury House, 900 Eastern Avenue
London IG2 7HH

and in the United States of America by
FRANK CASS PUBLISHERS
c/o ISBS, 5804 N.E. Hassalo Street
Portland, Oregon 97213-3644

Website http://www.frankcass.com

British Library Cataloguing in Publication Data:

Katz, Yossi
Partner to partition : the Jewish Agency's partition plan
in the mandate era
1. Jewish Agency   2. Palestine – History – Proposed partition,
1937
I. Title
956.9'4'04
ISBN 0-7146-4846-9 (cloth) 0-7146-4401-3 (paper)

Library of Congress Cataloging-in-Publication Data:

Katz, Yossi.
Partner to partition: the Jewish Agency's partition plan in the
mandate era/Yossi Katz.
    p.   cm.
Includes bibliographical references and index.
ISBN 0-7146-4846-9 (cloth). – ISBN 0-7146-4401-3 (paper)
    1. Palestine–History–Proposed partition, 1937. 2. Jewish Agency
for Palestine–History. 3. Zionism–Palestine–History. I. Title.
DS126.K38 1998
956.94'04–dc21   97-28250 CIP r97

Typeset by Vitaset, Paddock Wood
Printed in Great Britain by
Bookcraft (Bath) Ltd, Midsomer Norton, Avon

PARTNER TO PARTITION

To my son Avichai on the occasion
of his upcoming Bar–Mitzva

Contents

List of maps

Introduction

The Arab–Israeli dispute features prominently in Palestine's political history during the modern era, and attempts to solve it have continued for many years. A solution to the conflict based on partitioning the country into two nations has enjoyed currency. The partition idea emerged already in the 1930s and a number of plans were formulated to solve the dispute in such a fashion.[1] In fact, the partition of Palestine was on the verge of implementation only ten years later, when the United Nations General Assembly decided, in late 1947, to establish a Jewish and an Arab state.[2] However, the United Nations Plan was not realized. The cease-fire lines established following the 1948 War were those that divided Palestine between the newly arisen State of Israel and its Arab neighbors: a new Arab state did not arise in Palestine itself.[3] This reality was to prevail until the Six Day War in 1967. Following that war, Israel assumed control of all areas of Palestine and this situation obtained until implementation was begun in 1994 on the 'Declaration of Principles' between Israel and the Palestinians.

By the close of the 1930s plans for partitioning Palestine were already being awarded scholarly scrutiny, primarily by historians and researchers in the fields of international relations and political science. Special attention was devoted to the partition plan of 1937, which was elaborated by the British Royal Commission headed by Lord Peel. The reverberations that this plan touched off among the various parties connected to the dispute have also enjoyed scholarly interest. International bodies had already advanced plans for solving the Palestine problem via partition prior to the appearance of the Royal Commission's plan.[4] However, there is no doubt that the momentum behind solving the Jewish–Arab dispute via partition began gathering once the plan was advanced by this Commission. Most historical research on the contemporary Near East and Palestine, and the Jewish–Arab conflict makes reference to the Royal Commission's plan. However, the research literature that centers on the Royal Commission's plan – its formulation, the reverberations it touched off, the discussions on it until the plan was dropped from the political agenda at the close of 1938 – has been subsumed under two frameworks. The first views the plan in the context of an overall examination of British policy and activity in Palestine during Britain's mandatory rule.[5] The second focuses on the polemics and bitter debate that the plan set off within Palestine's Jewish community and within the Zionist Movement over the moral dilemma whether one should assent to the partition of Palestine, west of the Jordan, in return for obtaining a sovereign state.[6] Very little attention has been devoted towards examining the partition plan of 1937 in a comparative context together with other partitions that took place throughout the world during the 1920s.[7]

This book seeks to examine an additional aspect of the Palestine partition plan issue prior to the Second World War, which has not yet been awarded serious attention, namely the operative plans that the Jewish Agency Executive formulated in anticipation of partition. These plans were consonant with the Executive's current policy of supporting partition in return for getting a state. The Jewish Agency Executive was the central body within the network of Jewish national institutions. It was accredited as the representative of Palestinian Jews and enjoyed formal status vis-à-vis Britain and the League of Nations under the award of the mandate.[8] As it emerges, the Agency did not adopt a 'do-nothing' policy while passively awaiting the implementation of the British Partition Plan. The reverse is true. The Executive, a majority of whose membership endorsed the idea of partition in principle in return for obtaining a sovereign state took an active line. On the basis of the British Partition Plan advanced by the Royal Commission, or more aptly as a response to this plan, the Executive undertook the task of formulating its own basic partition plan between the years 1937–38. This, so it appears, was the first partition plan to be formulated at the initiative of an official Zionist body. The issue of boundaries, which is the central component of any partition scheme, formed the core of this plan, but it also encompassed additional elements, such as the status of Jerusalem and other cities, transfer of population, the status of the Arab minority in the Jewish state, the stages leading to the establishment of a Jewish State and more. The Jewish Agency entered into negotiations with the authorized British bodies on most components of its plan. This work will also attempt to demonstrate that the partition plan of the Agency Executive, even though it was not implemented, did not remain a mere episode from the Jewish standpoint but had both short-term and long-term repercussions. In the immediate term, it affected the direction of settlement policy, while in the long term it exerted an impact on various elements connected to the partition of

Palestine in the late 1940s, and on the first steps taken by the fledgling State of Israel.

The study of political partition the world over tends to view it as an amalgam of developmental stages, commencing with the pre-partition stage, continuing through the conflict leading to partition, partition itself, the separate development of the political units created in the wake of partition, the development of a normal framework of relations between the two political units, until the option of reunification of the two units becomes feasible.[9] Within this framework, our work will concentrate on the initial component of the partition stage itself: the stage when the formulation of an operative plan for partition crystallizes. However, this book does not devote its primary attention to the forces that were to implement partition (Britain and the League of Nations), but intends to focus and examine one of the forces expected to create and construct a political unit following partition (the Jewish Agency Executive). This force believed that it could influence the decisive power (Britain) when the latter elaborated an operative plan for partition, and for this reason it worked on formulating a plan of its own. Nonetheless, since the Jewish Agency Plan was composed on the basis of the anterior British Royal Commission Plan, we must first examine this plan and the responses which it elicited at the British political level and at the level of the League of Nations.

The book relies primarily on archival material, and first and foremost, the documents of the Jewish Agency Executive and its Political Department. This archival material, as well as material pertaining to other departments of the Jewish Agency, bodies affiliated to the Agency, the Inner Zionist General Council, the Zionist General Council, the Zionist Congress, material related to personages whose activity was associated with the Jewish Agency, as well as the archival materials of the Jewish National Fund, are all gathered at the Central Zionist Archives in Jerusalem. Other archives in Israel as well as the Public Records Office in London were tapped. This work was also facilitated by research devoted to the issue of partition schemes for Palestine and the general theoretical literature that addresses the issue of partition and boundaries.

The research upon which this book is predicated was made possible by the assistance of the Research Institute for the History of the Keren Kayemeth LeIsrael Land and Settlement. I would like to thank the institute's chairman, Mr S. BenShemesh and its academic director, Dr G. Alexander for their copious assistance. Dr Amiel Ungar did the translation and merits my deep gratitude. Thanks are also due to the workers of the Central Zionist Archives for all their help, to the Mapping Division of the Geography Department at Bar-Ilan University for preparing the maps, to

Mr Lior Petrover for preparing the jacket and to Daniela Ashur for preparing the index. I was able to make progress on the work during a sabbatical two years ago at York University in Canada. I would like to thank my colleagues there for both their guidance and the convivial work atmosphere which they provided. My most profound appreciation is tendered to Mr Frank Cass, to Mr Robert Easton, the Managing Editor, and to Ms Deborah Herit for the vast efforts which they expended in honing this book into shape for publication. Finally I would like to commend my wife Ruth, my mother, Mrs Hannah Katz, and my children, David, Yonatan, Michal, Merav, Avichai and Dan for their support and patience which allows me to devote the bulk of my time to research.

Yossi Katz
Efrat, Summer 1997

NOTES

1. See, for example, the article of Cohen, G. (1973); Dothan (1979), pp. 19, 20, 74–90. See also Palestine Royal Commission Report, 1937 (hereafter PRCR).
2. Year Book of the United Nations (1947–48), pp. 227–57.
3. See, for example, Shlaim (1988).
4. For details regarding such plans, see, for example, Eliash (1971), pp. 28–33; G. Cohen (1973).
5. See, for example, the works of Cohen, M. (1978), Katzburg (1974) Klieman (1983). See also Beeley (1937, 1938), Klieman (1980a), Rose (1970, 1971).
6. See, for example, the work of Dothan (1979) and the works of Geva (1980) and Eliash (1971). See also Galnoor (1991); Fraser (1988).
7. Fraser (1984).
8. See in detail the article by Rubinstein (1976), pp. 144–51.
9. For a sweeping theoretical discussion on the subject of 'Partition States', see Waterman (1987).

1

From the Partition Plan of the Royal Commission Until the Appointment of the Partition Commission

BACKGROUND TO THE PARTITION PLAN

The British Royal Investigation Commission, headed by Earl William Robert Peel, was appointed by the British government at the beginning of August 1936, and arrived at the close of that same year in Palestine. The backdrop to the Commission's appointment was the Arab general strike declared in April 1936, which had speedily escalated into riots, disturbances and acts of sabotage that were unprecedented in terms of their scope and force. In the course of these events, hundreds of Jews had been injured and heavy damage inflicted on property. Arab activity was marked by a hatred evinced towards British mandatory rule in Palestine in particular, and to British imperialism in general, and this hatred was no less venomous than the hatred manifested towards the Palestinian Jewish community and Zionism. The Arab camp had already voiced anti-imperialist slogans during the strikes of the early 1930s. What was novel in 1936 was that the Arabs presented demands for political independence, demands that were undoubtedly influenced by the changes taking place in neighboring Arab states and by the achievements of the neighboring Arab national movements.[1] Faced with these disturbing developments in Palestine, the British had, in May, already announced their intention to appoint a special investigation commission. Its task, as defined in the terms of reference that it received, was to examine the fundamental causes of the disturbances and to ascertain whether Arabs and Jews had legitimate complaints regarding the implementation of the British mandate in Palestine in the past and present. If it indeed became clear that there were grounds for these complaints, the Commission was requested to submit recommendations 'for their removal and for the prevention of their recurrence'.[2]

THE PLAN

The Commission, which, in addition to Peel, included five additional members, namely H. Rumbold, R. Coupland, H. Morris, M. Carter and L. Hammond, spent two and a half months in Palestine, established contacts with all parties relevant to the investigation, and in July 1937, less than a year after its appointment, officially published its findings.[3] Nonetheless, the principles underlying the findings of the Commission had already been formulated in the first months of 1937.[4] The Commission had decided that the mandate had lost its value; that the Jewish–Arab dispute in Palestine was deep and very bitter; and that the dispute could not be terminated or resolved within the existing political framework. In the Commission's view, the termination of the mandate and its replacement by a partition of the country into two states – a Jewish and an Arab one – offered the sole possibility for solving the Palestine problem in a peaceful manner and conferring peace upon the region. It also declared that the obligations towards the two peoples in Palestine, which Britain had undertaken upon receipt of the mandate over Palestine, were mutually contradictory. On the other hand, Britain's interest was to preserve peace in the region while maintaining friendship with both Arabs and Jews alike. The Commission emphasized that one could not maintain the existing situation in Palestine. However, after it became clear that 'the hope of harmony between the races has proved untenable', a solution could not be reached by transferring control in Palestine to either one of the parties, but only by partitioning the country. The Commission added that it viewed preserving the political unity of Palestine as of negligible moral value 'at the cost of perpetual hatred, strife and bloodshed and that there is little moral injury in drawing a political line through Palestine if peace and goodwill between the peoples on either side of it can thereby in the long run be attained … Partition seems to offer at least a chance of ultimate peace. We can see none in any other plan...' Although it was clear to the Commission that realization of the partition would encounter quite a few difficulties, it was persuaded that there were none that could not be overcome and that the continuation of the mandate and other solutions that the Commission examined (such as cantonization) were even more difficult, if not impossible.[5]

One member of the Commission, Reginald Coupland, steered the discussions towards embracing the partition proposal as the sole solution, and it was he who edited the final report of the Commission. As a Professor of Colonial History at Oxford, he was very proficient in the analysis of national conflicts in Canada and South Africa as well as in the measures adopted in the attempt to solve the Irish question. From his academic experience, Coupland understood that the national factor was a force that deserved respect, and he believed that Arab nationalism would gain further impetus. With this in mind, he thought that the dispute between the Jewish national movement and the Arab national movement would intensify if the British mandate were to continue. He saw no prospect of terminating the conflict and promoting Jewish–Arab co-operation in Palestine unless each side were made responsible for its own fate within the framework of a separate self-government. The fact of the matter was that a de facto partition in Palestine already existed, since Jewish settlement was generally not interspersed with Arab settlement. Concentrated in part of Palestine (the western part of the country and the valleys), the Jewish economy and society remained separate from the Arab one and maintained a ramified system of institutions as 'a state within a state'. All this confirmed Coupland's opinion, and subsequently that of other commission members that partition offered the most suitable and most practical solution. By the end of December 1936, Coupland had raised his proposal for a solution based on partition. Once he became aware that a personage as eminent as the President of the World Zionist Organization, Chaim Weizmann, supported the scheme in principle, he invested prodigious efforts to promote it.[6]

In practice, as we shall see in detail later, the plan of the Royal Commission described a geographic partition of Palestine into three political entities: an Arab, a Jewish and a British mandate – part in perpetuity and part temporary. The partition plan was based on three principles that the committee had postulated for itself: (1) the plan had to be realizable, (2) it had to accord with previous British obligations, and (3) it had to deal equally with Jews and Arabs alike. The plan itself encompassed five components: (1) the manner in which the new states would be established, and the transition stage preceding their establishment; (2) boundaries; (3) the status of the holy places and that of additional distinctive sites; and (4) the exchange of lands and populations.

Pursuant to the recommendations of the Commission, the first step towards the formation of the new states was to be implemented in the form of a British declaration. The declaration would announce the termination of the mandate and Britain's entry into negotiations with the government of Trans-Jordan and the representatives of the Palestinian Arabs on the one hand, and the representatives of the World Zionist Organization on the other, with a view towards concluding treaties following the precedents that had been established between Britain and Iraq in 1930, and between France and Syria in 1936 . A pledge that two sovereign and independent states would be established within a short time was to be enunciated in the treaties. The Arab State would embrace Trans-Jordan and part of Palestine and the second, the Jewish State, would embrace part of Palestine to the north and west of the Arab state (see Map 1). The treaties would incorporate guarantees to protect minorities within the areas of these states, and Britain committed herself to support any request submitted by the new states to join the League of Nations. The Commission recommended that during the transition stage, from the moment the plan was adopted by the British government until the states were established, the mandate would continue in force, but two measures would be adopted: the purchase of lands by Jews in the area planned for the Arab State would be prohibited as well as the converse, and Jewish immigration to the Arab area would be banned. The Jewish immigration quota would be determined by calculating the absorptive capacity of Palestine, from which the Arab sector would have been subtracted.[7]

Principles governing the boundary lines and their determination

The principle of separation between areas that the Jews purchased and settled and areas totally or mostly settled by Arabs constituted the guiding principle of the Commission when it fixed a boundary between the two states. This principle, in the opinion of the Commission, provided an equitable and practical basis for partition. An additional principle guiding the Commission was to place at the disposal of the Jewish State sufficient land for future demographic growth and settlement, thus meeting the spirit of the previous British obligation towards the Zionist Movement. The Commission viewed the Galilee as the territorial reserve for the development of the Jewish State, and therefore included it within the boundaries of the Jewish State, even though this contradicted the principle of separation because in the Galilee, and particularly in its mountainous region, a sizeable Arab concentration existed. The transfer of lands and population as recommended by the Commission (given in detail below) was intended to minimize the Arab population in the Galilee.[8] However, faced with the demographic situation of the Galilee and Arab ownership of lands in the region, the Commission, so it emerged, agonized at length over whether it would not be preferable to award only part of the Galilee to the Jewish State. The reserve earmarked for the development of the Jewish State would be satisfied by additions in the south and in the Negev (which, in the final recommendation, would remain in the confines of the Arab State). The issue remained open for a long time and was only decided subsequent to the publication of the Commission's report with the triumph of the 'Northern School'.[9]

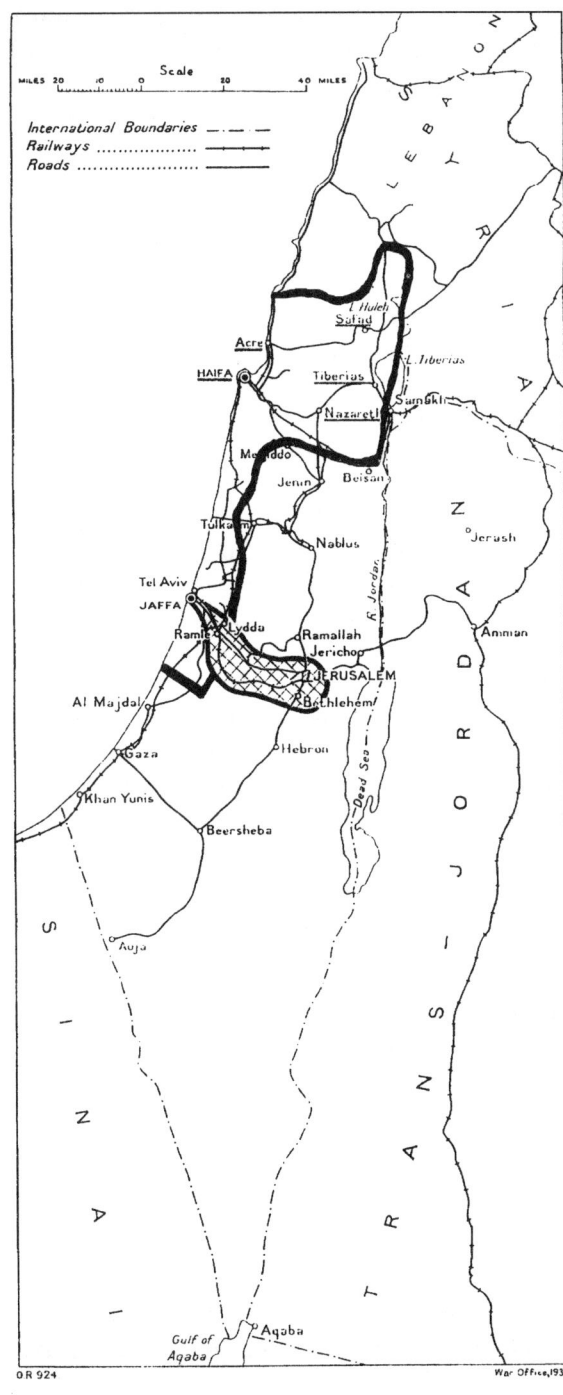

Map 1:
Partition Plans
of the Royal
Commission,
1937

A series of factors contributed to this outcome. Firstly, there was a strategic consideration. Britain's interest was to control Haifa to use the port, and to protect the oil pipeline from Iraq, which was to serve as a source of supply for the Royal Navy. It appears that a suitable defense line for protecting Haifa from the north was the descent from the mountains towards the Litani Valley. Jewish control of this entire area up to this line appeared to offer more security for the protection of British interests in Haifa than did Arab control.[10] There were also British intelligence estimates that the Jews were likely to induce the French to agree to a northwards boundary modification. Such a territorial arrangement would accrue to the advantage of the British. Secondly, ties of friendship existed between the Jews and the Maronites in Lebanon.[11] Thirdly, the Zionist leadership, headed by Weizmann, made efforts to influence the Commission and authorities within the British government to include the entire Galilee in the sphere of the Jewish State at the expense of the south and the Negev.[12] In the report itself, the Commission provides additional considerations for including the entire Galilee in the sphere of the Jewish state: 'It must be remembered that this is a part of Palestine in which the Jews have retained a foothold almost if not entirely without a break from the beginning of the Diaspora to the present day and that the sentiment of all Jewry is deeply attached to the "holy cities" of Safad and Tiberias. Until quite recently, moreover, the Jews in Galilee have lived on friendly terms with their Arab neighbors and throughout the series of "disturbances" the fellaheen of Galilee have shown themselves less amenable to political incitement than those of Samaria and Judea where the centers of Arab nationalism are located.'[13]

In its recommendations the Commission did not address the issue of whether the boundary between the states should be closed or open. Nonetheless, for the benefit of the trade and industry of the Arab State, it sought to guarantee an option for free transfer of goods from the Arab State to Haifa, which was Palestine's only deep-water port. In a similar fashion, the Commission requested that a free passage of goods from the Jewish State from the Egyptian border and the Gulf of Aquaba on the Red Sea Coast, connecting Palestine with the east, should be guaranteed.[14]

The mandatory enclave and limitations upon the sovereignty of the Jewish State

The Royal Commission believed that it was Britain's obligation to preserve the holy places, especially Jerusalem and Bethlehem, to prevent their desecration 'and of ensuring free and safe access to them for all the world. That in the fullest sense of the mandatory phrase is "a sacred trust of civilization" – a trust on behalf not merely of the people of Palestine but of multitudes in other lands to whom those places, one or both are Holy Places'.[15] The Commission therefore recommended the definition of a new and perpetual British mandate over an enclave that would include Jerusalem and Bethlehem and would link up to the Mediterranean shore in Jaffa (Jaffa itself was intended to be part of the Arab state since the majority of its population was Arab; its link to the Arab State was to be assured via the mandatory enclave, which was open to all). The enclave would also include the main highway and the railway connecting Jerusalem and Jaffa as well as the cities of Lydda and Ramle. In the enclave both Jews and Arabs would enjoy equal treatment, English would be the official language, and 'good and just government without regard for sectional interests would be its basic principle'.[16]

The Commission was aware of the fact that by transferring Jerusalem to the areas of the mandate, it was denuding Zionism of Zion, and detaching the clearly Jewish part of the city outside the walls, where 75,000 Jews resided, from the Jewish State, with all the repercussions that this would entail for the future of the Jewish State. In the deliberations that preceded the publication of the report, the Chairman of the Commission, anticipating Jewish claims on Jerusalem based on sentimental grounds, contended that 'while the sentimental reasons on the Jewish side were not really so strong, the Arabs also had the strongest sentimental ties to the city'.[17] Coupland transmitted a secret letter to Colonial Secretary Ormsby-Gore a short while after the Royal Commission's report was published, and criticism in British circles was voiced over stripping the Jewish State of Jerusalem. In his letter, Coupland raised the following arguments against including New Jerusalem within the borders of the Jewish State: the Jewish city would absorb appreciable waves of Jewish immigration, which would lead to administrative difficulties in the surrounding areas of the British enclave and would arouse suspicions among the Arabs; Jewish building would sprawl beyond the present boundaries of Jerusalem's Jewish neighborhoods, and in the course of time the Jews would also demand the inclusion of this construction within the areas of the Jewish State; one could not prevent a Jewish State from maintaining an army in Jerusalem; Jewish Jerusalem overlooking the Old City and especially those places sacred to the Moslems would intensify and aggravate Arab apprehensions, with all that this entailed, especially as the Jewish State would probably declare Jerusalem to be its capital; Jerusalem as a capital would constitute the core of Jewish political life in Palestine, and therefore one could foresee, at least during the first stage of the establishment of a Jewish State, politically related struggles, disputes and tensions accompanied by disorder and bloodshed.

Coupland saw no technical possibility of dividing the city. He was therefore prepared to provide Zionism with a symbolic foothold in Jerusalem
in the form of declaring Jewish Agency buildings in the western part of
the city and its immediate vicinity to be 'Jewish soil' and enjoying a status
similar to that of the foreign embassies.[18] Subsequently, prior to the arrival
in Palestine of the Partition Commission in 1938, Coupland wrote a
personal and secret letter to Weizmann, in which he suggested meeting
the Zionist demand for West Jerusalem in a manner that would allow the
Jewish residents of the mandatory enclave in Jerusalem to simultaneously
enjoy the status of 'nationals of the Jewish State so that they and their
business might function as part of the Jewish State'.[19]

The Commission also sought to include Nazareth in perpetuity within
the mandate, while allowing the mandate to maintain the sanctity of
Lake Tiberias and its shores. Nonetheless, the Commission was not as
determined on this issue as it was on the issue of the Jerusalem enclave.[20]
In contradistinction, with regards to the mixed cities of Tiberias,
Safad, Acre and Haifa, slated for inclusion within the area of the Jewish
State, the Commission sought to impose a temporary mandate. The
purported reason was that, since these cities comprised both Arab and
Jewish populations, friction between the parties would arise, and therefore: '[they believed] that it would greatly promote the successful
operation of partition in its early stages and in particular help to ensure
the execution of the treaty guarantees for the protection of minorities, if those four towns were kept for a period under mandatory
administration'.[21]

Nonetheless, it emerges that the Commission's recommendations
regarding the temporary mandate as well as the permanent ones also
reflected Britain's interest in maintaining a permanent presence in
Palestine in view of its strategic importance to the empire. We have already
noted the special interests of the British in Haifa. Because members
of the Commission lived and operated in the period following the
Ethiopian crisis, when Italian and German threats to Britain's position in the Middle East intensified, the strategic considerations were
pertinent in elaborating details of the partition plan. Members of the
Commission were also briefed by senior military authorities regarding the
strategic importance of Palestine, which could furnish Britain a foothold in the Middle East, a buffer between the Suez Canal and possible
enemies to the north, and an alternative area for deploying its forces when
after 20 years, the Anglo–Egyptian Agreement came up for review.[22]
In the words of Field Marshal Sir Cyril Deverell, Chief of the Imperial
General Staff:

From the military point of view, Palestine was of great strategic importance. It gave us a footing in the Eastern Mediterranean and without it we should be limited to Cyprus only in this area. Palestine was also of great importance as a 'buffer' state between our vital interests on the Canal and possible enemies to northward ... In twenty years time the Anglo–Egyptian treaty would be due for revision, and it might well be that after that time we should be no longer able to maintain troops in Palestine. Palestine was also a very important link in our communications to the East. The Haifa–Baghdad road was being developed as an all-weather road and it was always possible that at some time in the future a railway might also join these two places ...[23]

Although the Royal Commission determined that the Jewish and Arab States would be totally sovereign, it also stipulated that the ports of Tel Aviv and Jaffa would be subject to the supervision of a joint port authority of the Jewish and Arab States, which would be headed by an official appointed by the mandatory government. The Commission also decided that the Jewish State should permanently extend financial support to her Arab neighbor, for two reasons: firstly, the areas of the Jewish State would also encompass areas where there were no Jewish-owned lands or Jewish settlement (primarily in the Galilee); and secondly, once a Jewish State was established the population would be freed from the obligation (which currently existed for the Jewish population) to support territories outside the Jewish State via taxation. Tax collections in the ports of the two countries, the Commission determined, would be temporarily performed by the mandatory government.[24]

The boundary line between the Jewish and Arab State that the Royal Commission drew (see Map 1) stretched from the north-west edge of Palestine's international boundary along the northern and eastern boundary of the country until the Lake Tiberias. It crossed the lake and continued to the Jordan. From there the boundary continued along the Jordan River until north of the Arab town of Beisan (which, according to the principle of separation, remained in the Arab State) and from there to the Jezreel Valley, until north of Megiddo. From there, the boundary turned south-west along the coastal plain (while leaving Tulkarm in the Arab State, according to the principle of separation). It linked up to the northern boundary of the mandatory enclave, east of Lydda. Near Qazaza it joined the southern boundary of the mandatory enclave, and from there it passed in a straight line southwards until east of Jaladiya. From this point the boundary turned west until the sea (while including the Jewish settlement of Beer Tuvia in the Jewish State, but leaving Isdud within the Arab State). The British enclave bisected the Jewish State into two without any territorial contiguity between them. According to these boundaries, the Jewish State occupied 20 per cent of western Palestine and an area of five million dunams (1 dunam = 1,000m^2), the Arab State in Palestine was to occupy 20.5 million dunams; and the British enclave encompassed nearly 800,000 dunams.[25] Although the Royal Commission drew boundary lines and even attached the partition map to the report, it recommended that the exact boundary lines should be fixed by a special boundaries commission.[26]

Exchanges of land and population

Exchanges of land and populations between the two planned states were envisaged as necessary, complementary steps to drawing up the boundary lines because 'no frontier can be drawn which separates all Arabs and Arab-owned land from all Jews and Jewish-owned land'.[27] Without these exchange measures, the Commission believed that peace would prove unattainable. On the one hand, it considered the minorities problem in Europe and Asia, which had worsened since the end of the First World War, to be 'one of the most troublesome and intractable products of postwar nationalism; and nationalism in Palestine, as we have seen, is at least as intense a force as it is anywhere else in the world'.[28] On the other hand, the Commission was also aware of the precedent of forcible transfer between Turkey and Greece that had taken place in the early 1920s,[29] (given in detail in Chapter 4), which could serve as a possible model for implementing transfers in Palestine.

The deliberations of the Royal Commission took place 13 years after the signing of the Lausanne Treaty, which had stipulated the forced transfer of populations – a treaty that was concluded following the intervention of international forces (the League of Nations and the Great Powers). During the deliberations of the Royal Commission, the international community was aware of the positive achievements that had been obtained by virtue of the agreement. At the Lausanne Conference 'for the first time in history the international community accepted the forcible uprooting and the accompanying distress and hardship of hundreds of thousands of peaceful and law abiding citizens ...',[30] but after a short while it was demonstrated that the exchange of populations, as they affected the two peoples involved, had produced positive and striking results. As a result the international community was convinced of the utility of the population-transfer method for conflict resolution, even if such transfers were to be made on a compulsory basis.[31]

The positive and striking results of the Greco–Turkish precedent (if not the process itself), both in resettling Greek refugees and in the political repercussions it had on relations between the two peoples, encouraged the Royal Commission to recommend that transfer be implemented in Palestine as well. The Commission's own words as it summarized the results of the Greco–Turkish precedent attest to this: 'But the courage of the Greek and Turkish statesmen concerned has been justified by the result. Before the operation the Greek and Turkish minorities had been a constant irritant. Now the ulcer has been clean cut, and Greco–Turkish relations, we understand, are friendlier than they have ever been before'.[32] There was additional cause for optimism in the Palestine case, since one was dealing with immeasurably smaller populations and areas than in the Greco–Turkish case.[33]

As may be recalled, the Commission viewed the implementation of a transfer of lands and populations between the Jewish and the Arab States to be established in Palestine, as a necessary condition for obtaining total peace.[34] It estimated that the presence of minorities 'clearly constitutes the most serious hindrance to the smooth and successful operation of partition', and therefore favored even the imposition of a forced transfer. Britain was to supervise the transfer. Nonetheless, the Royal Commission was aware of the more problematic implications of the process, even noting that, next to the boundary issue, the issue of transfer was the most important and the thorniest of all the questions bound up in any partition. The statistics of the Commission revealed that the Arab population in the proposed Jewish State totaled 225,000 – a figure constituting nearly 50 per cent of the Jewish State's own population – whereas the Jewish population in the proposed Arab State was estimated at only 1,250 people. Hence, the Commission devoted greater attention to the problem of transferring and resettling the Arab population. The Jewish population to be transferred would not encounter any difficulties in finding a solution within the boundaries of the Jewish State, it was thought.

The Commission was also aware of the differences between the Balkan precedent and the Palestine case, especially in view of the fact that a surplus of arable had been available in Greece to provide for resettling Greeks leaving Turkey. Such a surplus did not exist within the confines of the Arab State proposed by the report for resettling the 225,000 Arabs resident in the proposed Jewish State, even if lands held by Jews in the Arab State were vacated. However, the Commission contended that 'such information as was available seemed to us, as we said, to justify the hope that the execution of largescale plans for irrigation, water-storage, and development in Trans-Jordan – and the same applies to Beersheba and the Jordan Valley – would make provision for a much larger population than exists there at the present time'.[35]

The Commission also determined in this fashion its recommendations regarding the target areas to where the Arab population from the proposed Jewish State would be transferred. The Commission recommended proceeding at once to an evaluation of the practical possibilities for irrigation and development of these areas in order to verify its estimates, because 'The provision of new land would bring the position in Palestine and Trans-Jordan closer to what it was in 1923, in Turkey and Greece'.[36]

Since the Commission's objectives were to recommend measures for solving the national dispute in Palestine, it believed that the coastal areas of Palestine where the population was mixed should be the area of origin for the populations to be exchanged. A mixed population heightened the probability of dispute between the two peoples. In contradistinction, the Commission felt that in the mountainous Galilee, since it was entirely settled by an Arab population, the dispute was non-existent and forced transfer should not be proposed. In this fashion, the Commission also pronounced that it was not proposing total transfer.[37] The Commission further recommended that land offered for sale by the minorities in both countries should not be sold on the open market, but only by the governments of the states in which the lands offered for sale were located.[38] This provision would be one means for accelerating the pace of transfer. The Commission imposed the burden of financing the development of the target areas primarily upon Britain.[39] As in other areas covered by its recommendations, on the subject of population and land transfers the Commission engaged in principles rather than in details. Thus, for example, the report provides no clear reference to the areas of lands to be exchanged and supplies no clear answer to the question of what would be the fate of minority populations in the cities.

THE RECOMMENDATIONS PASS THE CRITICAL SCRUTINY OF THE DECISION-MAKERS AND A PARTITION COMMISSION IS APPOINTED

At the end of June 1937 the report of the Royal Commission was submitted to the British government, which decided to adopt the recommendations.[40] In a communication presented to Parliament, together with the report of the Royal Commission, at the beginning of July, the government announced its decision to adopt the Royal Commission's partition plan and embark upon its implementation, because it had been impressed with the implicit advantages of partition for Arabs and Jews alike. Arabs would receive their national independence and would no longer fear a Jewish take-over of the land and the holy places. The Jews would obtain a state, where they would form the majority and where they themselves could supervise Jewish immigration. Treaties contracted with the states to be established would incorporate scrupulous guarantees for preserving the rights of minorities in both countries. Most importantly, fear and apprehension would vanish and a feeling of trust and confidence would follow in their stead. Nonetheless, the government added, that until such a partition plan would be implemented, a prohibition (as per the Commission's recommendation) would be imposed on land sales that could thwart the plan, and likewise Jewish immigration would be limited during the following eight months to only 8,000 persons.[41]

In contrast to the government, the British Parliament, when it discussed the plan at the end of July, raised a number of objections to the Royal Commission's plan. At the close of its deliberations, Parliament neither rejected nor approved the partition plan. It endorsed the principle of partition but obligated the government to return to Parliament following a proper investigation and present the House with a final partition plan in which all the details had been worked out, while taking account of the Royal Commission's recommendations. Parliament therefore awaited a more detailed partition plan, but nonetheless gave the government a go-ahead to continue with the timetable that it had set for itself on the partition issue, including among other things, the submission of its proposal to the League of Nations.[42]

The League discussed the issue within the framework of the Permanent Mandates Commission at the end of July and during the first half of August, and within the framework of a session of the League Council, which took place in September 1937. These bodies also voiced many criticisms of the plan. During the course of deliberations within the Permanent Mandates Commission, British Colonial Secretary Ormsby-Gore made it clear that the British government did not embrace the principle of forcible transfer of population postulated by the Royal Commission. In the end, the Permanent Mandates Commission agreed in principle to investigate the plan, which included partitioning Palestine, but expressed its reservation regarding the immediacy of such action. This reservation sought to solve the problem of Palestine on a momentary basis within the mandatory framework in one of the following two ways: temporary cantonization or partitioning of the country into two mandatory units, which in the course of time would turn into states.[43] The League Council, to whom the findings of the Permanent Mandates Commission had been referred, expressed its agreement with the intention of the British government with regards to investigating the status of Palestine and concentrating on partition as a solution. Likewise, the Council emphasized that the mandate remained in force until such time as it should be decided otherwise. In the course of discussions, the British Foreign Secretary, Anthony Eden, clarified that Britain's intention was to appoint a new body, which would visit the country and submit a detailed partition proposal to the government.[44]

Given the decisions of Parliament and the institutions of the League, public criticism regarding the Royal Commission's plan and the growing opposition to partition within the British government, for reasons that we will dwell upon later, the British government decided in December 1937 to issue a clarification: the government had not obligated itself in any manner to approving the Royal Commission's plan. It rejected the proposal of the Royal Commission regarding forced transfer, and announced its intention to undertake further investigations pursuant to formulating a detailed and precise partition plan. The implementation of this task would be entrusted to a special technical commission, which would be allotted the following tasks: (1) to propose boundaries for the Jewish State, the Arab State and the British enclave, which would meet the following conditions: the boundaries would be drawn to allow the Jewish State and the Arab State to sustain themselves in sufficient security; they would include the minimum number of Arabs and Arab enterprises in the Jewish State and the converse within the Arab State; they would allow Britain to fulfill its obligations under the mandate; (2) to investigate various economic and financial issues implicit in partition; (3) to examine the feasibility of voluntary land and population transfers; (4) to examine measures for providing tangible guarantees of the rights of minorities who would remain within the Jewish and Arab States. The government further clarified that if, as a result of the technical commission's investigations, the government were to find that the partition proposal was equitable and feasible, it would pass it on for consideration by the League Council. After the latter had granted approval measures towards the establishment of two independent states would commence. In March 1938 a technical commission headed by Sir John Woodhead was appointed. In contrast to the Royal Commission, the Partition Commission's terms of reference were extremely detailed. At the end of April 1938, the Commission arrived in Palestine,[45] tarried there until the end of August, and at the close of the year published its findings.[46]

NOTES

1. Cohen (1978), pp. 10–31; Klieman (1983), pp. 4–5; Ettinger (1969), p. 293.
2. *Palestine Royal Commission Report* (hereafter PRCR) (1937), p. vi.
3. See PRCR (1937).
4. See, for example, Public Record Office (hereafter PRO), file CO 733/346/9, note of an

informal discussion between the Chiefs of Staff Sub-committee and members of the Royal Commission on Palestine, 1 March 1937; Katzburg (1984).

5. PRCR (1937), pp. 370–96. The citations are from p. 275; PRO, file CO 733/346/9; Peel (1937).
6. Fraser (1984), pp. 130–5; Katzburg (1974), pp. 23–5; Geva (1980), pp. 97–211; Rose (1970); Fraser (1988); Klieman (1980a); Klieman (1983), pp. 29–36. In Klieman's opinion, the following factors worked in favour of partition: the tendency towards compromise characteristic of British culture and history; the accumulated stockpile of plans for solving the Palestine problem, through various methods of partition or cantonization, which had been drawn up on various occasions and with which the Commission and other British statesmen were acquainted. See also Central Zionist Archives (hereafter CZA), Protocols of the Jewish Agency Executive's meetings on 25 December 1936, 28 March 1937, 11 April 1937, 2 May 1937. Regarding segregation processes in Palestine, see Kimmerling (1976); The Problem of Palestine (1937).
7. PRCR (1937), pp. 380–1; 392–3.
8. PRCR (1937), pp. 380–6, 389–93. See also CZA, file S/25/10199, letter from Neumann to Shertok of 28 November 1937; Ofer (1983).
9. Ben-Gurion (1937), pp. 196, 198; Sharett (1937), pp. 208–9.
10. See PRO, file CO 733/346/9; Sharett (1937).
11. Sharett (1937), pp. 208–9.
12. CZA, file S25/10066, letter from Ben-Gurion to Shertok on 3 July 1937; Ben-Gurion (1937), pp. 198, 228; Sharett (1937), pp. 208–9; Ofer (1983); PRCR (1937), pp. 382–6, 389–93. Regarding Weizmann's endeavor to influence the final content of the Royal Commission's report, see Fraser (1988), especially pp. 665–6 and Ofer (1983), pp. 461–3.
13. PRCR (1937), p. 384.
14. Ibid., pp. 385–6.
15. Ibid., p. 381.
16. Ibid., pp. 381–2.
17. See PRO, file CO 733/346/9.
18. PRO, file CO 733/354, letter from Coupland to Ormsby-Gore on 29 July 1937. See also Sharett (1937), p. 344.
19. CZA, file S25/10.058, letter from Coupland to Weizmann on 17 April 1938.
20. PRCR (1937), p. 382.
21. Ibid., pp. 384–5.
22. PRO, file CO 733/346/9; Klieman (1983), p. 37.
23. PRO, file CO 733/346/9.
24. PRCR (1937), pp. 386–8.
25. Ibid., pp. 383–4; CZA, file S25/10054, memorandum by Ben-Gurion, 'Proposal for a Tripartite Partition', on 3 December 1937.
26. PRCR (1937), p. 383.
27. Ibid., p. 384.
28. Ibid., pp. 389–90.
29. Ibid., pp. 389–93.
30. Pentzopoulos (1962), pp. 61–3.
31. Katz (1992b), p. 59.
32. PRCR (1937), p. 390.
33. Katz (1992b), p. 61. It would appear that the arguments concerning the Greco–Turkish precedent were also related to the fact that a member of the Royal Commission, Sir H. Rumbold, participated as Britain's representative at the signing of the Lausanne Treaty in 1923, which stipulated the population exchange between Greece and Turkey. A short time afterwards, Rumbold served as Chairman of the Committee appointed by the League of Nations to handle the exchange of population between Greece and Bulgaria. See CZA, archives of the PLDC (Palestine Land Development Company), file 7, 1936, Studies and Professional Opinions, Section 9 – Population Exchanges.

34. PRCR (1937), p. 390.
35. Ibid., p. 391.
36. Ibid.
37. Ibid., pp. 391–2. In the personal opinion of the Commission's Chairman, Peel, total exchanges had to be implemented. On this, see PRO, file CO 733/346/9.
38. PRCR (1937), pp. 391–3.
39. Ibid.
40. Klieman (1983), pp. 39–42, levels strong criticism at the government regarding the approach and haste displayed in its decision-making. See also Klieman (1980a).
41. CZA, Publication No. 5865, Palestine Statement of Policy No. 11/37 of 7 July 1937. See also the document in Klieman (1983), Appendix 1, pp. 143–4.
42. See the parliamentary discussion in Klieman (1987), pp. 1–77; Klieman (1983); Geva (1980), p. 187; Klieman (1983), pp. 45–6; Katzburg (1974), p. 34; Rose (1970).
43. League of Nations, Permanent Mandates Commission, Minutes of the 32nd session (1937b); League of Nations, (1937a); Klieman (1987), pp. 91–321; *Palestine Partition Commission Report*, (hereafter PPCR) (1938), p. 52; CZA, file S25/3786, Ben-Gurion Memorandum; CZA, file S25/3786, Memorandum by Ben-Gurion 'Regarding the Ormsby-Gore Letter' (undated, but undoubtedly from the start of 1938).
44. Beeley (1937), pp. 558–60; League of Nations (1937a); Eliash (1971), p. 147.
45. Beeley, op. cit., pp. 560–3; PPCR (1938), pp. 7–9; CZA, file S25/10109, the Partition Commission's terms of reference; the journal *Ha'Olam*, 6 January 1938; Government Official Announcement No. 1/38 on 4 January 1938; CZA, file S25/3786, in note 43.
46. See PPCR (1938).

2

The Activism of the Jewish Agency Executive and the Formulation of Alternative Partition Boundaries

FROM OUTRIGHT REJECTION TO QUALIFIED ACCEPTANCE:
TOWARDS AN ALTERNATIVE PARTITION PLAN

The idea of partitioning Palestine in return for sovereignty was not novel to the World Zionist Organization and its leadership. Partition proposals had been broached since the 1920s by personages within the Zionist Organization. Thus, for example, Avigdor Jacobson, who had served since 1925 as the Zionist Executive's representative at the League of Nations and co-ordinated political activities in France and Italy, formulated during the years 1929–31 a series of models for solving the Palestine problem, and in 1931 arrived at the conclusion that the sole solution was the establishment of a sovereign Jewish State in part of Palestine. Haim Arlozoroff, who from 1931–33 headed the Political Department of the Jewish Agency, raised the proposal in 1931. Two years later, Mussolini, in conversation with Weizmann, raised the partition proposal but the latter refused to consider it as an operative plan. Generally, up to the beginning of 1937, Zionist official policy opposed any form of partition or cantonization. For this reason, Jacobson was forbidden to make reference to his plan in his diplomatic contacts. The official view of the Zionist leadership at the close of 1936 was that a solution of the Palestine problem should be reached within a framework of parity, i.e. within a framework providing Jewish–Arab equality in rule over Palestine, although this did not constitute a strategic retreat from the Zionist goal of a Jewish State.[1]

The Zionist leadership was therefore surprised when, at the beginning of 1937, it started to realize that the Royal Commission intended to achieve a solution via partition and the establishment of both a Jewish State and an Arab State in Palestine.[2] However, the leadership, which included the President of the World Zionist Organization, Chaim Weizmann, the Chairman of the Jewish Agency, David Ben-Gurion, and the Director of the Agency's Political Department, Moshe Shertok (Sharett), now supported partition in principle as opposed to the details spelled out in the Royal Commission's Plan. Some of the aforementioned personages had reached this position earlier, some would do so later. Weizmann was an early and vigorous proponent. From then onwards, the leadership, and first and foremost Weizmann, would seek to promote and realize the partition principle. Additional members of the Jewish Agency Executive, i.e. the embryonic 'Jewish Government', climbed aboard but there were also members of the Jewish Agency Executive who opposed the idea of partition.[3]

The support of the leadership for the partition principle in 1937 was motivated by the numerous advantages that sovereignty would confer once a Jewish State had emerged as a result of partition. These advantages appeared to the leadership to outweigh the preservation of the land's territorial integrity especially as the leadership contended that the present partition lines would not necessarily determine the final boundaries of a Jewish State in Palestine. Sovereignty provided advantages in the following areas: it would be possible to open the gates of Palestine before mass Jewish immigration and solve the difficult plight of European Jews; it would substantially intensify Jewish power in Palestine with all that this entailed and, most importantly, Arab acquiescence to the existence of a Jewish entity in the Middle East; the state would galvanize quantitative and qualitative change in the balance of forces in Palestine because it would create the accoutrements of power which the Jewish community in Palestine and the Zionist Movement, who lacked authority and were based on voluntary principles, could not establish on their own; it would accelerate and intensify the process of realizing Zionist goals not only in the realm of immigration and demographic power but in the social, cultural, economic and settlement spheres as well. In Weizmann's words: 'it would be possible to build a Jewish life as we described it to ourselves. To raise Jewish men and women erect in character, to foster agriculture, industry, language, literature, and art. In brief we could establish and build upon all those principles which constitute the holy and sanctified content of Zionism'; the attainment of government and the possibility of living our life 'according to our demands and in our own way'. It was assumed that partition and the loss of territory would not detract from the absorptive capacity, because the political and economic advantages obtained by sovereignty would compensate for the curtailment of territorial size. The leadership contended that the partition plan constituted an historic opportunity that should not be squandered and should be brought to fruition especially in light of the present reality and prospects for the imminent future. On the one hand, one had to consider the plight of Jews in eastern Europe and Germany, and on the other, the need to augment

Jewish power in the country. Unless mass immigration became possible, the numeric gap between Jews and Arabs would widen and this gap could determine the future of the country.

Additionally, the international situation could change for the worse with all the implications that had for attaining Jewish aspirations. Let us add that from the standpoint of institution-building and creating structural patterns, during the years 1931–36, most of the major processes of Jewish nation-building in Palestine had been completed. In those years the Jewish population in Palestine had doubled and reached 400,000, compared with 900,000 Arabs. In those years, Palestine became for the first time the principal haven for Jewish refugees from Europe. These were also years of appreciable economic development in the Jewish community, accompanied by an expansion in land purchases and settlement. For the first time since Zionism had begun, a feeling existed that a Jewish national home was soon attainable. All this contributed to a readiness to establish a Jewish State. In no small sense geographic separation already existed, for the Jewish community was concentrated along the coastal strips and in the valleys whereas the Arab community was located in the interior of the country.[4]

In the course of 1937, the leadership headed by Weizmann would do its utmost to influence the final report of the Royal Commission, and it would vigorously lobby the British Parliament and the League of Nations to accept the partition principle rather than the details of the Royal Commission's proposal.[5] It would also expend efforts on persuading the supreme authorized body of the World Zionist Organization – the Zionist Congress – to opt for a solution within the partition framework that would lead to the establishment of a state or at least to the granting of authorization to the Jewish Agency Executive to conduct negotiations with the British over the desired partition.[6]

In the Zionist Congress that took place during the first three weeks of August 1937, a series of decisions were adopted following fierce debate between those who supported the partition plan in return for obtaining a Jewish State in Palestine and those who rejected the idea.[7] The following three decisions are critical to our discussion:

The Congress declares that the partition plan as proposed by the Royal Commission is unacceptable; The Congress empowers the Executive to conduct negotiations with a view to clarifying the specific content of the British Government's proposal for establishing a Jewish State in Palestine; In these discussions the Executive is not authorized to obligate itself or obligate the World Zionist Organization. If as a result of these negotiations, a specific plan

for establishing a Jewish state should be agreed upon, the draft of the plan
should be submitted to the newly elected Congress for deliberation and
decision ...[8]

The leadership, which did not agree to details of the proposed Royal
Commission partition plan[9] and was aware of the report's tendencies even
before they became public,[10] began to devise an alternative formulation of
the partition details (or, in other words, amending the partition proposal
of the Royal Commission) in the first months of 1937. This activity
expanded at the close of summer 1937, given the decision of the twentieth
Zionist Congress and in view of the British decision to dispatch the
Partition Commission to Palestine to work out a detailed partition plan.
The deliberations and discussions of the British Parliament, as well as
those that ensued in the institutions of the League of Nations and within
the British Government itself, appeared to substantiate the assumption
that one could amend the partition details in the direction sought by
Zionism.[11] Those members of the Jewish Agency Executive and in the
Zionist General Council opposed to the partition idea, headed by
Menachem Ussishkin, strenuously objected to the leadership's activity.[12]
However, this did not prevent the continued activism of the leadership
and the Jewish Agency Executive geared towards elaborating a preferable
partition plan and establishing a Jewish State, who argued that this activity
fell within the purview of the Congress decision.[13] As Ben-Gurion
contended:

> The Executive must do its utmost ... so that a good proposal, ideal to the extent
> possible concerning the establishment of the Jewish State should be submitted
> to the forthcoming Congress. A large part of the Zionist Movement favors this
> and therefore the Congress granted its sanction that this position is not illicit,
> because it rejected the position which sought to negate this opinion and stated
> that the forthcoming congress would decide while the Executive for its part
> would see to a sound plan for a state ...[14] Congress entrusted the Executive
> with the conduct of negotiations regarding a Jewish State which would not
> arise in all of Palestine but only in part of the country ...[15]

Preparatory work was concentrated in the hands of the Jewish Agency's
Political Department, which consulted experts, set up a series of
professional committees to cogitate over the desired partition details and
formulate its findings. These findings, once they had been discussed in
the Agency Executive, were submitted at the beginning of 1938 as official
memoranda of the Executive to the Partition Commission as a supplement
to the personal testimony of the Executive and its experts before the
Partition Commission.[16]

DEFINING THE BOUNDARY LINES IN THE JEWISH AGENCY EXECUTIVE'S PARTITION PLAN

In mid-1937, the Executive had already begun dealing with the formulation of alternative boundary lines to those proposed by the Royal Commission, when the boundary lines of the Royal Commission began to emerge. As may be recalled, even prior to the publication of the Royal Commission's report, the Executive sought to exert influence on behalf of the inclusion of the entire Galilee in the proposed partition borders of the Royal Commission as well as on boundary demarcations in other areas.[17] In November 1937, the boundaries issue was submitted to the Boundary Committee, which was appointed by the Political Department of the Jewish Agency. The Committee included those experts on the subject who were at the disposal of the Political Department. On the basis of the Boundary Committee's findings and discussions on the issue within the Political Department and the Executive, the position of the Executive regarding the issue of boundaries was formulated and the Executive's partition map was drafted. The map and the Executive's position regarding the boundaries issue were presented to the Partition Commission at the close of 1938.[18] Let it be emphasized that when contacts between the Executive and the Partition Commission began, the Executive agonized over tactics. Was it preferable for the Executive to present the Commission only with a critique of the boundary lines defined in the Royal Commission's Plan as opposed to committing itself to the boundaries that the Executive desired? Alternatively the Executive could present the Commission with its own ideas regarding the boundaries.[19]

The Executive quickly decided not only to reject the Royal Commission Plan but to present the Partition Commission with its own views on the boundaries. This stance was not only the Executive's response to the demands of the Partition Commission that it present a precise map of the boundaries reflecting the Zionist position; first and foremost it conformed to the Executive's appreciation that such explicitness was also a clear Zionist interest, since only in this manner could one hope to persuade the Commission to back Zionist demands. In the words of Ben-Gurion:

> It is not possible for us to say to the Commission that we have come only to listen. When you or the government have a proposal we shall present it to the Congress and the Congress will decide. If we should do this ... we will be derelict in our Zionist mission which was entrusted to us ... to make every effort to obtain the optimal plan from the British Government ...[20]

It is clear that we have to show maps. If we say that we have to provide more strategic boundaries that will guarantee our defense, that will assure our water resources, we will have to demonstrate this to them. This is a Partition Commission. The principal issue is territory. All other things derive from territory. If we evade this negotiations are impossible. And we want to induce them to propose the optimal proposal …[21]

Bernard Joseph, who had begun in 1936 to serve as the legal adviser of the Zionist Executive, and Deputy Director of Political Department, headed the Boundaries Committee. Other members of the Committee were Moshe Smilansky, Gad Machnes, Elimelech Zelikovitz (Avner) – one of the early members and commanders of the 'Hagana' Organization[22] – the geographer Avraham Yaakov Brawer and Zalman Lifshitz (subsequently known as Lif).[23] The deliberations of the Committee were shaped to a great extent by Bernard Joseph and Zalman Lifshitz. The latter was an engineer, a surveyor and a cartographer. Thanks to his practical work, and the large theoretical knowledge that he had amassed, he was considered an expert in the field of land settlement, geography and Palestine lore. In the days to come (see the concluding chapter) Lifshitz would help shape the boundaries of the State of Israel. Lifshitz would summarize the deliberations of the Boundaries Committee and drew up the maps based on the various proposals raised in the Committee's deliberations. He also drew up the final map for partition boundaries that the Zionist Executive submitted to the British Partition Commission.[24]

The principles and goals of the Jewish Agency Executive in fixing the partition map

The stance of the Jewish Agency Executive regarding the partition boundaries was determined in the light of certain principles and objectives, but also took account of the directives that the British government gave to the Partition Commission in its terms of reference. The Commission was exhorted to recommend boundaries that would (a) afford a reasonable prospect of the eventual establishment, with adequate security, of self-supporting Arab and Jewish States; (b) necessitate the inclusion of the fewest possible Arabs and Arab enterprise in the Jewish area and vice versa.[25] Before we turn to an examination of the principles and objectives that guided the Executive in fixing the partition map, let us add that in the memorandum submitted to the Partition Commission the Executive also raised a number of rationalizations intended to buttress efforts to increase the overall area of the Jewish State.

The Executive contended that the Royal Commission's Plan contradicted its essential principles, since it did not preserve Britain's obligation towards the Jews and discriminated against the Jewish party to the dispute. The Executive also protested that this, in effect, was already the third partition of Palestine to the detriment of the Jewish side. In 1919, the land had been partitioned for the first time between Britain and France, and Jewish-owned territories had been severed from it. In 1922, the eastern portion of Palestine had been amputated from the national home, although the Balfour Declaration had intended to allow the Jews to immigrate and settle in the country, and establish a Jewish State in all its historic territory. Within the framework of a third partition, the Royal Commission now proposed to hand over to the Jews only one-eighteenth of the land originally included in the Balfour Declaration.[26] This area comprised only one-fifth of western Palestine. The Executive emphasized that the Commission had left only a limited area for the Jewish people who sought to rebuild their home in Palestine, whereas vast areas in the entire Arab milieu, and especially in places that had already obtained independence, lay at the Arabs' disposal. This injustice was particularly flagrant, given the persecution of the Jews in central Europe, the deterioration of the situation of the Jews in Eastern Europe and the fact that the world was progressively closing its doors to the Jews.[27] In general, a Jewish State was expected to provide a solution to the Jewish problem: it was intended for the entire Jewish people, and not for the Jews of Palestine alone. The problem was that the boundaries of the Jewish State proposed by the Royal Commission contained insufficient room to absorb the masses of the Jewish people who require refuge.[28] Indeed, Ben-Gurion emphasized that:

> the obligation to absorb a maximum number of Jews, and in this way promote the solution to the problem of the Jewish people, will determine the character, regime and mode of activity for the Jewish State, while the response of the Jewish people to the Commission's Plan and the proposals of His Majesty's Government will be determined by an examination of the extent to which the proposed Jewish State will be able to fulfill this purpose. In other words, to what extent will the area earmarked for the Jewish state afford not only an independent and secure existence, for the Jews already residing in the country, but would adequately allow for immigrant absorption and additional settlement consistent with the spirit of the obligation undertaken by the British Government towards the Jewish People ...[29]

The Zionist Executive also contended that, from the standpoint of the British interests:

1. The Royal Commission's plan had failings since including the Negev within the Arab State surrendered the strategic key to Egypt and the Gulf of Eilat to

British forces and imperils the free passage of England to India and other Asian countries.

2. The corridor will not be capable of sustaining itself and will require financial assistance from the British Exchequer.

3. The military weakness of the Jewish State and the anticipated dangers emanating from the new Arab State and other neighboring Arab countries would impose a severe moral responsibility upon Britain.[30]

Six principles and goals guided the Executive and the Boundaries Committee that it appointed in determining the partition boundaries. The first principle was that one should present boundary lines that had reasonable prospects of British acceptance; as Shertok opined, 'we must consider what is possible and what is impossible to obtain ...'[31] '[W]e must choose only those things which are vital for us and which enjoy good prospects for success and we must fight for all these things together ...'[32] Similar sentiments were voiced by Weizmann[33] and Gruenbaum. Gruenbaum said: 'We must refrain from demanding things which are not a necessity for achieving our goals';[34] and Ben-Gurion added: 'we won't make ourselves into a laughing stock by stating that all of Palestine on both sides of the Jordan should be included within the Jewish State'.[35]

On the basis of this principle, Bernard Joseph rejected the proposal suggested by the Boundaries Committee to propose constricting to a very minimum the actual area of the Arab State in Samaria (the Jenin–Ramallah line), for 'in this fashion the Arabs will receive only the mountainous areas of the country, and the British won't assent to the proposal which is unfair from the Arab standpoint'.[36] In similar fashion, Ben-Gurion contended that it was impossible to demand the inclusion of the Negev within the area of the Jewish State if the Galilee was to be included in it.[37] Likewise, the Zionists raised no demand to abrogate the British mandate enclave, although that enclave would harm the Jewish State by cutting it in two. Only amendments to the enclave boundaries were proposed.[38] Within the framework of the 'reasonable demands' guidelines, an effort was made to prove that the desired amendments in favor of the Jewish State (at the expense of the Arab State) would not actually harm the Arab State.[39] Thus, for example, a reiterated contention denied that a transfer of the Negev to the area of the British enclave would impair the Arab State since there was no possibility that the Arabs could make the desert bloom.[40] Similarly, A. Y. Brawer, a member of the Boundaries Committee, argued that moving the eastern boundary further east into Samaria, in order to include the water resources within the boundaries of the Jewish State, would not harm the Arabs in Samaria.[41]

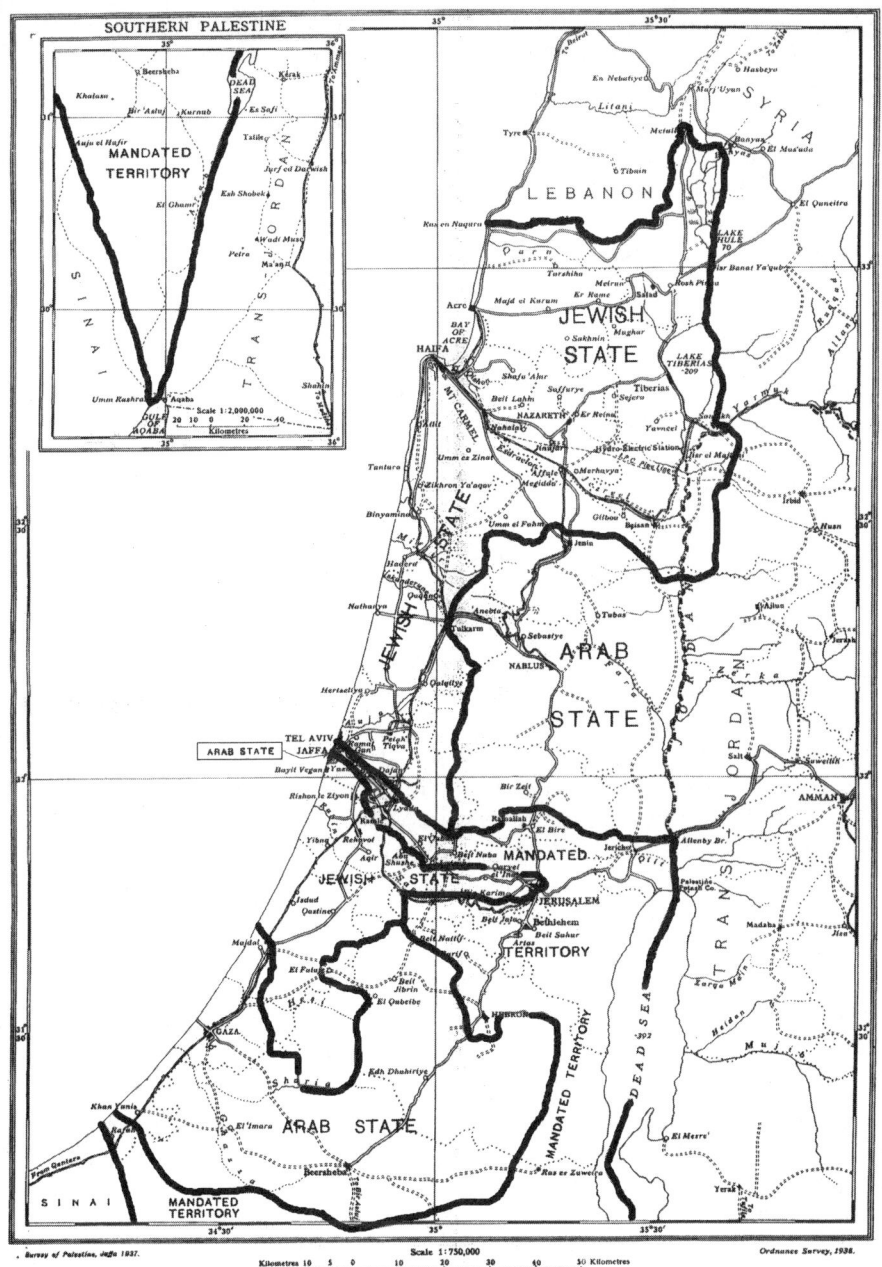

Map 2: Proposal of Jewish Agency Executive for the Partition of Palestine, 1938 (Original Map)

The second principle dealt with the Jewish State's necessity for defensible boundaries and security. Defensible boundaries were needed, given the ugly tenor of relations that prevailed between Jews and Arabs, the ceaseless acts of provocation on the part of the Arabs, and the assumption that indefensible boundaries would only invite aggression and lead to boundary disputes.[42] Furthermore, one had to take into account not only the likelihood that rifles and machine guns would be used in the event of war but also 'sophisticated equipment on both sides, heavy artillery, planes, etc.'.[43] The Jewish State would be an island surrounded by an Arab sea, and it was necessary that the area of the state should be sufficiently large in order to provide strategic depth and to settle a population large enough to protect the boundaries.[44] In this context, Ben-Gurion emphasized that:

> A Jewish State in such a limited area could not withstand a neighboring Arab State. The area of the new Arab State … is 17 times larger than the area of the Jewish State and is settled by a population nearly double that of the Jewish State (850,000 versus 591,356) and one cannot overlook that the Jewish State includes a population of nearly 300,000 Arabs and at a time of crisis the residents of the neighboring states (Syria, Iraq, Saudi Arabia) would come to the assistance of the Arab State.[45]

Given security needs, it was decided that the boundary line would not separate Arab villages from their agricultural territories. This would obviate the need to award the frontier villages special privileges, which could damage the Jewish State.[46] Another corollary of security requirements was the ambition for a maximal territorial increase in areas with a negligible Arab population.[47]

Economic security, a self-sustaining state, and a suitable destination for absorbing Jewish immigration from the diaspora were additional guiding principles for the Agency Executive. These goals could be obtained first and foremost if the size of the Jewish State were sufficiently large. This would facilitate the future increase in the size of the Jewish population, and in particular the absorption of mass immigration, an appreciable part of which would be channeled to agricultural settlement and a portion to industry. In the opinion of the Executive, the proposed area of the Jewish State (about 5 million dunam) would not suffice for these needs. This argument was buttressed by the fact that the Royal Commission's recommendation of forced transfer of population, which was intended to facilitate Jewish settlement on areas vacated within the Jewish State, had, as may be recalled, been rejected by the British government and the

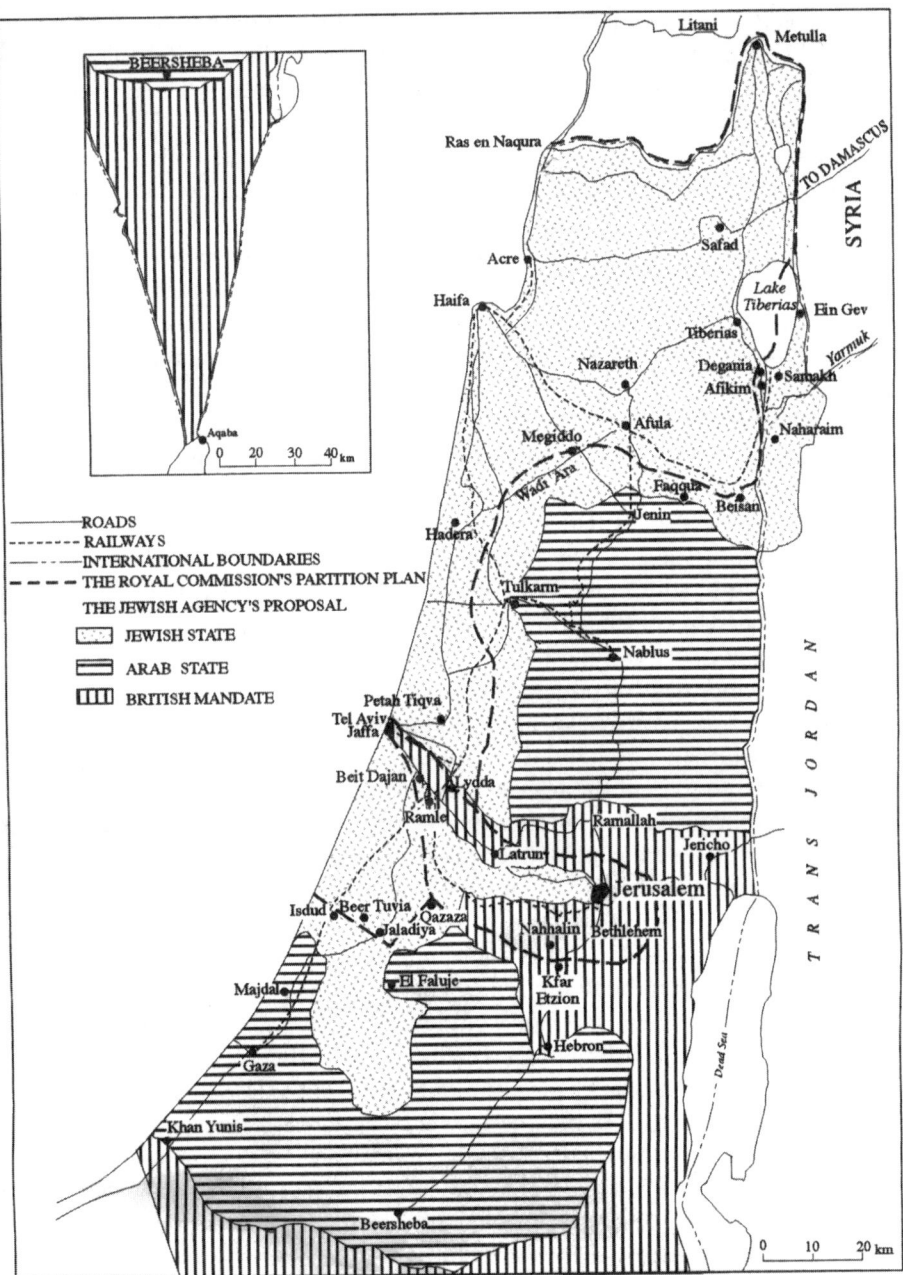

Map 3: Proposal of Jewish Agency Executive for the Partition of Palestine, 1938
        (Redrawn Map by the Author)

prospects for voluntary transfer were dim. The Executive believed it should demand at least a 1 million dunam increase in the area of the Jewish State. The economic–financial considerations necessitated the retention of areas rich in natural resources and economic enterprises, as well as places with economic demographic potential, such as Haifa (which was assigned a temporary mandatory status) and West Jerusalem, within the boundaries of the Jewish State.[48]

The fourth principle was maximum control over water resources. This was indispensable to dense settlement based on intensive farms, which required irrigation (the Royal Commission had already dwelt on this point), and to the very existence of the Jewish State in general. First of all, there was apprehension that water resources that lay outside the control of the Jewish State would be poisoned. Secondly, a special experts commission appointed by the Boundaries Committee dwelt on the importance of the run-off water from the Samarian hills westwards, which would serve the needs of dense settlement in the coastal plain. In the opinion of the committee, 'it was possible that the water resources accruing from the exploitation of subterranean water by drilling or springs could become impoverished by continual and perhaps prodigal use'. Therefore, the run-off waters of Samaria should be collected, either by damming them up in the mountains or by introducing them into the depths of the soil. Likewise, control over the entire Lake Tiberias and both banks of the Jordan in the area of the Jordan Valley and the Galilee heights, which incorporated half the water resources of the Jewish State, had to be maintained.[49]

Two other principles guiding the Jewish Agency in determining the boundary lines were control over the main transportation arteries[50] and the annexation of lands that were not settled by Arabs.[51] This latter principle was primarily dictated by security and political considerations. Likewise, it was noted that the Zionist position on this point was identical to the directive that the Boundaries Commission had received in its terms of reference. Only in this fashion would a real Jewish majority be obtainable within the future Jewish State, especially in view of the fact that, according to the Royal Commission's plan, the boundaries of the Jewish State would include many Arabs. As may be recalled, the forcible-transfer proposal had been ruled out by the British government.[52]

The historical–symbolic and sentimental importance of particular areas did not induce the Executive to demand their inclusion within the Jewish State, with the exception to some degree of Jerusalem – an issue that we will address in the following chapter. Thus, in response to Berl Katznelson's (one of the Labor movement's leaders) criticism of the fact that the Jewish State was to include neither Hebron nor Modiin, 'the cradle of the Hasmoneans', and not Mazada, 'the shrine of our tragedy under the Hasmoneans',[53] Shertok responded that

> it is inconceivable that simply because of these arid names which I use symbolically, we should forfeit the acquisition of new tangible and possible acquisitions [i.e. a state] ... We have shed blood throughout the country, we have created spiritual values and we have constructed monuments. However, when we presently confront the possibilities of becoming a dominant force in the country without obtaining all our shrines, we have to find the moral strength to decide ...[54]

Later, we will examine how these principles and the Zionist goals that we surveyed influenced the shaping of the boundary line incorporated in the Jewish Agency's proposal. It emerges that the reality on the ground posed dilemmas and obligated the Executive to decide between principles that were mutually contradictory. Thus, for example, 'the necessity to include at various places Arab settlements within the Jewish region for reasons of security, transport or economics (for example, the water resources in the mountains)' became clear.[55] What follows is an examination of the Zionist boundary lines, according to the country's various regions from north to south.

The Galilee and the refusal to concede parts of it in return for compensation in the Negev

The Royal Commission recommended the incorporation of the entire Galilee within the borders of the Jewish State. Prior to the publication of the Commission's report, the Agency Executive had already sought to clarify how vital the entire Galilee, including its mountain region, was to the future Jewish State. Emphasis was put on the Galilee's importance to the network of Jewish settlement, the achievements of the Zionist settlement project in the region; the land purchases that had been consummated and that were on the verge of consummation by Jewish bodies in the Galilee; the strategic importance of the mountainous Galilee for protecting the valleys; and the political and security importance that would be conferred, provided that the Jewish State's neighbor in the north were Lebanon and an Arab buffer were not to intrude between Lebanon and the Jewish State. Likewise, the historic value of the Galilee in Jewish national consciousness was noted.[56]

In summing up the importance of incorporating the entire Galilee within the Jewish State, Shertok wrote to the British High Commissioner in June 1937:

I would sum up the value of the Galilee to the Jews as follows: 1. Our patrimony in the Eastern boundary of the Galilee extends over the entire length of this area from north to south ... now we are progressing northwards along the coast. There we have established Nahariya which has put us close to the border point of Ras en Naqura and we have prospects for purchasing additional areas in this coastal area. To excise and extract from this area, which the Jews can settle, the entire portion of the Galilee between the Jordan and the coast, will place our defensive positions in both our eastern and western regions in serious danger. It will shut us out of a vast area rich in water resources and orchards whose settlement potential even if yet unrealized is vast; 2. The Galilee includes Lake Hule and all that surrounds it. We have already taken steps to enlarge our patrimony in this region where the appropriate use of waters from the Hule and the Jordan guarantees the possibility of irrigation, intensive agriculture and dense settlement. More distant possibilities do not exclude the use of the Litani River waters; 3. It is indispensable for the Jews to have a settlement area bounding upon Lebanon. Ties of friendship have already germinated between us and the Maronites. Thinkers in both areas share a deep hope that this friendship will be reinforced to provide for economic and political alliance on behalf of both communities and both nations. Any wedge dividing us from Lebanon will lessen the prospects for stability of the welfare of the two states and the entire coastal region of the Mediterranean; 4. Thanks to Jewish–Maronite friendship and other factors which operate in the region, there are fair prospects for Jewish agricultural settlement in the border regions of Lebanon and Syria which will be a great blessing to the Jews and to these two countries. These prospects can be realized only if boundary access to which I have referred in the previous passage will be maintained ...[57]

The Executive therefore made efforts to influence the Royal Commission to include the entire Galilee within the boundaries of the Jewish State. However, it did not expect that this would actually occur, especially not with regard to the mountainous area, given its dense Arab population. Ben-Gurion himself found it difficult to believe Weizmann's reports, on the eve of the report's official publication, that the Commission had actually included the entire Galilee within the area of the Jewish State.[58] Upon the official publication of the report, Ben-Gurion wrote in his diary:

The Commission has earned no small measure of merit in determining the boundaries. To award the entire Galilee to the Jews is an act of great courage and great generosity. This merit can atone for a number of the Commission's transgressions ... All the realistic conditions contest a Jewish take over of the country's entire north. The density of the Arab community, the mountainous region, its propinquity to Syria – all these factors would have stood as an iron wall against Jewish colonizatory conquest. In this conquest, I detect the center of gravity of the Commission's findings in practice ...[59]

However, circles within the British government did not look favorably upon the recommendation of the Royal Commission regarding the Galilee. A letter sent by the Colonial Secretary to the High Commissioner at the beginning of January 1938 even hinted that it would be necessary to constrict appreciably the area of the Jewish State in the Galilee, and in recompense the Jewish area would be widened in the south. Another proposal spoke of constricting the Galilee in return for including the Negev within the area of the mandate and granting the Jews permission to settle there.[60] The Agency Executive rejected any concession on areas in the Galilee ('without the Galilee one cannot even begin to describe a Jewish State'[61]) and even refused to discuss the issue (without any connection to Zionist demands regarding the Negev, on which we will dwell later). Indeed, in response to a question posed by a member of the Royal Commission to Weizmann, Ben-Gurion and Shertok, as to what in their opinion would be adequate compensation for the Galilee, all three elected not to respond.[62] The Executive therefore believed that the receipt of the Negev did not constitute compensation for the loss of the Galilee. The arguments were primarily those already noted and now these were joined by the Royal Commission's decision to include the entire Galilee within the Jewish State. Ben-Gurion added: 'We would have lost the Galilee if it had become part of an Arab State since it is densely settled, whereas the Negev within an Arab country would remain desolate and sooner or later the dynamic pressure which stands behind Jewish settlement would have overcome the obstructive constraint of barren Arab patriotism ...'.[63]

Following water tests that the Water Committee (which was a sub-committee of the Boundaries Committee) conducted, the argument was raised that the principal water resources of the future Jewish State were located in the Galilee. The northern Galilee alone accounted for half the water required by the Jewish State.[64] It appears that the vehement decision of the Executive not to concede portions of the Galilee in recompense for the Negev, was also influenced by a report by Joseph Weitz, the Director of the Lands Division within the Jewish National Fund (JNF – the instrument of the World Zionist Organization for redeeming lands in Palestine) and an expert on settlement in Palestine. Weitz examined the prospects for agricultural settlement in the Upper Galilee as opposed to those in the Negev and decided unequivocally in favor of the Galilee. Weitz estimated that the Upper Galilee could absorb still an additional 110,000 persons, even if no transfer of Arab population occurred in those areas. He further emphasized:

To demand the Negev as an addition to a Jewish State or as a reserve for Jewish settlement under a British Mandate – that's all well and good. To pay for this with a generous portion of the Upper Galilee which comprises a quarter of the Jewish State's total area according to the boundaries of the Royal Commission – by no means whatsoever. An exchange of the Upper Galilee for the Negev is an exchange of something definite for something chancy. Even if they enjoyed the same political status, the upper Galilee with its hills and valleys, is from an agricultural standpoint something concrete and healthy. It is concrete because any place you plant a tree or sow a seed it will bear fruit – some places more and some places less – even in places where there are stones and boulders. We don't have to dynamite them and remove them to build terraces and prevent soil erosion. The rest has been seen to from the time of Genesis: a good climate and sufficient water. The Negev is just the opposite. It carries a large question mark from this standpoint with regards to its future, and it is clearly a minus from today's perspective … We can definitely not assent to such an exchange for even if they don't give us the Negev now we haven't abandoned hope for obtaining it in the future because its desolation will preserve it for us. Neither the Arabs nor the English will redeem it from its ruinous state … The answer in my opinion is sufficiently clear. From a settlement–agricultural perspective and in terms of absorption potential, the Galilee today is much more important to us than the Negev. Even if the former appears already populated and the second is empty of population. We must further note that precisely in this very same Galilee there are many many tens of thousands of dunams which belong to absentee owners and therefore it will prove easier to purchase them …

Weitz also emphasized the strategic importance of the Upper Galilee, its historical value to the Jewish people, and its culture and the contribution of the mountainous region for the quality of life of the residents of the Jewish State. In conclusion, he wrote:

Once the Upper Galilee is severed from the Jewish State it will be necessary to connect it to the Arab State via a corridor which will bisect the Jewish State. This will be still an additional corridor to the proposed corridor on the Jerusalem–Jaffa road which will carve up the Jewish state into bits and pieces and turn it into a ridiculous plaything. We can only be compensated for forfeiting the Galilee in Jerusalem and the Judean Hills and by the cancellation of the Jaffa Corridor plus part of the Hills of Ephraim. Although from an agricultural standpoint the latter is inferior to the Galilee mountains.[65]

In a concluding memorandum, which the Executive presented to the Woodhead Commission, the demands for amendments to the partition proposal of the Royal Commission were detailed. No reference at all was made to the Galilee.[66] It appears that the consideration was tactical – a quasi-declaration that there was nothing to be discussed concerning the Galilee and it belonged to the Jewish State in accordance with the recommendations of the Royal Commission. Nonetheless, as we shall see, the Executive adopted measures in order to increase the prospects for the retention of the entire Galilee within the Jewish State by stepping up land purchases in the Galilee and accelerating settlement in this area.

Lake Tiberias and the Jordan Valley

The Royal Commission decided that the boundary line would cross Lake Tiberias and continue along the length of the Jordan. The position of the Jewish Agency Executive was that one should include Lake Tiberias in its entirety, even its eastern shores, within the boundaries of the Jewish State. The boundary line would pass along the mountains at a distance of a number of kilometers east of the Jordan to the Beisan Valley, south-east of the town (see Map 4). According to this proposal, a number of kibbutzim severed under the original proposal of the Royal Commission, as well as the power station at Naharaim, would now be included within the Jewish State.

The demand of the Jewish Agency Executive to include all of Lake Tiberias and its eastern banks within the Jewish State stemmed from a number of reasons. First of all, the French, within the framework of the Sykes–Picot Treaty had assented to this, and 'it was inconceivable that a boundary which had been drawn at the time in favor of a Jewish national home should not remain the boundary of the Jewish State'.[67] Secondly, Lake Tiberias served as a water reservoir whose importance ranged beyond its immediate vicinity, and dividing the sea between two states would encumber the possibility of using it for this purpose. Thirdly, apprehension was felt that frequent disputes and clashes with the Arab state regarding the exact location of the boundary within the sea would arise and this would then require allocating forces to protect the boundary in the sea and prevent infiltration and smuggling. Fourthly, dividing Lake Tiberias would hinder fisheries. It was also noted that the British had an interest in preserving the integrity of the sea: 'A British Airline would be interested in the water area for its needs and it was therefore in the British interest that this area should not be divided between two countries...'.[68]

The demand to include the eastern bank of Lake Tiberias within the Jewish State up to the international boundary line with Syria stemmed first and foremost from strategic considerations. The mountain crest of

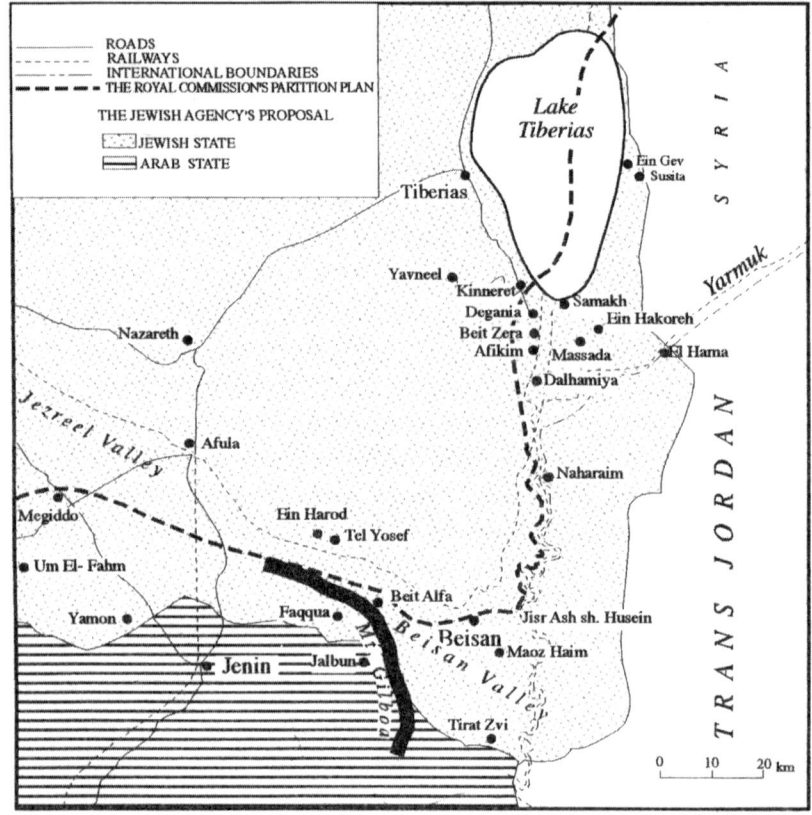

Map 4: Partition Proposal of Jewish Agency Executive for Northern Palestine, 1938

Susita served as a natural defense line for the region, and overlooked the Horon and the approach to Lake Tiberias as well. Additionally, Jewish-owned lands were located there, and, on the eve of the Royal Commission Report's publication, kibbutz Ein Gev settled in this region. Additionally, from the standpoint of the interests of the Arab State, these areas had no tangible importance.[69]

The area of the triangle spanning Lake Tiberias, the Yarmuk River and the Jordan River, held great importance, especially to the Jewish State. First of all, in Shertok's words, 'this corner is entirely Jewish in practice'.[70] Thirty-three thousand dunams, more than half of the area, were Jewish-owned and further purchases were planned. There were already seven Jewish agricultural kibbutzim in this area: Degania A, Degania B, Beit Zera,

Afikim, Dalhamiya (Gesher), Massada, Ein Hakoreh (Sha'ar Hagolan) and the power station in Naharaim (Tel Or). Fourteen hundred people lived there, and the farms had registered impressive achievements in intensive agriculture while exploiting the many advantages of the area. The development potential of the entire area was high. It was therefore logical that the region should be included within the Jewish State, especially as, in 1922, when the British fixed the boundary line between Palestine and Trans-Jordan they had already included the area in Palestine.[71]

This area contained the highest concentration of Jewish settlements fated to be severed from the Jewish State. Ben-Gurion contended that the proposal of the Royal Commission regarding this region was absurd and scandalous. None the less,[72] he expressed his readiness in principle to consider allowing the Jewish settlements to remain within the borders of the Arab State:

> If the plan of the Royal Commission will be implemented ... it is totally clear to me that this will not be the final arrangement. We will tear through these boundaries and not necessarily by force of the sword. More than at any other time I believe in a Jewish–Arab agreement in a non too distant future. If we will eventuate the immigration of hundreds of thousands Jews and fortify ourselves from an economic and military standpoint, we will lay the basis for a free agreement regarding the annulment of boundaries between us and the Arab State. This will bring to the Arab State not only material benefit – for it is possible that material benefit alone will not suffice to break down Arab patriotic opposition to our immigration into their state but raison d'etat will prod the Arabs into compromise with us in return for a mutual use and benefit in the areas of the two countries. The location of Jewish settlements within the Arab state will make it easier for Arab leaders and rulers to compromise and will pave the road for our expansion into their state.[73]

However, when he directly addressed the issue of the Lake Tiberias region and the Jordan Valley, Ben-Gurion added: 'It is difficult to make peace with this amputation, given our special sentimental attachment to the settlement points but also from a strategic standpoint.' In particular, he could not be consoled about the surrender of the electric power plant, which it was envisaged, would pass under state ownership in the foreseeable future.[74]

Indeed, it was the power plant in Naharaim that induced the Agency Executive to turn the boundary line eastward. This power plant was founded at the initiative of Pinhas Rutenberg in 1927 in the territory of Trans-Jordan, and was of supreme importance to the Jewish State because it supplied an appreciable portion of the electricity of the coastal region, including industrial and irrigation projects. Furthermore, 'Palestine is impoverished in natural fuels such as coal and oil and the Jewish State is dependent to a large extent and will be in the future, especially in times of emergency, on the supply of power from the aforementioned hydro-electric power station.'[75] Allowing the station to remain in the Arab State would therefore endanger the regular supply of electricity from the plant. Likewise, an area in the vicinity of the plant would be required for housing quarters for the workers, since they would patrol it in times of necessity.[76]

For security reasons as well, the Executive demanded that the boundary line be moved eastward. The water depth in the Jordan in the aforesaid region was shallow and the river could be forded without any difficulty. The dense plantations between the Jordan and the Yarmuk could facilitate infiltration. In contradistinction, the Yarmuk was much wider and deeper, and its flow of water was much stronger and it could therefore serve as an effective barrier against penetration. If the triangle was to be handed over to the Arabs they would quickly populate it and employ it as a base for attacking the Jewish State. A frequently voiced opinion expressed fear that the Yavneel–Kinneret road would be exposed to cannon and machine-gun fire. There was also talk of possibly reinforcing the Jewish settlement belt between the Jordan and the Yarmuk in order to buttress the region.[77] The members of the Boundaries Committee attached special importance to the inclusion of the important railway station at Samakh within the boundaries of the Jewish State.[78] The need for water also influenced the demand to move the boundary. In order to permit efficient exploitation of the Jordan water, dam up the Yarmuk at El Hama and divert its waters to Lake Tiberias during the rainy season, the boundary had to pass east of El Hama.[79] In the light of these points, the general tendency of the Boundaries Committee was to transfer the boundary line east of Lake Tiberias and from El Hama until south of Naharaim along the Yarmuk river bed (see Map 4).[80] A further plan was to permit the Arabs to use the Jordan waters, thus demonstrating that the Arab economy would not be harmed if the boundary line were moved eastward.[81]

The boundary line in this region, according to the Jewish Agency Executive's final proposal, differed from what the Boundary Committee proposed. It passed through the mountain line about 5–11 kilometers east of the Jordan. The goal of the Executive was to obtain additional territory for the Jewish State in a region that was easy to settle, possessed only small concentrations of Arabs, and whose mountain line also afforded the requisite defense.[82]

The Beisan Valley, the Gilboa and south-east Jezreel Valley

Pursuant to the proposal of the Royal Commission, the majority of the Beisan Valley, the Gilboa mountain ridge and the southern portion of Jezreel Valley remained outside the boundaries of the Jewish State. The boundary line following this proposal departed from the Jordan north of the city of Beisan and crossed the Beisan Valley (south of the Hijaz rail line) to Megiddo. According to the proposal of the Jewish Agency Executive, the entire Jezreel Valley, the Gilboa mountain ridge, and the Beisan Valley to the west and east of the Jordan River, including the city of Beisan (see Map 4), were included within the Jewish State.[83] The demands for modifications in the Beisan Valley in the region of Beisan stemmed also from economic–settlement considerations and security grounds. The area that the Agency Executive demanded in the Beisan Valley included about 100,000 dunams of crop-lands, rich in springs and subterranean waters, which could support an extensive and dense Jewish settlement. By the estimates of the Boundaries Committee, it would be possible to exploit the water resources in the valley for use in other areas. Of these territories, 17,000 dunams were Jewish owned and the kibbutzim Maoz Haim and Tirat Zvi were established upon them in 1937 with a view towards influencing the boundary lines of the Royal Commission (see in detail below). These settlements were to be located within the area of the Arab State. Likewise, negotiations were conducted concerning the purchase of additional lands in the area.[84] The Boundaries Commission contended that the Arabs were totally incapable of developing the region: 'This area is now sparsely settled and the Arab residents have an appreciable surplus of land which they cannot cultivate and it is not feasible for them to cultivate and they have offered it for sale.'[85] In a concluding memorandum sent to the Partition Commission, the Executive emphasized that many lands belonged to absentee landlords. The Executive cited the words of the Royal Commission which was also aware that the Arabs had not managed to develop the region. Among other things, the Royal Commission based itself on the statement of Sir John Hope-Simpson, who, in 1930, had criticized the Ghor-Mudawara Agreement between the mandatory government and the Bedouins of Beisan because it had 'taken from the government the control of a large area of fertile land, eminently suitable to development and for which there is ample water available for irrigation ... The grant of the lands has led to land speculation on a considerable scale ... It [the agreement] was made in order to provide the Arabs with a holding sufficient to maintain a decent standard of life, not to provide them with areas of land with which to speculate'.

The Royal Commission had endorsed these criticisms, and added: 'The original agreement in 1921 was hastily made without sufficient examination. There was a disregard of possible development and unduly generous terms were given to Arabs, who were not in a position to take advantage of them, without sufficient safeguards against abuse ...'. In the opinion of the Executive this criticism should have obligated the Royal Commission to include the Beisan land in the areas of the Jewish State, especially since the mandatory government was obligated to allow Jewish settlement on state land. The executive expressed its astonishment that the Royal Commission was contradicting itself on one of the principles that it had itself established, namely, keeping faith with previous British obligations.[86]

Security considerations also dictated important changes in the boundary line. First and foremost, it was necessary to demand the inclusion of the northern slopes of the Gilboa and its upper crest within the Jewish State, for

> the Jewish state would not have any possibility of protecting itself in boundaries if it does not have strategic position on the mountain looking southward from which it will be possible to hold up an attack developing from the side of the Samarian hills. Only from the high peaks which spread in the direction of the villages of Jalbun and Faqqua can one survey the mountain region to the south and monitor every movement and events that come from there. These peaks command the entire vicinity and have served from time immemorial and in all periods as watchtowers and fortified points of the valley. The nature of the land therefore makes it incumbent that they too should belong to the land to which the Jezreel Valley and the Jordan Valley will belong to and they will serve as fortified frontier points in times of necessity ...[87]

Likewise, the Beisan Valley and the Jezreel Valley should be kept out of reach of Arab artillery range.[88] Nonetheless, the Zionist proposal emphasized that the Gilboa Crest had no agricultural value and, therefore, its inclusion within the Jewish State would not harm the Arab State.[89]

From the security standpoint, it was necessary to move the boundary southwards from the vicinity of the town of Beisan and the Hijaz rail line in order to protect the rail line and prevent the transformation of Beisan

> into a strong military base with easy communications to Trans-Jordan through the Ash Sheikh Husein Bridge and from the South via the Beisan–Jericho Road. In this manner the swift and easy connection with the Jordan Valley through the Jezreel Valley would be terminated. Likewise, this fortified

position would require us to expend efforts in order to guarantee the southern portion of the Jordan Valley which would remain in our hands and we would have to invest many efforts in order to guarantee the southeast portion of the Jezreel Valley which would lie open on the Beisan side ...'[90]

This was the reason for including the town of Beisan within the boundaries of the Jewish State, although this would add about 3,000 Arabs to the Jewish State.[91] As may be recalled, one of the principles of the Executive in planning the boundary line was to refrain to the maximum extent possible from adding Arabs to the Jewish State, and indeed Shertok proposed leaving the town of Beisan, as an Arab salient, outside the Jewish State.[92] However, given the security considerations, his proposal was not adopted by the Executive. The fate of the recently established Jewish kibbutzim (plural of kibbutz) was another consideration for moving the boundary line southwards.[93]

The inclusion of the south-east Jezreel Valley south of Afula towards Jenin within the boundaries of the Jewish State was intended first and foremost to secure the expansion of the area earmarked for Jewish settlement, because it concerned an increment of 125,000 dunams to the Jewish State.[94] A further intention was to prevent the Arab State from establishing control over entry to the Jezreel Valley from the east,[95] and guarantee the Hijaz railway and the valley road – the two major transportation arteries of the valley – and keep the boundary line sufficiently away from the kibbutzim Beit Alfa, Ein Harod and Tel Yosef.[96] The proposal raised by one member of the Boundaries Committee to place the boundary line at a distance from Jenin for security considerations, and thus diminish the areas of the Jewish State (according to the Executive's proposal), was not adopted in the Committee or in the Executive. Opponents of the proposal believed that this would diminish the areas intended for settlement in the south-east Jezreel Valley,[97] a region that was sparsely settled and where land purchases were easy.[98]

The coastal plain and the eastern boundary

According to the proposal of the Royal Commission, the boundary line ran through the southern Jezreel Valley as far as Megiddo, and twice bisected the Wadi Ara road. From there it joined the coastal plain through the southern tributaries of the Carmel, crossed the Petah Tiqva–Tulkarm–Haifa road twice, and the railway to Haifa. East of Lydda it met up with the mandatory enclave (see Map 3). The boundary proposed by the Agency Executive ran from Jenin through the northern and western tributaries of Samaria, by-passed Tulkarm and connected with the mandatory enclave west of Modiin. Under this proposal, the Wadi Ara road, the railway to Haifa and the road east of it were included in their entirety within the Jewish State (see Map 3).

The boundary line proposed by the Executive was based on security considerations, control of water sources and important transportation arteries. In determining this boundary line, no considerations of expanding the area of the Jewish State for settlement purposes applied: 'From an agricultural standpoint the land on these slopes is of no great value.'[99]

The Boundaries Committee arrived at the conclusion that the northern peak of the Samarian Hills in the vicinity of the villages of Yamon and Um El-Fahem controlled the mountain area in its vicinity. From there and from nearby Mount Gilboa enemy incursions from the south could be blocked (see Map 4).[100] Members of the Committee attached great importance to the inclusion of the Wadi Ara road in its entire length within the boundaries of the Jewish State. This road connected the coastal plain with the Jezreel Valley and the Galilee, and would function as one of the principal transportation arteries of the Jewish State. In contradistinction, the Arab State had no need of this artery.[101] In the light of these considerations, the Boundaries Committee pondered the exact siting of the boundary line, because the desired siting from a strategic standpoint included within the area of the Jewish State five large Arab villages, including Um El-Fahem, which meant the addition of more than 5,000 Arabs. Joseph Weitz, in a special memorandum that he prepared along with Lifshitz, recommended leaving the large Arab villages of Um El-Fahem and Yamon within the Arab State but including the entire Wadi Ara axis within the Jewish State.[102] In the final analysis, the Agency Executive decided to move the boundary along a line that would be desirable from a defense standpoint, although this meant that the Arab villages would be included in the Jewish State. It appeared that in addition to the desire to control the hills to the south, the need to distance the border from the Wadi Ara axis proved decisive.

With regards to the eastern boundary of the Jewish State, strategic considerations again took center stage. The preservation of the narrow and densely settled strip of the coastal plain made it necessary to keep the border away from the eastern tip of the plain, at least towards the slope descending from Samaria. Then perhaps it would be possible to prevent attacks from the mountain region in the area of the Arab State, and occupy a sufficient number of positions 'from which one could peer into the hilly convolutions facing Nablus and Ramallah and from where one could protect the border against incursions from the East'.[103] Nonetheless, doubts were raised about the boundary's utility against artillery attack.[104] In any case, it was clear to the Agency Executive that it would be unrealistic to demand moving the boundary eastwards into the interior of Samaria and the very heart of Arab settlement.[105] The line which the Executive's proposal sought represented the indispensable minimum.

No less central to the determination of the eastern boundary was the need to control the water resources. The boundary line proposed by the Executive, afforded control over appreciable amounts of subterranean waters, and the source of the springs that flowed from the hills towards the plain; in addition, it allowed for the erection of dams to store upper run-off water that flowed down from the slopes, or to introduce it into the depths of the soil as subterranean waters. In such a fashion one could exploit the upper run-off waters that flowed down to the sea as well as subterranean waters for the purpose of Jewish settlement in the coastal plain. Control over water resources was of immense importance, given the apprehension that sources in the coastal plain would be depleted owing to increased water usage in an intensive agricultural economy. This difficulty could thwart the plan of predicating future settlement in the coastal plain on intensive agriculture as well. There was also fear that the Arabs would poison these water resources if they were to remain within the areas of their state. In a concluding memorandum presented to the British Partition Commission, the Executive emphasized that the water flowing from the mountains could not be used to irrigate territories in the Arab State, and therefore the proposed boundary line did not do harm to the Arab State.[106]

Two additional principles influenced the definition of the eastern boundary line: the first principle was to add territories containing a sparse Arab population. Owing to this consideration, Tulkarm was left in the area of the Arab State. The second principle was to avoid dividing major transportation arteries and therefore the Wadi Ara road, the Lydda–Haifa rail line and the Petah Tiqva–Tulkarm–Haifa road were left within the Jewish State. The inclusion of important longitudinal roads within the Jewish State was important for strategic, administrative and economic reasons. As may be recalled, under the Royal Commission's proposal, the boundary would have cut across these roads twice.[107]

The Boundaries Committee recommended to the Executive two alternatives regarding the eastern boundary line. Following the eastern alternative, the boundary line would pass through the Samarian slopes in a series of hills east of the boundary line proposed by the Royal Commission. The Committee emphasized that the eastern alternative was superior from a strategic standpoint. According to the western alternative, the boundary line ran three kilometers west of the other proposal at an inferior topographical height. This was proposed as a compromise in the event that the British proved unwilling to accept the eastern alternative.[108] The Executive decided to embrace the eastern alternative and presented this demand to the Partition Commission (see Map 4). Lifshitz leaned towards recommending the eastern alternative, whereas Brawer and Weitz feared the addition of Arab residents in the Jewish State implicit in this alternative.[109] It would appear that more than the issue of a bargaining counter, the strategic consideration proved decisive. Thus, for example, Ben-Gurion repeatedly emphasized over that period that the need to place the eastern boundary at a distance, up to the hilly line, stemmed from strategic considerations.[110] The choice of the eastern alternative did indeed result in the addition of 30 Arab villages to the Jewish State, but these were sparsely settled.[111] Nonetheless, the boundary line proposed by the Executive separated a number of villages from their areas of cultivation, and detached the villagers south of Tulkarm from their work places,[112] and the market for their produce.[113]

The southern boundary of the Jewish State

According to the Royal Commission's proposal, the mandatory corridor cut the Jewish State into two. The southern half of the state included the coastal plain until the Beer Tuviah–Isdud line (see Map 5). The Executive's proposal for this part of the Jewish State called for widening the area of the Jewish State northwards, eastwards and southwards – both at the expense of the mandatory corridor and at the expense of the Arab State (see Map 5). The main expansion was south to Ruhama and until the northern coast to Majdal.

The Executive's proposal concerning the Jewish State's southern portion was intended to achieve four goals: (1) restricting to a minimum the salient that divided the Jewish State into two; (2) obtaining to the extent possible a defensible border; (3) territorial expansion for economic settlement purposes; (4) the inclusion of Jewish settlements and Jewish-owned land within the Jewish State and avoiding cutting off the Jewish settlements from their land.

According to the Royal Commission proposal, the western portion of the mandatory corridor running from the coast until the Qazaza–Gimzo line caused the Jewish State to be divided into two parts separated from each other by two to six kilometers. Some Jewish settlements were removed from the Jewish State and had been transferred to the mandatory corridor. Other settlements were severed from their lands.[114] The southern portion of the Jewish State stretched over more than half a million dunams, (10 per cent of the total area of the Jewish State). Only about 40 per cent of

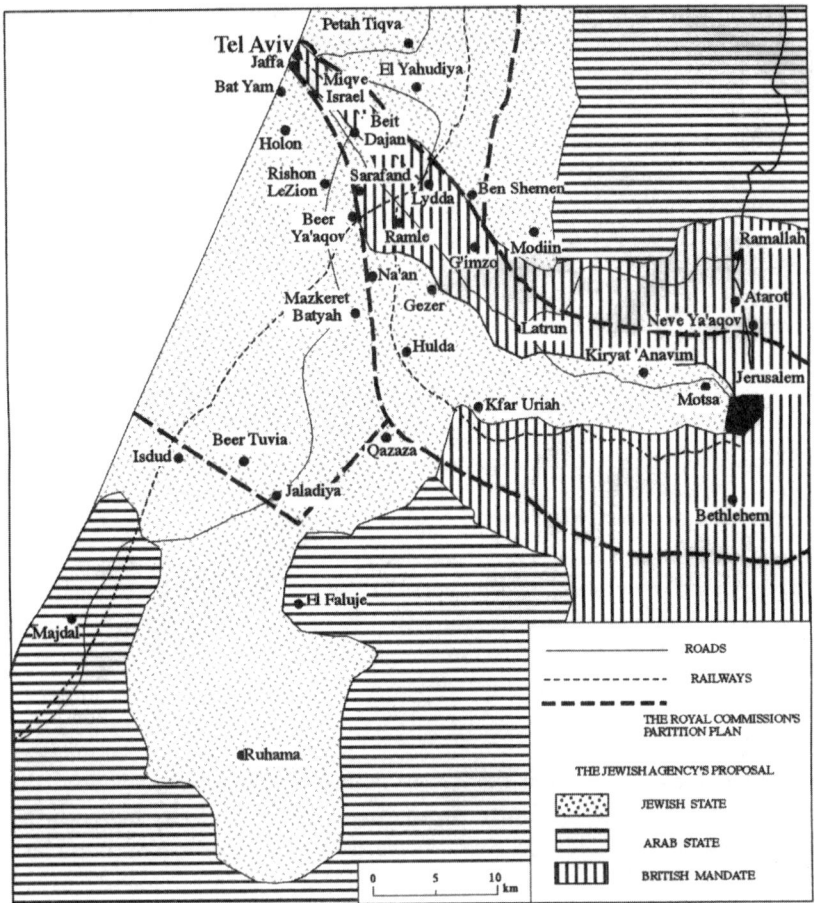

Map 5: Partition Proposal of Jewish Agency Executive for Southern Palestine, 1938

its inhabitants were Jews (about 19,000 out of 47,000).[115] Lifshitz warned of the harmful repercussions that would result if the Jewish State were divided into two parts:

> The portion of the Jewish State that extends south of the British Corridor is according to the official proposal of such minuscule portions and area and in such a case the number of its inhabitants will be limited. It will therefore find it difficult to survive in times of emergency should it be separated from the main portion of the state. This area from an economic standpoint and in terms of supply and sales is connected by a strong and vital bond to the city of Tel Aviv. Therefore the creation of an artificial separation with a broad territorial

expanse between them can exert a harmful influence on their future development. Undesirable elements can settle in the corridor area who would not be subject to the authority of the Jewish State since the corridor will be under a special mandatory jurisdiction. They can develop settlement forms and economic activities that are detrimental to the interests of the Jewish State and will thus exert a harmful influence upon it. These elements will also constitute a perpetual internal danger to the Jewish State. The social and economic harmony of the Jewish State will be hindered by this interposed barrier if its area within the state's borders will be of sizable proportions ...

The salient would have an especially harmful influence on the development of Tel Aviv and its daughter cities to the south: Holon and Bat Yam. Lifshitz expounded on this point:

The city of Tel Aviv has displayed in recent years a tendency to expand and grow to the south and to the southeast where many of the areas were purchased by Jews and earmarked for expanding the city limits. Appreciable sums have been invested by companies and individuals towards purchasing and preparing these lands. A wide and divisive corridor will cut off this entire bloc of lands from Tel Aviv and the city will be unable to expand and progress vigorously in this direction and it will be forced to turn northwards where the territorial opportunities are far more restricted ...[116]

Including Jaffa within the borders of the Jewish State[117] would have provided some alleviation for Tel Aviv and would have prevented the intrusion of a dangerous buffer belonging to the Arab State between the two portions of the Jewish State, since Jaffa was to be an Arab enclave under the Royal Commission proposal. However, such a demand was not realistic. It was obvious that the British would reject it, even on the sole ground that they could not consent to establish a Jewish State that from the day of its establishment would host an Arab majority. Furthermore, if such a request were granted, the Executive would have forfeited its principal argument for retaining the western portion of Jerusalem within the boundaries of the Jewish State (see below).[118] The proposal to demand the abolition of the corridor from the west to Ramle, and thus to unify the two parts of the Jewish State, was similarly not a realistic one. It was clear to the Boundaries Committee that the British could not forgo free passage subject to their control from Jerusalem to the coast. For this reason, the proposal formulated by one of the Boundary Committee's sub-committees, which demanded the cancellation of the corridor running west of Ramle to the sea but transferred to British ownership the road from Ramle to Jaffa, was also rejected.[119] The solution that crystallized in the Boundaries Committee and the Executive was to whittle the corridor down to the very minimum in the areas where it passed through the Jewish State. The width of the corridor was narrowed to seven kilometers in the area south-east of Ramle and to only 400 meters north-west of Lydda and to the sea (see Map 5). In this area the corridor included the railway and a strip of 200 meters on either side. South of the railway a new road was to be laid within the confines of the British enclave. A system of bridges or tunnels would have connected the two parts of the Jewish State from the Ramle region to the sea, and thus 'both parts of the Jewish State located north and south of the corridor would constitute a contiguous bloc separated by an artificial obstacle which one could regard as only a topographical obstacle'.[120]

The proposal to narrow the corridor served a number of purposes. First of all, it was designed to achieve a unification of both portions of the Jewish State. Secondly, it solved the problem of the development of Tel Aviv, Holon and Bat Yam. Thirdly, it was to provide additional land for settlement (some of which was already Jewish owned) north of Rishon LeZion and south of the moshava Yehudiya and primarily in the Judean plain, south-east of Ramle (part of which such as the lands of the abandoned settlements of Kfar Uriah and Gezer, were already Jewish owned). Fourthly, the area of the Jewish State would include settlements that originally would have formed part of the British corridor (Naan, Hulda and Ben Shemen), or areas belonging to agricultural settlements that remained in the Jewish State under the original plan but lost their lands to the corridor (Miqve Israel, Beer Ya'aqov, Mazkeret Batyah).[121]

In this region, a strategic consideration also guided the planners to situate the boundary line as a feasible defense line at the foot of the Judean Hills:[122] 'However, heeding the principle of not introducing a surplus Arab population into the Jewish State, if there was no special need to so, the boundary line was diverted diagonally to the southwest to leave the populated Arab community of El Faluje on the other side of the border.'[123] The villages north of El Faluje were not included within the Jewish State, and neither were the town of Majdal and the villages east of it.

The southern boundary lines of the Jewish State were determined by economic–settlement considerations of adding a generally unsettled land reserve that was considered suitable for settlement.[124] As Lifshitz adds:

In this part of the country major land purchases have not occurred and the process of additional crowding of residents has not manifested itself. In addition, this part of the Beersheba District east and north of Ruhama is totally barren of permanent settlement and is in the possession of a not too sizable

Bedouin tribe. This area can therefore serve as a natural reserve for expansion
and hence should be included within the Jewish area ...[125]

The areas added included Jewish-owned lands (such as the areas of
abandoned Ruhama and the lands of Beer Tuvia).[126] Wadi Sharia served
as a natural boundary for the proposed Jewish State on the southern side.[127]

The boundaries of the permanent British mandate

The Royal Commission limited the size of the permanent British Mandate
to a corridor that stretched from the vicinity of Jerusalem until the
Mediterranean Sea. The Jewish Agency Executive, with the intention of
securing Zionist goals, proposed that the British mandate should cover
more extensive areas. Nonetheless, when it came to West Jerusalem the
Executive sought its inclusion within the Jewish State (see the following
chapter for details). Areas of the corridor as proposed by the Royal Commission were constricted in the Executive's counter-proposal to benefit
the Jewish State, but they were broadened to the north and south of
Jerusalem and to its east. The most important expansion was suggested
in the Negev and in the Dead Sea area. As a result, the original mandatory
territory was transformed from a limited enclave into a capacious state.
All the expansions in favor of the mandatory state were to come at the
expense of the areas allotted to the Arab State (see Map 3).

The expansion of the areas remaining under the British mandate was
intended to restrict the areas of the Arab State following the assumption
that areas of the mandate would be open to Jewish settlement. This gave
rise to the hope that over time these areas would be added to the Jewish
State. Furthermore, the expansion of the mandatory areas allowed for the
inclusion of Jewish settlements and Jewish-owned land that otherwise
would have fallen within the Arab state, since there was no way of incorporating them within the boundaries of the Jewish State.[128]

We have noted the Zionist demand to restrict the width of the area of
the mandate west and east of Ramle. Despite the difficulties and special
limitations that the mandatory corridor imposed upon the Jewish State,
the Executive did not propose the abolition of the corridor, since there
were no prospects for securing this request. In the Boundaries Committee,
certain proposals were actually made to call for the abrogation of the
corridor proposed by the Royal Commission (while adding Lydda and
Ramle to the Arab State under one proposal, or joining them to the Jewish
State once a population transfer had been effected, according to the other
proposal) and to limit the British enclave to Jerusalem and Bethlehem
alone. In this context, the possibility was suggested that the British outlet

to the Mediterranean Sea should be via Hebron and Gaza. Moshe Smilansky, a Committee member, went even further and proposed surrendering the Galilee in return for the abolition of the corridor. However, as already said, the Committee reached the conclusion that from the Zionist standpoint, as well, the existence of the corridor was positive, although it should be limited to the contours described above.

For two reasons the Boundaries Committee viewed the existence of the corridor with favor. First of all, it excluded Lydda and Ramle with their Arab residents from the areas of the Jewish State but did not include them in the Arab State – a proposal that reduced the danger to the Jewish State. Secondly, the corridor diminished the size of the Arab State by a million dunams, and members of the Committee assumed that in a large portion of this area Jewish settlement would be permitted.[129]

The intention behind the northwards expansion of the mandate's beyond Jerusalem until the north of Ramallah was to include the Jewish agricultural villages of Atarot and Neve Ya'akov within the confines of the mandate as well as 7,000 dunams of Jewish-owned land north of Jerusalem. Atarot airfield was also included in the mandate's area to the north. According to the Royal Commission's proposal, all these areas fell to the Arab State.[130] It is nearly certain (as Lifshitz hints) that fixing this boundary north of Ramallah was intended to facilitate the inclusion of the road from Jaffa that linked up to Jerusalem from the north and was located entirely within the area of the mandatory corridor. The northern road entering Jerusalem from the coast passed through Ramallah (nonetheless, the avowed reason for including Ramallah was that most of its inhabitants were Christians). Members of the Executive assumed that this would make it easier to persuade the British to accept a demand for a Jewish corridor running south of Ramle until Jerusalem, which would encompass Jewish agricultural settlements (including Motsa and Kiryat 'Anavim at the approaches to Jerusalem). The Jerusalem–Jaffa highway passed through this corridor up to Latrun, as did the railway to Jerusalem from the southwest to Kfar Uriah and until south of Ramle – two transportation arteries that were vital to the British (see Map 5).[131]

An expansion of the mandatory areas south of Jerusalem until Hebron was intended first and foremost to exclude Jewish-owned Kfar Etzion and Jewish-owned lands in Nahhalin from the area of the Arab State. In total, the issue concerned about 8,500 dunams of primarily Jewish-owned land that had been purchased during the 1920s and 1930s. The Executive additionally contended that the inclusion of Hebron, holy to the Jews, within the Arab State was inconceivable and therefore demanded the transfer of these areas to the mandate (see Map 3).[132]

The expansion of the area of the mandate east of Jerusalem and up to the Dead Sea was intended to include the potash works north of the Dead Sea and to its south within the boundaries of the British mandate, thus allowing Jewish organizations to continue exploiting the Sea's resources and coasts. The Executive attached great economic importance to these projects, because they could serve as a basis for developing a large and diversified chemical industry, especially as 'Jewish Palestine will in large measure have to be based economically on the development of industry'.[133] There was even talk of the possibility of oil discoveries in the vicinity of Mount Sodom. To justify its demands, the Executive contended that the inclusion of the region within the area of the Arab State penalized Jewish entrepreneurs and deprived the Jewish State from enjoying the fruits of the Jewish labor that had been expended to this date. It was emphasized that only Jewish–Zionist entrepreneurship was interested in the continued exploitation of the Sea's treasures. This hinted that if the region was allowed to remain within the area of the Arab State it would result in the liquidation of the existing plants. British investors who had invested capital in the potash works would also be injured.[134]

The Negev south of the Beersheba–Khan Yunis line was the principal region located in the Arab State that the Agency sought to transfer to the area of the British Mandate. This request was accompanied by a demand to receive a charter for Jewish settlement in the region. The Executive identified three spheres where the Negev was important from the Zionist standpoint: as a territorial reserve for Jewish settlement; as a potential source of raw materials, including the possibility of oil discoveries; and as a link to the Gulf of Aqaba – 'Palestine's gateway to the Red Sea, the Indian Ocean and beyond' – which could serve as a substitute for the Suez Canal.[135] The Executive was also aware of the implicit difficulties in developing the Negev as a settlement region, especially given the shortage of water. To this, it countered that only Jewish bodies would have both the interest and the ability to invest huge amounts of capital and exploit scientific know-how and skilled labor in order to overcome these difficulties.[136] In contradistinction, if these areas were left within the Arab State: 'It would consign a vast area to doom ... which is almost totally devoid of settlement. There is no prospect or possibility that the Arabs could develop this waste and make it blossom.'[137]

The Executive contended that from a British standpoint also it was worthwhile to include the Negev within the area of the mandate, as it would gain a Jewish population favorably disposed to Britain at the entrance to Aqaba and in the vicinity of British concentrations in Egypt. Furthermore, this population in the Negev would guarantee the alternative transportation artery (a railway which crossed the Negev), which would connect the Red Sea with the Mediterranean. This would remain functional even if Britain's position on the Suez Canal became threatened.[138] In addition, 'the importance of Aqaba to the British Empire as a port and perhaps as a naval base could be realized at a minimal expense if the Jews would be allowed to exercise their energies in the development of Aqaba and the adjacent region'.[139]

Let us note that the Executive was aware that the British government was pondering the question of the Negev within the framework of partition, and was inclined to retain it in British hands. Among other reasons, the Egyptian government was opposed to having as its neighbor an Arab State 'which would serve as an additional place for Italian and German intrigues against the Egyptian government. Egypt had a bitter experience regarding her borders with Libya which were in Italian hands'.[140] Thoughts were mooted within the Executive about including the Negev within the areas of the Jewish State. However, in the end, the Executive waived this demand, for two principal reasons. Firstly, there was no chance, once the Royal Commission had awarded the entire Galilee to the Jewish State, and the Executive had vigorously decided that one should not yield portions of the Galilee in favor of the Negev. There was also concern that, if the Executive vigorously demanded the Negev, the British might award the Galilee to the Arabs in return for the Negev. Secondly, anxiety was expressed over the absence of real Jewish settlement in the Negev. As long as this situation prevailed, control of the region would prove burdensome to the Jewish State, which would become embroiled with the Bedouin, and perhaps with the ruler of Saudi Arabia. As was the case with other areas of the Arab State that the Executive sought to transfer to the British mandate, the Executive hoped that the Negev would also in the course of years be turned over to the Jewish State.[141]

SUMMARY OF THE JEWISH AGENCY EXECUTIVE'S PARTITION BOUNDARY PROPOSALS

The proposals of the Jewish Agency Executive for partition boundaries were subjected to criticism to ensure that they would appear plausible and logical to the British and would seek what was compulsory from a Jewish standpoint in security, economic-settlement and political terms. In order to achieve this, the Executive sought to demonstrate that the modifications that it proposed did not harm the Arab State and coincided with British interests. The security, economic-settlement and political considerations influenced the Executive in its deliberations on the boundaries in the various regions, although each of these considerations was not necessarily factored equally in every region. Nonetheless, the fact emerges that the security consideration occupied a central position in the considerations of the Executive, especially in comparison with the place that the Royal Commission assigned it in crafting the boundaries.[142]

The Royal Commission assumed that the very act of political partition and separation between the two populations, to be further abetted by population transfers, would produce peace between Jews and Arabs. The Executive, it becomes clear, did not share the prognosis of the Royal Commission regarding the prospects for 'peace and goodwill between the peoples on either side of it [the boundary line]' even after partition. It seems that the Executive's gut feeling that the future was uncertain was fueled by the Arab disturbances of that time and by the British government's rejection of forced transfer of the Arab population. In view of all these circumstances, there remained a need for defensible boundaries, strategic depth and guaranteed transportation arteries.[143]

The Executive did not actually express a clear position on the question of whether the boundaries of the Jewish State with its neighboring Arab State would be open or closed. However, in one of its deliberations on the issue of boundaries, a member contended that 'free movement on the boundaries should not be allowed. In all states this freedom was granted only when permanent relations existed and there was no fear of traitors. In the initial stage the boundaries were closed.'[144] Members of the Executive did not express opposition to these words. There was also agreement that Arab settlements should not be allowed to remain in the frontier area: 'The question of who would sit on the frontier is one of the main strategic and security problems of the Jewish State. If Arab settlements are to remain in the frontier, then no patrol can be of any avail and no army could prove of assistance. One of the strategic conditions of the country must be the placement of Jewish settlements on the frontier.'[145] In response to a question from the British Partition Commission, the Executive followed the recommendations of the Security Committee that it had appointed. The Executive made it clear that, for strategic considerations, Jewish settlements would be established along the boundary lines[146] and that the boundary line itself would be fenced.[147]

NOTES

1. Cohen, G. (1973), pp. 346–82; Geva (1980), pp. 105–9; Kimmerling (1976), pp. 45–7; Heller (1984), pp. 19–21; CZA, Protocols of the Jewish Agency Executive's Meetings on 10 July 1936, 21 October 1936 (morning session), 21 October 1936 (afternoon session),

22 January 1936, 23 November 1936, 10 January 1937, 11 April 1937.

2. Heller (1984), p. 20; Fraser (1984), p. 659.

3. PRO file CO 733/348, letter from Weizmann to Ormsby-Gore on 15 June 1937; see Protocols of the Jewish Agency Executive's Meetings on 6 June 1937, 17 June 1937; Geva (1980), pp. 97ff., 110, 167; Fraser (1988); Rose (1970, 1971); CZA, Protocols of the Jewish Agency Executive's Meetings on 21 June 1937 and 8 July 1937.

4. See, for details, the twentieth Zionist Congress, stenographic report, 1937, the addresses of Weizmann, Ben-Gurion, Shertok, Ruppin and Gruenbaum. The first citation is from Weizmann's address, ibid., p. 32; the second from Gruenbaum, ibid., p. 130; Galnoor (1991); Kimmerling (1976); Shapira (1984); Eliash (1971); Reichman, *et al.* (1997); CZA, file S25/272, Horowitz's Memorandum 'Economic Aspects of Partition', May 1938; CZA, file S25/10110, Horowitz's Memorandum: 'Scheme for the Industrial Development of Palestine', July 1937; CZA, file S25/5113, letter from Horowitz to Kaplan on 2 August 1937; Elazari (1955), Vol. 4, pp. 154–7.

5. Fraser (1988), especially pp. 657–66; Geva (1980), pp. 187–9, 204; CZA, file S25/993, letter from Weizmann to Bernard Joseph of 22 July 1937; PRO, file CO 733/348, letter from Weizmann to Ormsby-Gore on 15 June 1937 where he writes, *inter alia*: 'As I told you, I am not in any sense committed to any partition scheme, but I am anxious as always to be helpful to H.M. Government, and in accordance with your suggestion, I here set out very briefly what, in my view, would be the minimum requirements for a Jewish State ... It is in my view unlikely that the scheme would prove workable, and I doubt whether any responsible Jewish leader could ask his people to consider it'; CZA, Protocols of the Jewish Agency Executive's Meetings on 17 July 1937, 1 August 1937; ibid., Protocols of the Meeting of the Inner Zionist General Council on 21 June 1937 and 3 November 1937.

6. CZA, Protocols of the Jewish Agency Executive's Meetings on 17 June 1937, 4 July 1937, 8 July 1937 and 1 August 1937; CZA, Protocol of the Meeting of the Inner Zionist General Council on 21 June 1937; the twentieth Zionist Congress, stenographic report, 1937, pp. 23–33, 57–8, 70–4, 95–122, 128–31, 170–7, 192–200, 348–52 (addresses at the congress by Weizmann, Ben-Gurion, Shertok, Ruppin and Gruenbaum).

7. For details regarding the deliberations of the congress, see Dothan (1979); Geva (1980); Shapira (1984); Eliash (1971); Galnoor (1991); Beeley (1937), pp. 545–8.

8. The twentieth Zionist Congress, stenographic report, pp. 359–60. See also Beeley, (1937), p. 546.

9. The twentieth Zionist Congress, stenographic report; CZA, Protocols of the Jewish Agency Executive's Meetings on 8 July 1937, 1 August 1937, 25 October 1937, 2 November 1937; CZA, Protocol of the Meeting of the Inner Zionist General Council on 3 November 1937.

10. CZA, Protocols of the Jewish Agency Executive's Meetings on 10 January 1937, 7 February 1937, 2 August 1937, 19 April 1937, 2 May 1937.

11. CZA, Protocols of the Jewish Agency Executive's Meetings on 17 October 1937, 2 November 1937; 21 November 1937, 29 November 1937, 12 December 1937, 2 January 1938, 13 February 1938, 16 February 1938, 8 May 1938, 29 May 1938, 14 July 1938; CZA, Protocols of the Inner Zionist General Council's Meetings on 3 November 1937, 18 May 1938, 11 July 1938; Eliash (1971), p. 92.

12. See, for example, CZA, Protocols of the Jewish Agency Executive's Meetings on 2 November 1937, 21 November 1937 (morning session), 21 November 1937 (afternoon session), 29 November 1937; CZA, Protocols of the Inner Zionist General Council's Meetings on 20 June 1938 and 11 July 1938.

13. Political Report of the Jewish Agency Executive for Palestine, 1939, pp. 8–10; see, for example, CZA, Protocols of the Jewish Agency Executive's Meetings on 21 November 1937, 12 December 1937; CZA, Protocol of the Inner Zionist General Council's Meeting on 3 November 1937.

14. CZA, Protocol of the Inner Zionist General Council's Meeting on 3 November 1937.

15. CZA, Protocol of the Inner Zionist General Council's Meeting on 20 June 1938.

16. The twenty-first Zionist Congress, stenographic report, 1939, p. 35; CZA, Protocols of the Jewish Agency Executive's Meetings on 2 November 1937, 21 November 1937 (morning), 21 November 1937 (afternoon), 29 November 1937, 8 May 1938, 16 May 1938, 23 May 1938, 25 May 1938, 29 May 1938, 7 June 1938, 14 July 1938; CZA, Protocols of the Inner Zionist General Council's Meetings on 18 May 1938, 20 June 1938; CZA, Protocol of the Jewish Agency Executive's Meeting with the Political Committee of the Inner Zionist General Council on 12 June 1938.

17. See pp. 4–6.

18. One should note that this was not the first time that the World Zionist Organization had drawn up political boundaries in the context of Palestine. Nineteen years previously, in 1919, the World Zionist Organization had submitted its demands to the Peace Conference regarding the boundaries of Palestine. These expressed its outlook regarding the ideal boundaries for a Jewish State: in the south – the Egypt–Aqaba line; in the east – along the Trans-Jordan desert; and in the north – along the line extending from the Mediterranean south of Sidon until Beit Jan. For these boundaries and the inherent logic governing their determination, see in detail Gelber (1960); Report of the Executive of the Zionist Organization (1921), pp. 33–9. In the years 1937–38, the Political Department employed the material that had accumulated in the archives of the World Zionist Organization on Zionist demands at the Peace Conference regarding the boundaries of Palestine. On this see CZA, file S25/5143, letter from Gelber to Shertok on 30 August 1938.

19. CZA, Protocol of the Jewish Agency Executive's Meeting on 16 May 1938.

20. CZA, Protocol of the Inner Zionist General Council's Meeting on 18 May 1938.

21. CZA, Protocol of the Jewish Agency Executive's Meeting with the Political Committee of the Inner Zionist General Council on 12 June 1938 – Ben-Gurion's address. See also CZA, Protocols of the Jewish Agency Executive's Meetings on 8 May 1938, 16 May 1938, 29 May 1938, 7 June 1938, 4 July 1938. See also Protocols of the Inner Zionist General Council's Meetings on 18 May 1938, 20 June 1938 and 11 July 1938.

22. Dothan (1993), pp. 201–2.

23. CZA, file S25/10109, List of of the Boundaries Committee's members and a précis of its activity.

24. Zalman Lif (1953); CZA, file S25/5143, Protocol of the Boundaries Committee's Meeting on 1 December 1937; CZA, file S25/5120, letter from Simon to Shertok on 27 January 1938. The final map that was prepared and presented to the Partition Commission was appended to a report of the Partition Commission. See PPCR (1938), Map No. 17.

25. CZA, file S25/10110, letter from Simon to Shertok on 27 January 1938.

26. CZA, file S25/5156, memorandum submitted to the Palestine Partition Commission by the Executive of the Jewish Agency for Palestine: (1) the Resolutions of the Governing Bodies of the Zionist Organization and the Jewish Agency on the Conclusions of the Royal Commission; (2) The Partition Scheme of the Royal Commission, Jerusalem, 23 May 1938 (hereinafter CZA, The Executive's Memorandum to the Partition Commission); Ben-Gurion (1937), pp. 190, 274, 455 (the quotations are from there).

27. CZA, The Executive's Memorandum to the Partition Commission; CZA, file S25/3786, Ben-Gurion's comments on the Ormsby-Gore letter (undated, but undoubtedly from the start of of 1938).

28. CZA, The Executive's Memorandum to the Partition Commission; CZA, file S25/3786, Ben-Gurion (1937), p. 124 (citations from there); see also pp. 226, 323, 398, 455.

29. CZA, Protocol of the Jewish Agency Executive's Meeting on 7 June 1938.

30. Ben-Gurion (1937), p. 456.

31. CZA, Protocol of the Jewish Agency Executive's Meeting on 4 July 1937.

32. Sharett (1937), p. 259.

33. The twentieth Zionist Congress, stenographic report, 1937, p. 166.

34. CZA, Protocol of the Jewish Agency Executive's Meeting on 7 October 1938.

35. CZA, Protocol of the Inner Zionist General Council's Meeting on 20 June 1938.

36. CZA, file S25/5143, Protocol of the Boundaries Committee's Meeting on 1 December

1938.

37. Ben-Gurion (1937), p. 322.
38. CZA, file S25/6654, Zalman Lifshitz's Summary Report: 'The Boundaries Committee – Proposals for Partitioning the Country' on 14 April 1938 (hereinafter CZA, Lifshitz – Concluding Report).
39. CZA, The Executive's Memorandum to the Partition Commission.
40. Ben-Gurion (1937), p. 455.
41. CZA, file S25/5138, Protocol of the Water Committee, 19 May 1938.
42. CZA, The Executive's Memorandum to the Partition Commission.
43. CZA, file S25/5154, Report of an Appraisal of the Boundaries from a Security Perspective, on 26 July 1937 (the report was apparently authored by A. Zelikowitz and the citations are from there). See also CZA, file S25/5143, letter from Simon to Zelikowitz, 18 April 1938; CZA, file S25/10054, letter from Zelikowitz to Simon, 23 April 1938; CZA, file S25/10109, A Précis of the Boundaries Committee's Activities; CZA, file S25/10066, letter from Ben-Gurion to Shertok, 3 July 1937; CZA, file S25/5143, Protocol of the Boundaries Committee, 10 November 1937; CZA, file S25/5120, letter from Simon to Shertok, 27 January 1938; CZA, Lifshitz – Concluding Report; CZA, file S25/3786, Ben-Gurion's comment on Ormsby-Gore's letter; Ben-Gurion (1937), pp. 131, 254, 323, 398, 455.
44. CZA, The Executive's Memorandum to the Partition Commission.
45. CZA, file S25/10054, Ben-Gurion's proposal for a tripartite partition, 3 December 1937 (also published in Ben-Gurion [1937], pp. 455–7). See also CZA, file S25/5145, letter from Berl Katznelson to Weizmann, 27 April 1937, which deals in detail with the subversive potential of the large Arab minority scheduled to remain in the Jewish State. See the letter in Heller (1984), pp. 190–3.
46. CZA, Lifshitz – Concluding Report; CZA, file S25/5143, Lifshitz's report submitted to the Executive: 'On the Question of Villages Located on the Frontier'.
47. CZA, file S25/10054, comments on a partition proposal apparently written by J. Weitz, 19 July 1937; CZA, file S25/5143, Protocol of the Boundaries Committee, 10 November 1937; CZA, file S25/5120, letter from Simon to Shertok, 27 January 1938; CZA, Lifshitz – Concluding Report; CZA, file S25/3786, Ben-Gurion's comments on the Ormbsy-Gore letter; Sharett (1937), p. 316; Sharett (1938), p. 126. This was also the directive given to the Partition Commission: to draw up boundaries that would require the inclusion of the minimum number of Arabs and Arab enterprises possible in the Jewish area, and vice versa. On this see PPCR (1938), pp. 7–8. Nonetheless, the Zionist position on this issue would have been presented in the same manner in any event.
48. CZA, file S25/8121, letter from Dr. Avnimelech to the Political Department of the Jewish Agency, 11 July 1937; CZA, file S25/5143, Protocol of the Boundaries Committee, 10 November 1937; CZA, file S25/5120, letter from Simon to Shertok, 27 January 1938; CZA, Lifshitz – Concluding Report; CZA, file S25/8122, letter from Picard to the Political Department, July 1938; CZA, Memorandum of the Executive to the Partition Commission; CZA, file S25/10109, a précis of the Boundaries Committee's Activities; Ben-Gurion (1937), pp. 61, 67, 131, 207, 243, 266, 455. See also PRO, file CO 733/348, letter from Weizmann to Ormsby-Gore on 15 June 1937; Ibid., letter from Pinhas Rutenberg to Sir John Maffey on 5 June 1937.
49. CZA, Lifshitz – Concluding Report (citation is from there). See also CZA, file S25/5143, Protocol of the Boundaries Committee's meeting on 22 November 1937; CZA, letter from Simon to Vilenstuck, on 11 May 1938; CZA, file S25/5138, Protocols of the Water Committee's meetings on 19 May 1938, 27 May 1938; CZA, file S25/5143 Protocol of the Boundaries Committee's meeting on 10 November 1937; CZA, file S25/5138, Report on the Partition Problem from the Hydrological Point of View, apparently composed by the Water Committee, undated. See also PPCR (1938), pp. 251–5, especially 254–5.
50. CZA, file S25/10054, Report of Zalman Lifshitz 'Possible Boundaries of the Jewish State as a Result of the Partition of Western Palestine into two Separate Authorities' on 15 July

1938 (hereinafter: Lifshitz – Preliminary Report); CZA, Lifshitz –Concluding Report; CZA, file S25/10109, a précis of the Boundaries Committee's Activities.

51. CZA, file S25/10054, Comments on the Partition Proposal, apparently written by Weitz, 19 July 1937; CZA, file S25/5143, Protocol of the Boundaries Committee's meeting on 10 November 1937; CZA, file S25/5120, letter from Simon to Shertok, 27 January 1938; CZA, file S25/10109; CZA, file S25/3786, Ben-Gurion's comments on the Ormsby-Gore letter; CZA, Lifshitz – Concluding Report.

52. CZA, S25/5145, letter from Berl Katznelson to Weizmann, 27 April 1937; CZA., Lifshitz – Concluding Report. See also Gruenbaum's comments on this issue in CZA, Protocol of the Jewish Agency Executive's meeting on 1 August 1937.

53. See the twentieth Zionist Congress, stenographic report, 1937, pp. 74–5, Katznelson's statement.

54. See the twentieth Zionist Congress, stenographic report, 1937, pp. 174–5, Shertok's statement.

55. CZA, file S25/5120, letter from Simon to Shertok, 27 January 1938. See also CZA, Lifshitz – Concluding Report; CZA, file S25/10054, comments apparently written by Weitz for a partition proposal; CZA, file S25/5143 Protocol of the Boundaries Committee on 10 November 1937.

56. Ben-Gurion (1937), pp. 65, 197, 206–7, 211, 222; CZA, file S25/5145, letter from Berl Katznelson to Weizmann, on 27 April 1937; Sharett (1937), p. 197; see also CZA, file S25/5150, Memorandum of Dr. S. Hareli: 'The Jews in Galilee'; CZA, file S25/3791, the Executive's Memorandum: 'Jewish Settlement in Galilee', August 1938.

57. Sharett (1937), pp. 220–1; see also PRO file CO 733/348, in note 48.

58. Ben-Gurion (1937), pp. 198, 264, 276.

59. Ibid., p. 293.

60. CZA, file S25/3786, Ben-Gurion's comments on the Ormsby-Gore letter; CZA, file S25/5138, Protocol of the Water Committee, 19 May 1938. See also Shertok's statement at the Inner Zionist General Council on 3 November 1937, noting, *inter alia*: '... to the extent of what we have heard from circles in the British government, various modifications are being considered, some for good and some for ill. Regarding boundaries, the main point where the ill favored modifications are concentrated is the question of the Galilee'.

61. CZA, Protocol of the Jewish Agency Executive's meeting on 29 May 1938.

62. Sharett (1938), p. 116. Already in June 1937, Shertok responded on the question of priorities posed by the High Commissioner and stated: '... I regret that I cannot respond to this ... from my point of view, it is the equivalent of being asked would you prefer to lose an eye or a leg? In order to answer this type of question you have to agree at first to be maimed and this is something that I cannot and do not have to do ...' On this, see Sharett (1937), p. 220.

63. See, for example, Ben-Gurion (1937), pp. 278 (citation from there), 308, 331, 367.

64. CZA, file S25/5143, Protocol of the Boundaries Committee's meeting on 1 December 1937; CZA, file S25/5138, Protocols of the Water Committee's meetings on 19 May 1938, and 27 May 1938.

65. CZA, file S25/7673, letter from Weitz to Bernard Joseph, on 5 December 1937. When the members of the Partition Commission asked the representatives of the Jewish Agency how they expected to settle the Galilee hills, they replied that the Jewish State would operate through governmental authorities to exploit the full potential of every corner in the country. On this, see Sharett (1938), p. 116.

66. CZA, file S25/10055, letter from Simon to Dr. S. Hareli, on 17 March 1938; a draft of the proposal was indeed prepared but it was not presented. On this see CZA, file S25/3791, Memorandum 'On Jewish Settlement in Galilee', August 1938.

67. Ben-Gurion (1937), p. 363. One should note that the boundary delineated by the Royal Commission for bisecting Lake Tiberias had already been proposed in the Sykes–Picot Treaty; but, pursuant to the French government's agreement to include Lake Tiberias in its entirety within the area of the British mandate and the Jewish national home, the

international boundary passed east of Lake Tiberias. On this, see CZA, file S25/5143, the Executive's Memorandum to the Partition Commission; CZA, file S25/5143, letter from Rutenberg to Ormsby-Gore, 29 July 1937.

68. CZA, file S25/5143, Protocol of the Boundary Committee's meeting on 10 November 1937; CZA, file S25/5143, Protocol of the Boundaries Committee's meeting on 22 November 1937 (citation from there); CZA, file S25/5143, letter from Rutenberg in note 67; CZA, file S25/5143, The Executive's Memorandum to the Partition Commission; CZA, Lifshitz – Concluding Report; CZA, file S25/10054, letter from Zelikowitz to Simon, 23 April 1938.

69. CZA, The Executive's Memorandum to the Partition Commission; CZA, Lifshitz – Concluding Report; CZA, Lifshitz – Preliminary Report; Sharett (1937), p. 243; Weitz, (1951), p. 54.

70. Sharett (1937), p. 243. See also Shertok's statement at the Jewish Agency Executive's meeting on 8 July 1937.

71. Ben-Gurion (1937), pp. 283, 289, 331, 355, 362–3, 455; Sharett (1937), pp. 144, 229; CZA, The Executive's Memorandum to the Partition Commission; CZA, Lifshitz – Concluding Report; CZA, file S25/5145, letter of the Jordan Valley Settlements to the Executive, undated; CZA, file S25/8932, Report of the PLDC Regarding the Lands of Samakh, 19 June 1938; CZA, file S25/10054, data on the Jewish settlements that were to remain within the Arab State or in the mandatory enclave, according to the Royal Commission's Report.

72. Ben-Gurion (1937), p. 289.

73. CZA, file S25/10066, letter from Ben-Gurion to Shertok, 3 July 1937 (appears also in Ben-Gurion [1937], pp. 276–80). Shertok opposed this fundamental position. See Sharett (1937), p. 259.

74. See Ben-Gurion (1937), p. 277.

75. CZA, Lifshitz – Concluding Report.

76. Ibid.; CZA, The Executive's Memorandum to the Partition Commission; CZA, file S25/5145, letter from Shertok to Rutenberg, 30 November 1937; CZA, file S25/5143, Protocol of the Boundaries Committee's meeting on 22 November 1937; CZA, letter from Rutenberg to Ormsby-Gore, on 29 July 1937. See also PRO in note 48, letter from Pinhas Rutenberg to Sir John Maffey, on 5 June 1937, who writes, *inter alia*, regarding the necessity to include the present Hydro-Electric Power House with the immediately surrounding territory: '... Independent of the cheap cost of power as an instrument of economical development in the country, the power houses would become the sole source of supply of power in case of emergency, when fuel could not be imported to Palestine'.

77. CZA, Lifshitz – Concluding Report; CZA, file S25/10054, letter from Zelikowitz to Simon, 23 April 1938; CZA, file S25/10066, letter from Ben-Gurion to Shertok, 3 July 1937.

78. CZA, file S25/5143, Protocol of the Boundaries Committee's meeting on 22 November 1937.

79. CZA, Lifshitz – Concluding Report; CZA, The Executive's Memorandum to the Partition Commission; CZA, file S25/5143, Protocol of the Boundaries Committee's meeting on 22 November 1937; CZA, file S25/5138, Protocol of the Water Committee's meeting on 19 May 1938.

80. CZA, Lifshitz – Concluding Report; CZA, The Executive's Memorandum to the Partition Commission; CZA, file S25/5143, Protocol of the Boundaries Committee's meeting on 22 November 1937.

81. CZA, file S25/5138, Protocol of the Water Committee's meeting on 19 May 1938.

82. PPCR (1938), pp. 111–14.

83. Sharett (1937), p. 229.

84. All of the area was government land, and it was turned over to the Arabs in the framework of the Ghor–Mudawara agreement. See CZA, Lifshitz – Concluding Report; CZA, The Executive's Memorandum to the Partition Commission; CZA, file S25/10054, Weitz's comments on the partition proposal; CZA, file S25/5138, Protocol of the Water

Committee's meeting on 19 May 1938; PPCR (1938), pp. 111–14; Ben-Gurion (1937), p. 455.

85. CZA, Lifshitz – Concluding Report.
86. CZA, The Executive's Memorandum to the Partition Commission; PPCR (1938), pp. 111–14; Ben-Gurion (1937), pp. 363–4. The citations are from PRCR (1937), pp. 259–62.
87. CZA, Lifshitz – Concluding Report. See also CZA, Lifshitz – Preliminary Report; CZA, file S25/5143, Protocol of the Partition Commission's meeting on 10 November 1937; CZA, file S25/10054, Report by Lifshitz and Zelikowitz, 12 November 1937.
88. CZA, file S25/10054, letter from Zelikowitz to Simon on 23 April 1938. According to this source, the effective range of the field artillery was 7–8 kilometers.
89. CZA, Lifshitz – Preliminary Report; CZA, The Executive's Memorandum to the Partition Commission.
90. CZA, file 25/10054, Report by Lifshitz and Zelikowitz, 12 December 1937.
91. PPCR (1938), pp. 113–14. It is unclear why Brawer contended in the Boundaries Committee during the session which took place on 22 November 1937 (CZA, file S25/5143), that the city totaled only a few hundred people.
92. CZA, Protocol of the Jewish Agency Executive's meeting on 4 July 1937.
93. See CZA file S25/10054, report by Lifshitz and Zelikowitz.
94. See CZA, Protocol of the Jewish Agency Executive's meeting on 4 July 1937; CZA, Lifshitz – Concluding Report. See CZA file S25/10054, in note 90.
95. According to the Royal Commission's Proposal, the village of Zirin, which controlled the south-eastern approaches of the Jezreel Valley, was to stay within the area of the Arab State and this hostile presence menaced entry to the valley from this region. On this see note 90.
96. CZA, file S25/5143, Protocol of the Boundaries Committee's meeting on 22 November 1937; CZA, file S25/10054, Report of Lifshitz and Zelikowitz, 12 December 1937.
97. CZA, file S25/10054, Protocol of the Boundaries Committee's meeting on 22 November 1937; CZA, Lifshitz – Concluding Report.
98. CZA, file S25/10054, Weitz's comments on the partition proposal, 19 July 1937; See also Katz (1994b).
99. CZA, Lifshitz – Concluding Report.
100. See CZA, file S25/10054 and CZA, Lipshitz – Conclusing Report.
101. Ibid.; CZA, The Executive's Memorandum to the Partition Commission; CZA, file S25/5143, Protocol of the Boundaries Committee's meeting on 22 November 1937; Sharett (1938), pp. 126–7.
102. CZA, Lifshitz – Concluding Report; CZA, file S25/10054, Weitz's comments on the partition Proposal, 19 July 1937.
103. CZA, Lifshitz – Concluding Report. See also CZA, file S25/5154, Report on an Appraisal of the Boundary Line from a Military–Security Standpoint, 26 July 1937 (it is not clear who drew up the report); CZA, file S25/10054, Lifshitz and Zelikowitz's Report Following 'Survey D', undated; CZA, Weitz's comments on the partition proposal, 19 July 1937. See also CZA, file S25/993, letter from Weizmann to Bernard Joseph on 22 July 1937. See also Shertok's comments, CZA, Protocol of the Jewish Agency Executive's meeting on 21 November 1937.
104. CZA, file S25/5154 (in note 103).
105. See Machnes's proposal in the Boundaries Committee's meeting on 1 December 1937 (CZA, file S25/5143), to transfer the boundary to the Jenin–Ramallah line, and Bernard Joseph's reply that the British would not agree to such a monstrous proposal, from the Arabs' standpoint.
106. CZA, Lifshitz – Concluding Report; CZA, The Executive's Memorandum to the Partition Commission; CZA, file S25/5143, Protocols of the Boundary Committee's meetings on 22 November 1937, and 10 November 1937; ibid., letter from Simon to Wilenshtuck, on 11 May 1938; ibid., letter from Simon to Weitz and Wilenshtuck, 18 April 1938; CZA, file S25/5138, Protocols of the Water Committee's meetings on 19 May 1938, and 27 May 1938.

107. CZA, Lifshitz – Concluding Report; CZA, The Executive's Memorandum to the Partition Commission; CZA, file S25/5143, Protocol of the Boundaries Committee's meeting on 10 November 1937; CZA, Protocol of the Jewish Agency Executive's meeting with the Political Committee of the Inner Zionist General Council on 12 June 1938.
108. CZA, Lifshitz – Concluding Report; CZA, Protocol of the Jewish Agency Executive's meeting on 8 May 1938, Shertok's statement.
109. CZA, file S25/5143, Protocol of the Boundaries Committee's meeting on 1 December 1937.
110. Ben-Gurion (1937), pp. 207, 277, 289, 295, 323; Ben-Gurion (1938), p. 200. It appears that Shertok was willing to content himself with the western alternative. On this see Ben-Gurion (1937), p. 283; Sharett (1937), pp. 258–9, in which he did not view the modification of the eastern boundary as indispensable.
111. CZA, file S25/10054, Report by Lifshitz and Zelikowitz, following Survey D, undated. Compare with Brawer's comments, CZA, file S25/5143, Protocol of the Boundaries Committee's meeting on 1 December 1937, and with Weitz's comments, CZA, file S25/10054, comments on the partition proposal, 19 July 1937.
112. CZA, file S25/5143, Protocols of the Boundaries Committee's meetings on 10 November 1937 and 1 December 1937.
113. Sharett (1938), pp. 126–7.
114. CZA, Lifshitz – Concluding Report; CZA, The Executive's Memorandum to the Partition Commission; CZA, file S25/5143, Protocol of the Boundaries Committee's meeting on 22 November 1937; CZA, file S25/10054, Ben-Gurion's proposal for a tri-partite partition 3 December 1937; CZA, data on the Jewish Settlements and the Jewish land-holdings that were to remain in the area of the Arab State or within the areas of the mandatory enclave.
115. Ben-Gurion (1937), pp. 455–6.
116. CZA, Lifshitz – Concluding Report. See also CZA, file S25/5143, Protocol of the Boundaries Committee's meeting on 22 November 1937; Ben-Gurion (1937), pp. 455–6.
117. Ussishkin raised such a proposal. See Sharett (1937), p. 316.
118. See ibid., as well as Ben-Gurion (1937), p. 277.
119. CZA, Lifshitz – Concluding Report; CZA, file S25/5143, Protocol of the Sub-Committee for Determining the Boundaries of the Mandatory Cities, meeting on 14 March 1938.
120. CZA, Lifshitz – Concluding Report. See also CZA, file S25/5143, Protocol of the Boundaries Committee's meeting on 22 November 1937; Sharett (1938), p. 126.
121. CZA, Lifshitz – Preliminary Report; CZA Lifshitz –Concluding Report; CZA, file S25/5143, Protocol of the Boundaries Committee's meeting on 1 December 1937; CZA, file S25/10054, data on the Jewish Settlements and the Jewish land-holdings that were to remain in the area of the Arab State or within the areas of the mandatory enclave. For the Executive's proposal regarding the boundary between Jaffa and Tel Aviv, see Map 12, appended to PRCR (1937). See also CZA, letter from Shertok to Crosbie on 4 February 1938.
122. CZA, Lifshitz – Concluding Report.
123. Ibid.
124. Ibid.; CZA, Lifshitz – Preliminary Report; Sharett (1937), pp. 228, 258; Ben-Gurion (1937), pp. 295, 455–6.
125. CZA, Lifshitz – Preliminary Report.
126. CZA, Lifshitz – Concluding Report; CZA, file S25/10054, data on the Jewish Settlements and the Jewish land-holdings that were to remain in the area of the Arab State or within the areas of the mandatory enclave.
127. CZA, Lifshitz – Concluding Report.
128. CZA, Lifshitz – Concluding Report. In response to Rabbi Fishman's statement at the Jewish Agency Executive's meeting on 4 July 1937, where he called for efforts to include Jewish settlement points around Jerusalem in the Jewish State, Shertok responded: '... We have to consider what is possible and what is impossible to obtain ... we cannot demand that every isolated Jewish settlement point should be recognized as a separate cell of the

Jewish State. The Moshav Atarot will be imperiled should it remain within the Arab area because Arab villages interpose between Atarot and Jerusalem and it is impossible to demand that these Arab villages should be included within the Jewish area. What we can do is to seek an expansion of the Mandate's area to the aerodrome so that it includes Atarot as well'. See Sharett (1937), p.230; Ben-Gurion (1937), pp. 282–3.

129. CZA, file S25/5143, Protocols of the Boundaries Committee's meetings on 10 November 1937, 22 November 1937, and 1 December 1937; CZA, Lifshitz – Concluding Report.

130. CZA, Lifshitz – Preliminary Report; CZA, file S25/5143, Protocol of the Boundaries Committee's meeting on 1 December 1937; CZA, Lifshitz – Concluding Report; CZA, The Executive's Memorandum to the Partition Commission; CZA, file S25/10054, data on the Jewish Settlements that were to remain in the area of the Arab State or within the areas of the mandatory enclave as per the Royal Comission's Report; Sharett (1937), p. 283.

131. CZA, Lifshitz – Concluding Report.

132. Ibid.; CZA, The Executive's Memorandum to the Partition Commission; CZA, Lifshitz – Preliminary Report; CZA, file S25/5143, Protocol of the Boundaries Committee's meeting on 1 December 1937; CZA, file S25/10054, data on the Jewish Settlements that were to remain in the area of the Arab State or within the areas of the mandatory enclave as per the Royal Commission's Report. See also Katz (1990), pp. 109–35. In Shertok's report to the Executive, on his and Ben-Gurion's testimony before the Partition Commission, Shertok observed the following on the issue of Hebron: '[they asked] Why is Hebron holy? We replied that this was the city of the Patriarchs, the location of the Tomb of the Patriarchs, one of the four holy cities, according to Jewish tradition the second most in importance. They asked if we thought that the Arab State would prohibit Jews from praying and prostrating themselves at the Tomb of the Patriarchs? We answered that this is not a question of visiting and prayer, but this is a holy city, sacred to the Jews and the Jew should be given permission to settle there.' On this see CZA, Protocol of the Jewish Agency Executive's meeting with the Political Department of the Inner Zionist General Council on 12 June 1938. See also CZA, Protocol of the Inner Zionist General Council on 12 June 1938. See also CZA, Protocol of the Inner Zionist General Council on 20 June 1938, testimony of Rabbi Herzog, Chief Rabbi of Palestine, on the matter.

133. See PRO, file CO 733/348, letter of Weizmann to Ormsby-Gore and the letter from Rutenberg to Sir J. Maffey.

134. CZA, The Executive's Memorandum to the Partition Commission; CZA, file S25/8122, letter from Leo Picard to the Political Department, on July 1938; Ben-Gurion (1937), pp. 207, 221, 295; Sharett (1937), pp. 222, 243.

135. CZA, file S25/10006 Ben-Gurion's letter to Shertok on 3 July 1937; CZA Lifshitz – Preliminary Report, CZA, The Executive's Memorandum to the Partition Commission; Sharett (1937), pp. 209–10, 221–2 (the citation is taken from there), 243, Ben-Gurion (1937), pp. 211, 221, 228. See also various studies that the Jewish Agency Executive specially commissioned in order to determine its position regarding the Negev in CZA, file S25/9237 'A Report Embodying the Data at Present Relating to the Negev', undated; CZA, file S25/182/1, Memorandum on the Negev District of Southern Palestine, compiled by A. L. Zissu and J. M. A. Gwyer, evidence submitted to the Palestine Partition Commission 1938; CZA, file S25/10057, The Negev – a Preliminary Memorandum authored by Avi-Yonah (undated); CZA, file S25/10057, The Negev – a Second Memorandum authored by L. Picard (September 1938); CZA, file S25/10057, A Memorandum Regarding Water in the Negev, authored by L. Picard, on 13 July 1938. See also Protocol of the Jewish Agency Executive's Meeting on 8 July 1937, statement by Kaplan.

136. CZA, The Executive's Memorandum to the Partition Commission; Sharett (1937), p. 197; See also CZA, Protocol of the Jewish Agency Executive's Meeting with the Political Committee of the Inner Zionist General Council on 12 June 1938; CZA, Protocol of the Inner Zionist General Council's Meeting on 20 June 1938; CZA, Protocol of the Jewish Agency Executive's Meeting on 14 July 1938.

137. CZA, file S25/10054, Ben-Gurion's Proposal for a Tripartite Partition, 3 December 1937. See also note 45.
138. Sharett (1937), p. 222. Ben-Gurion (1937), pp. 254–5, 278, 289; Porat (1989), p. 170.
139. Sharett (1937), p. 222.
140. CZA, Protocol of the Jewish Agency Executive's Meeting on 12 December 1937 – Statement by Weizmann.
141. Porat (1989), p. 172; Ben-Gurion (1937), pp. 222, 291, 322.
142. PRCR (1937), pp. 374–6, 389–90, 394–6.
143. See also PRO, file CO 733/346/9, where Peel himself notes how critical the security issue was to the considerations of the Jewish side. See also CZA, Protocol of the Jewish Agency Executive's Meeting on 23 May 1938 and especially the words of Mrs. Jacobs and Ben-Gurion, from which it emerges that the Executive assumed that when the two states would arise, 'these two states would be hostile to each other'. See, in detail, CZA, file S25/81109, Memorandum of the Security Committee, 'A Proposal for the Organization of the Security Forces in the Jewish State', from 15 May 1938, especially the introductory chapter and the section on the frontier forces.
144. CZA, Protocol the Jewish Agency Executive's Meeting together with the Political Committee of the Inner Zionist General Council on 12 June 1938, statement by S. Zuchovitzky.
145. Ibid., Statement by B. Katznelson. Similar words were uttered by Zuchovitzky.
146. CZA, Protocol of the Jewish Agency Executive's Meeting on 29 May 1938 – statement by Shertok; CZA, file S25/8119 in note 43, especially the summary of the chapter on the frontier forces.
147. CZA, Protocol of the Jewish Agency Executive's Meeting on 24 July 1938. See also CZA, file S25/42, Protocol of the Security Committee's Meeting on 10 November 1937; CZA, file S25/5119, Protocol of the Security Committee's Meeting on 7 February 1937; CZA, file S25/8119, especially the chapter on the frontier forces.

3

The Proposal for Partitioning Jerusalem

THE NECESSITY TO PARTITION THE CITY

As mentioned previously, under the Royal Commission's Plan, Jerusalem in its entirety and its environs, was incorporated within the boundaries of the permanent mandatory enclave. Even prior to publication of the Royal Commission's Plan, a majority on the Executive believed that it would prove necessary to swallow the amputation of the Old City, including the Jewish holy places (such as the Western Wall), from the territory of the Jewish State. There was no chance that the British would assent to a demand to incorporate the Old City, or at least the Jewish holy places, within the boundaries of the Jewish State. Furthermore, the Jewish Agency Executive assumed that a Zionist demand for the Old City, i.e. 'control over the holy places ... the Holy Sepulcher, the Mosque of Omar, etc',[1] would provoke an Arab uprising on the one hand, and stir up Christian criticism on the other. This could seriously endanger the possibility of implementing the partition proposal. Additionally, whether the Jews demanded the entire Old City or merely the sites within it that were sacred to Judaism, such a *démarche* would elicit a similar Arab counter-demand. Ben-Gurion did not even hesitate to state, that in the unlikely event that all of Jerusalem were offered to the Jews, he would have attempted to persuade them to spurn acceptance of the Old City.

The Executive believed that under the existing circumstances 'it would be impossible to partition the old city of Jerusalem between various authorities and the only way out of the morass of demands [in the Old City] created of by the various religions was to preserve the Old City in its entirety as a single unit and entrust it to a single Authority disposing of international clout'. The Executive therefore made peace with the reality that part of the city would remain within the permanent mandatory enclave.[2] With the promulgation of the Royal Commission's Report, Weizmann wrote to Ormsby-Gore: 'We fully recognize and even desire that the Old City of Jerusalem and parts of the city remain under British control'.[3] The Executive even announced before the Partition Commission that 'there could be no question of the necessity of entrusting the Holy Places of Jerusalem to the custody of the Mandatory Power as an international trustee'.[4] In a 1934 conversation with Mussolini[5] Weizmann had already alluded to the Agency's readiness to award the Old City a special international status, while Jacobson's partition plan in the early 1930s enunciated that Jerusalem would be recognized as an autonomous city enjoying international status.[6] At the close of 1936, Shertok raised the possibility of a tripartite municipal partition of Jerusalem: 'The Old City as a place sacred to all religions should remain exclusively under British control. The Arabs would receive only a narrow strip in the new city whereas all other parts of the city would be in the hands of the Jewish municipality.'[7]

However, the position of the Executive, as well as those who supported the partition plan within the Zionist Congress, was totally different with regards to the New City – that area located west of the Old City, where the bulk of the Jewish population resided. The Executive demanded that Jerusalem be partitioned in a manner that would include the Jewish portion of the New City within the boundaries of the Jewish State. First of all, the Executive grasped the demographic importance of New Jerusalem with all that it portended for the fate of the Jewish State. In the period discussed, nearly one-fifth of the country's Jews resided in this city (about 75,000 out of 400,000). West Jerusalem's inclusion within the confines of the mandatory enclave would inflict a major loss of political and economic strength on the Jewish state. The repercussions of this situation could exert a destructive influence on the fate of the Jewish State in general.[8] An analysis which the Institute for the Study of the Economy affiliated with the Jewish Agency, conducted on behalf of the Political Department, found, for example, that the exclusion of Jerusalem from the Jewish State would cause moral and economic harm to the Jewish public, the economic catalyst of the city. Consequently, the Jews in the rest of the country, who were influenced economically and spiritually by Jerusalem, would also suffer harm. The Arabs, who also benefited from Jewish economic activity, would also be injured, and the same would apply to the projected mandatory state which predicated a balanced budget on the Jewish economy and proceeds from taxes levied upon it.[9] It was clear that in the normal course of development Jerusalem would grow into a Jewish city and attract myriad forces; whereas, if it were extracted to become a British enclave the growth of the Jewish population would be minimized and the Jewish character of the city would be lost.[10] Apprehension was expressed[11] regarding the future of Jewish settlements and Jewish-owned land in the vicinity of Jerusalem if the New City were severed from the Jewish State.[12]

Jerusalem's symbolic character, its centrality to the history of the Jewish people and the esteem that it commanded among the Jewish people in general, buttressed the demand to include the New City within the boundaries of the Jewish State.[13] The Agency Executive believed that the Jewish people would not be prepared to accept the loss of Jewish Jerusalem even as the price for attaining a Jewish State. The Jewish people's delegates at the Zionist Congress, which was to decide whether or not to ratify partition, would reject the partition of Palestine outright if Jerusalem were not included. In a discussion with the Colonial Secretary, Ormsby-Gore, on the eve of the publication of the Royal Commission's partition plan, Weizmann emphasized that: 'Jerusalem is the soul of the Jewish people. If any possibility exists for us to accept the partition it is necessary that the Jewish people be with us, and for the Jewish people, Jerusalem is the token of redemption.'[14] In that period, Ben-Gurion wrote on the same subject:

From a colonizing standpoint, the matter is not decisive – Jerusalem would not be the center of mass absorption. However, the future of the entire partition plan possibly hinges on the inclusion or non-inclusion of Jerusalem in the Jewish State. Even if we were to receive the optimal conditions from the standpoint of territory, boundaries, authority and security, we would confront enormous difficulties ... a war waged by a number of faithful Zionists who will perhaps bolt the World Zionist Organization. Within the Jewish community we will have a Spanish [civil war] situation ... The Arabs within our country and within the Arab State and the Arab countries will rampage against us. We will be able to weather all these calamities only if we can muster all our latent and profound enthusiasm and provided the Jewish people stands by us. There is only one thing capable of arousing the enthusiasm of the Jewish people – *a Jewish Government in Jerusalem* [emphasis in the original]. A Jewish State has no magic without Jerusalem. Amongst the irrational forces, to which we owe our survival and which sustain our current activities, the name Jerusalem surpasses everything ... England (and we) need authority over the holy places, i.e. the Old City. Control over Rehavia [a prestigious Jewish neighborhood in West Jerusalem] won't add a thing whereas for the Jew – the millions of Jews who have no inkling what the Sharon and the Valley are and have no understanding in investment and agriculture, in calculating the number of dunams and absorptive capacity – the name Jerusalem is everything. With Jerusalem, partition will succeed. Without it partition can wind up as a catastrophe for the Jewish People and a disgrace for Great Britain. If England desires an honorable solution and a hopeful solution, it must grant us Jerusalem, part of Jerusalem ...[15]

In his address before the Zionist Congress in August 1937, Berl Katznelson, one of the leaders of the Labor Movement, added the following words regarding Jerusalem:

> this is one of the subjects that it is hard to talk about. I am not speaking now about old and holy Jerusalem, where many bask in its holiness, but of simple Jerusalem, the secular Jerusalem which is sacred only to us. It is sacred by virtue of the holiness of labor and construction. If they take this Jerusalem as well away from the Jewish State, they will making the Jewish State a nullity from a psychological, political and cultural standpoint. People should not denigrate this as a matter of sentiment. A Jewish State, even a truncated one with Jerusalem, will be accepted by the Jewish people as a harbinger of redemption. A Jewish State without Jerusalem would be a decapitated body. Jerusalem within a Jewish State would be dynamic force, a force for attracting people, means, ideas and cultural enterprises. Jerusalem within a Jewish State would be the capital of Israel, a center of world Jewry. Jerusalem outside of our boundaries means not only the loss of 71,000 Jews, a lodestone for world Jewry. Jerusalem outside the boundaries portends the danger of destruction for the Jewish State. Jerusalem will not remain a no-man's land without owners, it will belong to the British corridor, it will merge with the British state which will arise in the heart of the country. There the Balfour Declaration will be rescinded. There the English language will totally prevail. The political trend will be clear – to transform Jerusalem into the citadel of the modern crusaders. Such a Jerusalem will turn into a center for the enemies of the Jewish State – non-Jews and Jews alike. Such a Jerusalem will be the capital of assimilation and indiscipline. All those elements who look askance at the Jewish people will concentrate there. The presumed Jewish aristocracy which is unwilling to accept the discipline of the Jewish State ... whoever seeks to evade paying taxes to a Jewish State, whoever wants to take a swipe at Zionist culture ... will turn towards Jerusalem and abet our foes. Jerusalem will become hostile to us just as occurred during the Hellenistic Period. There is no greater danger for the Hebrew language and our national culture than this: a Jerusalem that has been expropriated from the Jewish people ...[16]

Indeed, Weizmann, Ben-Gurion and Shertok emphasized that in the event that New Jerusalem would not be incorporated within the boundaries of the Jewish State, there was no further point in negotiating with the British government on partition.[17] The assumption shared by most members of the Executive was that, from the standpoint of ethical and symbolic needs, the Jewish people would content itself with New Jerusalem.[18]

To buttress this contention, the Executive argued that the British had no real reason to include New Jerusalem within the British mandatory enclave because no holy places were located there.[19] The Executive emphasized that, in the light of the decision of the Royal Commission regarding Jaffa, it was only fair that New Jerusalem should also be incorporated within the boundaries of the Jewish State. Although Jaffa was removed from the heart of the Arab State, the Royal Commission still saw no obstacle to declare it a part of the Arab State. Additionally, Jerusalem's situation was less complicated, since it would prove possible to link West Jerusalem to the Jewish State via a corridor.[20] Furthermore, 'the right of 70,000 Jews in Jerusalem and the right of the entire Jewish people to Jewish Jerusalem was much greater than the right of 50,000 Arabs in Jaffa'.[21] The Executive drew vast encouragement from articles in the British press, statements made by Members of Parliament and in the House of Lords (some of whose members were acting at the behest of the Executive), deliberations of the League of Nations, and statements by cabinet ministers. All voiced support for the Jewish Agency Executive's position regarding the partition of Jerusalem and the incorporation of the western portion within the Jewish state.[22]

FUNDAMENTAL ISSUES PREPARATORY TO DRAFTING THE EXECUTIVE'S PROPOSAL FOR PARTITIONING JERUSALEM

The Agency's Political Department entrusted the handling of Jerusalem's partitioning to a special committee of experts, which was given the sobriquet, 'the Jerusalem Committee'. Their task was to prepare, for the Executive, 'persuasive arguments in favor of incorporating Jewish Jerusalem within the proposed Jewish State'. They would also provide evidence based on historical sources that Jerusalem had been created by the Jewish people, had formed an inseparable part of its consciousness from that time onwards, and constituted a symbol of national rebirth to this date. The Committee would draw up a map that would emphasize the proposed boundaries or a series of alternative boundaries, for the Jewish political unit in Jerusalem. The members would amass examples of other divided cities the world over to demonstrate that the geographical situation of the city allowed partition into two separate cities and that the technical difficulties arising from partition could be solved. Finally, the committee was expected 'to work out a concrete plan for including Jewish Jerusalem within the Jewish State'. The members of the Committee were Bernard Joseph, the attorneys Olshan and Auster, Dr. Eliash, Dr. Bonne, Yitzhak Ben Zvi, Professor David Yellin, Professor Klein and Haim Salomon.

These personages, in addition to their expertise on matters pertaining to Jerusalem, also represented the central bodies in Jewish communal affairs in Jerusalem.[23]

A series of questions and numerous complicated dilemmas had already arisen during the deliberations of the Jewish Agency Executive and the Political Department, which antedated the formation of the Jerusalem Committee. These carried over to the Jerusalem Committee's first meeting and reflected the profound complexity of the Jerusalem partition issue. Paramount among all the questions pondered was whether, given the geographical structure, partition of Jerusalem was at all feasible. While there were marked Jewish concentrations, many neighborhoods and important sites were scattered over the four corners of the city. The heart of the new modern city was not notably Jewish but, rather, characterized by an appreciable ethnic *mélange*, which was further complicated by a crazy quilt of economic and government institutions, which the British would not want to leave in the Jewish area. Another fundamental issue was who was the real partner to partition – the British or the Arabs. There was apprehension that if the Jews were to demand part of the city, the Arabs would demand a similar part, leaving only the city within the walls remaining under the mandate, which would further complicate the management of the city. An additional problem was to decide by which criteria an area would be adjudicated as 'Jewish' – a determination that was crucial to any partition plan. Would one work according to a Jewish population density higher than a certain percentage, or would one apply more rigid criteria, such as Jewish land ownership? Perhaps Jewish land utilization would more faithfully reflect the Jewish population distribution.

Another type of problem was represented by the planning aspect. Should the partition plan deal only with the municipal area of the city (which did not include most of the western neighborhoods), or should the city limits be determined as the boundary guidelines for discussion? In this latter event, a non-Jewish population would have to be incorporated. An opinion was voiced that perhaps a geographic grouping of lands purchased by Jews around the city should constitute the guiding line. The fact that Jerusalem was sacred to Christianity and Islam, on the one hand, and both symbolic and holy to the Jewish people, on the other, created a seemingly insuperable conflict and in tandem touched off an internal debate within the Jerusalem Committee itself. Committee members asked what was the point of fighting for Jerusalem if one had conceded the holy places in advance, including the pivotal Western Wall as well as other historic places such as David's Citadel. However, most committee members believed that there were no prospects that the British would respond favorably to a Jewish demand to incorporate the holy places of Jerusalem within the Jewish State. The question examined was whether to pose maximal demands concerning the western part of the city or to present a plan that offered the possibility of securing British acceptance. On this matter as well as on the attitude to be adopted towards the Old City, including the places sacred to Judaism, Bernard Joseph contended that 'it is quite obvious that we won't demand things that we cannot be sure in advance of receiving them. Our demands must be moderate and in the realm of the possible.' A plethora of technical questions also arose for discussion, as did security issues. Thus, for example, the future fate of the Jewish population left behind the partition line and who would protect them in the event of an Arab attack, was an issue that surfaced. Economic and financial questions also vexed the committee members, centering around the issue of what would be the political–economic structure of the city.[24]

Following the gamut of questions that were raised in the discussions, and the interdependence between them, it was decided to split the Jerusalem Committee into four sub-committees. The Historical Committee's role was to amass material and draft a memorandum concerning the continuous tie existing throughout all the generations between the Jewish people and Jerusalem, how Jerusalem became the capital of the Land of Israel, and its significance to the Jewish renaissance movement.[25] The Economic Committee was to elucidate the Jewish contribution in building New Jerusalem, to demonstrate the possibility that the proposed Jewish city could survive as an economic unit and to prove that the exclusion of the city and its Jewish population from the area of the proposed Jewish State would simultaneously wreak economic damage to the Jewish City, the Jewish State and the mandatory state. The Legal sub-committee's job was to amass comparative material, comprising evidence from other politically divided cities throughout the world, in order to 'demonstrate to the British that these things do exist in the world and they can be implemented', and to formulate, on the basis of examples the world over, the network of relations between the neighboring parts of the city regarding the issues of passage of goods and persons, custom duties, police, municipal services, etc., and co-operation between both sides of the boundary. The task of the Geographic Committee was to formulate in practice the proposed boundaries between Jewish Jerusalem and mandatory Jerusalem, while taking into consideration the data amassed by the other sub-committees and the geographic, symbolic, security, operative, economic and political criteria.[26]

PRINCIPLES AND DETAILS INVOLVED IN DETERMINING
THE MAP FOR JERUSALEM'S PARTITION

The Geographic sub-committee confronted two types of problems. First of all, it had to determine the criteria and the definitions for identifying land separating the 'Jewish' region and the 'non-Jewish' region. Secondly, it had to create a solidified Jewish expanse while at the same time minimizing the damage to British interests, namely the protection of the holy places.[27] The engineer Max Hecker was co-opted onto the sub-committee. He was an expert on the city's affairs and he was tapped to prepare the first draft of the partition map. In the discussion on his proposal, Hecker explained that it was based on three principles: creating a contiguous Jewish bloc; security considerations, and the historical tie to the location. In order to define the areas of the Jewish bloc, Hecker prepared, in conjunction with the Institute for Economic Research of the Jewish Agency, a detailed survey on the distribution of the Jewish population and the grouping of Jewish land resources. He also examined the distribution of Jewish taxpayers in order to receive a fuller picture of land-use distribution, as many Jews used apartments and office buildings owned by Arabs. For security considerations, and on the basis of experience acquired during the riots of 1929 and the disturbances that began in the year 1936, Hecker's proposal expanded the municipal boundary in the north-western margins of the city, in order to create a more easily defended boundary. For this reason he also annexed the small Arab neighborhood that dominated the Jewish neighborhood of Romema (see Map 7). Likewise, Hecker postulated in this plan that the boundaries of Jewish Jerusalem should incorporate those lands where negotiations with Arab sellers were in progress, and which were necessary for the future development of existing Jewish neighborhoods. Hecker did not anticipate opposition to the plan regarding the first two principles, and he therefore focused his main arguments on the importance of retaining the historic and religious sites for the Jewish city including the area of the Western Wall, the Jewish quarter, the Mount of Olives, the Yemin Moshe Quarter, which is 'the most veteran outside the wall', and additional historic sites (see Map 7). In general, Hecker's plan was not embraced by the committee. However, the map which he prepared served as a basis for the committee's decisions in all that pertained to the first two principles.[28]

The central problem confronting the Geographic sub-committee was how to preserve Jewish interests in the partition without harming important British interests. The distribution of the Jewish community and of the British interests was such that partition would of necessity harm one side or the other. It was clear that, in any Jewish attempt to achieve some sort of territorial unification, the Jews would necessarily harm or amputate a British interest or an approach artery to the eastern city and to the walled city. The existence of free and secure arteries was vital to the British, and this accounted for the Royal Commission's proposal to establish a British corridor to the city extending from the Mediterranean, instead of contenting themselves with securing Jerusalem proper. This was evident to the Geographic sub-committee, which scrounged for a partition proposal that would create a substantial and contiguous Jewish bloc that would not encounter immediate British opposition. On the other hand, if a clash of interests with the British were totally avoided, the Jewish concentrations would be splintered into molecules, which was equally unacceptable to the sub-committee. The sole possible solution to this impasse lay in compromise and mutual concessions, which would obligate both sides – the British and the Jewish – to make concessions, and this was the Geographic sub-committee's point of departure as it began work. The discussion revolved around setting an order of priorities within the city: what was crucial to the Jews, and for the British, and what could be waived *in extremis*. It was also necessary to create an order of priorities that would reflect the demographic weight of population distribution, as well as the security needs, future development contingencies and the symbolic value of the locations. Simultaneously, there was also a need to draw up a parallel hierarchy of interests for the British side, and thus it was possible to identify peak areas of conflict, on the one hand, and areas that were open to negotiation and concessions, on the other. This calculus could be used to rank three areas as paramountly important for the city's future from a Zionist standpoint, while correspondingly low in terms of the damage to British interests. Two additional areas were relegated to low priorities, since they were highly laden with conflict. The five areas (ranging from the easiest to the most complicated) were as follows: the Rehavia–Beit Hakerem bloc; the bloc of neighborhoods north of Jaffa Road and west of Nablus Road; the Mount Scopus crest; the bloc of southern neighborhoods; the Old City (including the Western Wall) and its vicinity (see Maps 6, 7).

The Rehavia Beit–Hakerem bloc was considered by the committee to be the nucleus of the new Zionist city, and a conflict-free region from the British standpoint. It extended from south of Jaffa Road and west of King George Road and stretched out contiguously to the new western neighborhoods of the city, including four out of the five modern important garden neighborhoods of New Jerusalem, and the 25,650 Jews already resident there. Between the two neighborhoods of Rehavia and Beit–Hakerem

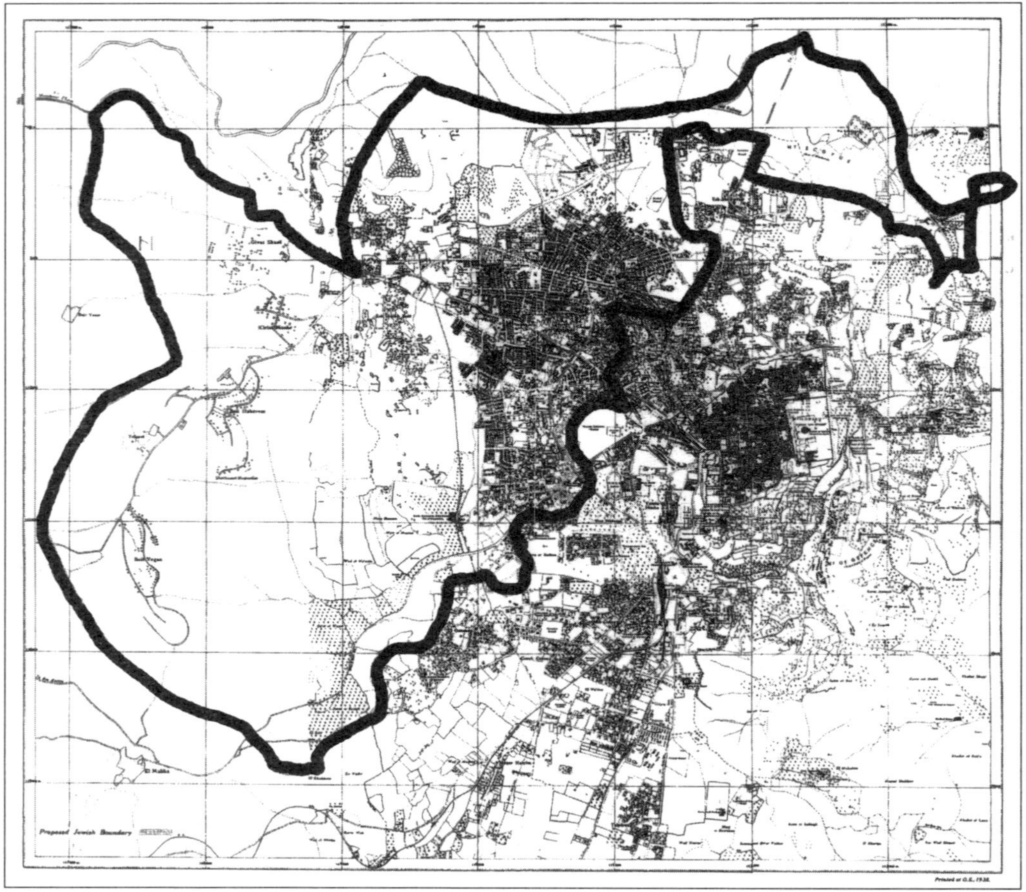

Map 6: Proposal of Jewish Agency Executive for the Partition of Jerusalem, 1938 (Original Map)

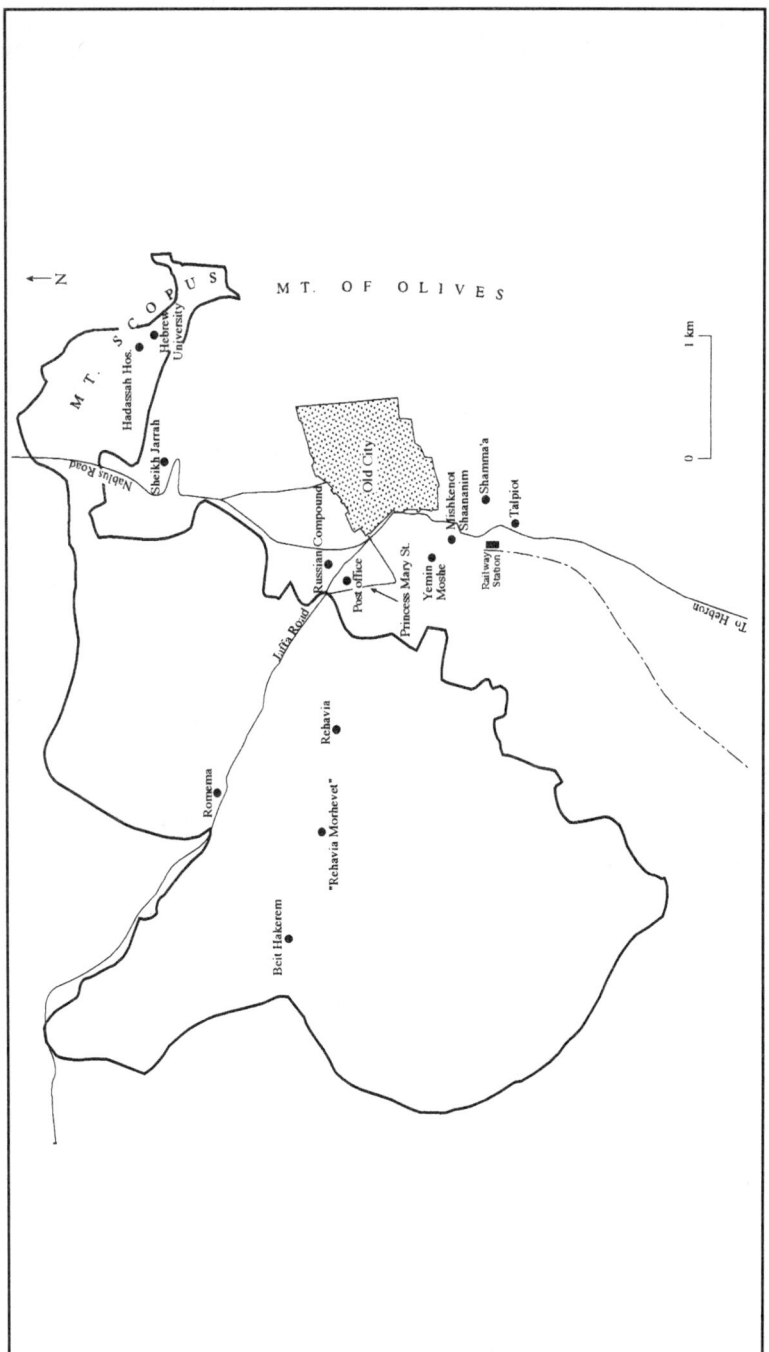

Map 7: Proposal of Jewish Agency Executive for the Partition of Jerusalem, 1938 (Redrawn Map by the Author)

stretched a wide empty expanse that was called 'Rehavia Morhevet' (Greater Rehavia), which had already been partially purchased by Jewish bodies while outstanding commitments of more than one thousand additional dunams existed. 'Rehavia Morhevet' was considered to be the heart of Jerusalem's future development. The prestigious Zionist neighborhoods of Rehavia and Beit Hakerem also epitomized New Jerusalem. The national institutions (the Jewish Agency and its various departments, the Jewish National Fund and Keren Hayesod), which had recently transferred to their new headquarters in Rehavia, as well as the prestigious Hebrew Teachers Seminary in Beit Hakerem, left a very important Zionist imprint on these neighborhoods and on the entire area. Near Rehavia, a new Jewish commercial center on the axis of Jaffa and Ben Yehuda Streets was taking shape, and its future course of development lay westwards. The architect Richard Kaufmann prepared an impressive building plan for the area of 'Rehavia Morhevet' and a feeling existed that this would be Jerusalem's equivalent to Tel Aviv. It was therefore clear that this area was the hard nucleus of any Jewish partition plan and without it there was no realistic basis for any partition plan. This area was also the least problematic from the standpoint of the British, because it did not cut off any roads and did not conflict with any major British interests.[29]

The second most important area from the Jewish perspective was the large bloc of neighborhoods north of Jaffa Road and west of Nablus Road. In this area the greatest Jewish population mass (45,650 out of 75,000 Jews) resided. Its demographic importance was of the first order. The process of building and development had also continued there. The major obstacle to annexing this region to the Jewish city was anxiety over harming a most vital British interest, in the form of an unimpeded territorial link between Jerusalem and the sea (i.e. the Jaffa Road). The various proposals put forth by members of the committee and the affiliated experts could not provide a real answer to this problem.[30]

The third area of importance from the Zionist standpoint was the area of Mount Scopus and the institutions established there – the Hebrew University and Hadassah Hospital. Their importance was not demographic but they constituted an important symbol and were the pride of the Zionist enterprise in Jerusalem and in Palestine as a whole.[31] Forfeiting Mount Scopus was akin to surrendering the symbol and the banner of the new city. In such an event the Zionist enterprise in Jerusalem might become devoid of symbols, especially as it was already clear that the symbolic holy places in the Old City and its vicinity would have to be relinquished. Indeed, in his international contacts, Weizmann, following the publication of the Royal Commission's proposal, emphasized 'the incorporation of

New Jerusalem *including the University* within the Jewish State' [emphasis added].[32] On the other hand, as a result of Zionist insistence on Mount Scopus's inclusion within the Jewish city, the British would be cut off from the northern entrance to the city: the artery by-passing Jaffa Road from the north and the Nablus–Ramallah–Jerusalem road. In addition, one could assume that the Jewish presence on the crest commanding the old City, and the roads to it, would arouse British resentment and would not encourage them to support the proposal. Nonetheless, it appears that the symbolic character of Mount Scopus proved decisive and the area would not be relinquished. The Jewish link with the mountain would have to be maintained through a bypass road to the west and north of the Sheikh Jarrah neighborhood, and the damage to British interests by severing Nablus Road as well as Jaffa Road would be offset by granting permission for monitored passage through the Jewish city by creating crossing points and customs control.[33]

The fourth region, which included the southern Jewish neighborhoods, was finally left in the non-Jewish area. This decision overrode opinions in the committee that the neighborhoods should be connected and linked to the Jewish city for security reasons. The demographic status of the seven neighborhoods whose population did not surpass 900 people was negligible. Their location, severed as they were from Jewish contiguity and east of the Jerusalem–Bethlehem road, was problematic. These reasons effectively dictated their non-inclusion within the boundaries of Jewish Jerusalem, according to the proposal of the Jerusalem Committee.[34] It is possible that the decision was also related to a plan that surfaced in the Boundary Committee, and in the Jerusalem Committee, proposing a corridor to the sea – an alternative artery to the one proposed by the Royal Commission – in the form of a Jerusalem–Gaza artery. The logic was to avoid bisecting Jewish territory on the coastal plain. However, the British corridor would then have to enter Jerusalem along the Hebron Road artery, which would then intervene between the bulk of the Jewish city and the southern neighborhoods. On the other hand, this alternative was of immense advantage to Jewish Jerusalem because it obviated the problem of British passage through the Jaffa Road, the heart of the Jewish bloc. It is entirely possible that the Jerusalem committee was preparing the groundwork for a southern corridor plan at the cost of yielding the southern Jewish neighborhoods, including the garden suburb of Talpiot.[35]

The fifth area, the Old City and its surroundings, was the most problematic and sensitive to the Jews, the British and the Arabs alike. This area was sub-divided into a number of sub-areas, which deserve to be treated separately. The first was the area of the 'city', the contemporary

confluence of the Jaffa Road and Princess Mary Street, which was considered to be the heart of the central business district (CBD). Located
there were a number of very important financial and commercial institutions
belonging in a jumbled fashion to Jews, Arabs and the mandatory
authorities. Among the most important institutions were the centers of
authority in the Russian Compound; the New Central Post Office
Building; the World Zionist Organization's Anglo–Palestine Company
Bank; the Mayoralty Building and the Palace Hotel, which housed the
government offices. Also located in this area, in a similar haphazard
fashion, were business edifices, hotels, entertainment structures – which
were owned by various ethnic groups and were geographically mixed. This
encumbered any attempt to draw a partition line that would prove
satisfactory to everybody. Additionally, uncertainty prevailed as to whether
the center would continue to be a central business district common to both
parts of the city or whether each part would develop its own alternative
central business district at a new focal point.[36] In its final proposal, the
Jerusalem Committee, following prolonged deliberations, attempted to
formulate a boundary line, which implied the surrender of Jewish property
that lay adjacent to it, including the 'Shamma'a' Jewish Commercial
Center.

Additional sub-areas surrounding the old city and adjacent to it were
the two venerable Jewish neighborhoods, Yemin Moshe and Mishkenot
Shaananim, which symbolized the departure of the Jews from the Old
City walls and the start of the construction of the new city. They were
located at a point that controlled the access roads to the Old City from the
direction of Bethlehem and the area of the Jewish cemetery on the slopes
of the Mount of Olives, east of the Old City. The latter area had been
sacred to Jews from time immemorial, and was where Jews from all over
the world sought to find their final resting place. Nonetheless, the cemetery
was located at a distance from any Jewish neighborhood and in a direction
counter to the development trends of the Jewish community. Additionally,
most of the area was east of the Jerusalem–Jericho road, and controlled
that and the south-east wing of the Temple Mount.

The sub-area within the walled city was undoubtedly the most sensitive
for all the parties. Even if there was room for discussion and compromise
with regards to the Old City's surroundings, when it came to the Old City
itself, including the Western Wall and the Jewish Quarter, it was certain
that the British would not relinquish even a portion of it and would not
agree to a partition. Indeed, during the deliberations of the Jerusalem
Committee, Bernard Joseph argued 'that we should already adopt a decision
to limit our proposals exclusively to the New City because there is no hope

for obtaining part of the Old City. We shouldn't ask for things which we know in advance to be unobtainable.'[37] The engineer Max Hecker attempted to persuade members of the committee to avoid deciding in haste over such a sensitive issue to the Jewish people. He demanded that he be allowed time to prepare a detailed memorandum and a map that would demonstrate to members of the committee that a specific partition of the Old City was in the realm of the possible, and added: 'Let us not disparage dreams and let's not be modest in our demands ...'.[38] His request was granted, and in his memorandum Hecker attempted to demonstrate that one could partition the Old City and incorporate part of it into Jewish Jerusalem, with part outside of the wall, such as the Jewish neighborhoods of Mishkenot Shaananim and Yemin Moshe. He also proposed another radical change – to give up the present Western Wall (which, according to his examinations, had become holy to Jews only in the previous 400–700 years) and utilize as a substitute part of the Western rampart (which in the past had been entirely sacred to the Jews) and construct a luxurious synagogue there.[39] Hecker's plans did not receive the backing of the committee which also saw no point in being stubborn and demanding the other areas adjacent to the Old City, such at Mount Zion and the Mount of Olives, which were much less important than the Western Wall itself.[40]

The partition map of Jerusalem that the Jerusalem Committee formulated in the end and that the Jewish Agency Executive presented to the Partition Commission (see Maps 6, 7) was based on the principles described above, and divided Jerusalem into two regions. The western region was typified by Jewish demographic and territorial concentration, and the eastern region was typified by non-Jewish demographic and territorial concentration. The exception, as stated, was Mount Scopus; despite the fact that it had no demographic importance, it was included in the boundaries of Jewish Jerusalem for national–symbolic reasons. In order to enhance the possibility that the British would accept the proposal, every effort was made to insure that the municipal boundary line would not harm British interests in places that were crucial from their stand-point. Nonetheless, there was no evading the fact that the boundary line would bisect the Jaffa Road and the Nablus Road, and thereby impair British interests. The suggestion proposed by the Jerusalem Committee was to sign a treaty granting the right of free passage to the holy places via these arteries. The Old City, including the places sacred to Judaism with all their religious and symbolic importance, was not included in the area of the proposed Jewish City.[41] The scholarly memoranda of the Historical Committee regarding the perpetual tie between all of Jerusalem and the Jewish people, which were also submitted to the Partition Commission,[42] lost their significance to a large measure by virtue of the forfeiture of Old Jerusalem, a concession which stemmed from clear political realism. However, these memoranda still retained a general explanatory importance.

Regarding the external boundaries of the city and the definition of the Jewish area, Hecker's approach, which assigned decisive importance to the criteria of strategic depth, space for development, contiguity and Jewish ownership, was accepted.[43] According to the proposal of the Boundaries Committee, West Jerusalem was linked to the heart of the Jewish State via a corridor, which was also included in the area of the Jewish State. The corridor passed alongside the railway (that remained within the area of the mandatory enclave) to the south and alongside the Jerusalem–Jaffa road to the north (see Map 5). In this manner, the Executive also sought to include the Jewish agricultural settlements of Motsa and Kiryat 'Anavim on the outskirts of Jerusalem within the area of the Jewish State.[44]

A DIVIDED CITY MAINTAINING CO-OPERATION AND OPEN BORDERS: THE APPLICATION OF PRECEDENTS THE WORLD OVER

The crafting of a partition map predicated on the assumption that its general features would prove acceptable to the British did not suffice. It was necessary to persuade them, as well as the international bodies associated with partition, that Jerusalem's partition could be implemented from a technical standpoint while allowing the sound operation of both cities – the Jewish and the mandatory city – despite partition. The contentions of the Jerusalem Committee that partition could feasibly be implemented rested on the assumption that extensive co-operation between the two municipalities – the municipality of mandatory Jerusalem and the municipality of Jewish Jerusalem – would exist and the borders of the two cities would be drawn in a manner that would allow free traffic between the two cities. To prove this was possible, the Jerusalem Committee cited examples from various places around the world where political borders cut through urban regions.

To demonstrate the feasibility of co-operation on municipal services such as electricity, street lighting, sewage, water, etc., the committee cited the example of co-operation between the towns of Milltown and Calais in the state of Maine on the northern border of the United States with the towns of St Stephen and Milltown in New Brunswick on the Canadian border (see Map 8). A single water plant located in St Stephen, utilizing the spring at the site, supplied water to all four towns. This spared the

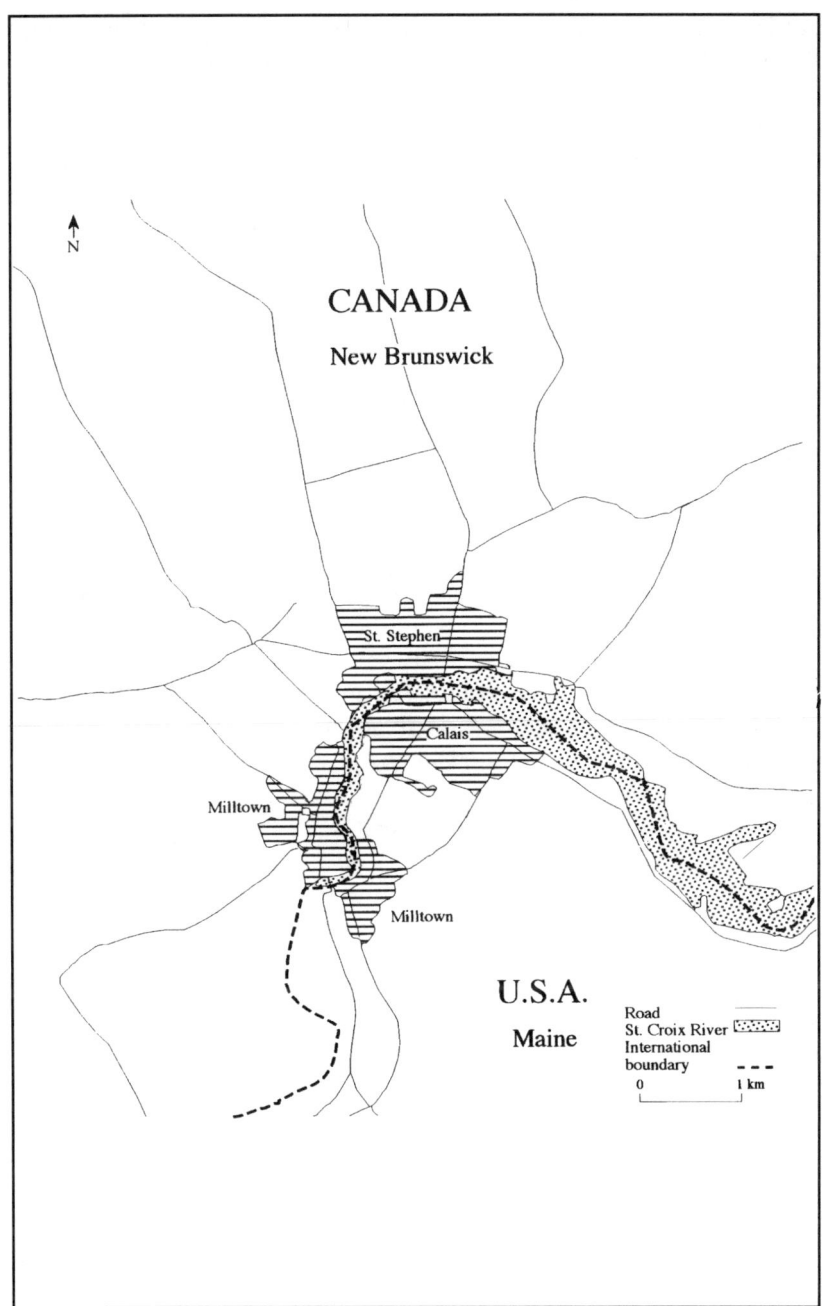

Map 8: US–Canadian Border at the St Croix River

need for establishing water projects on both sides of the border. In a similar fashion, Milltown in New Brunswick supplied gas to all four towns. This close co-operation between the four towns on both sides of the border also existed in fire fighting, and the central hospital in St Stephen served the other three towns as well. The customs and immigration offices located on both sides of the bridge connecting the towns provided the sole evidence that a border existed. A similar model for supplying central services to Jerusalem would, it was hoped, develop between the two municipalities in Jerusalem, thus obviating the need to establish separate networks of services and avoiding the technical problems that would arise from the creation of new and separate services for both cities.[45]

The border between Konstanz in Germany and Kreuzlingen in Switzerland which bisected municipal areas (see Map 9), and similarly the border between Basle in Switzerland and Stetten-Lourrach in Germany and St Louise in France, served as an example of a boundary that allowed free passage of people and vehicles from one country to another and fostered close economic relations between the two cities, without harming customs collection or challenging the legality of people from one state (such as workers) who resided within the boundaries of the other state. The residents of the two cities carried special certificates that allowed them free passage, and the customs checks in public transportation took place during the in-transit stage from one city to the other. This created a virtual unity in the economic and cultural life and in the day-to-day transportation between both sides.[46]

The Jerusalem Committee proposed that, similar to the above-mentioned cities, the Jewish city and mandatory Jerusalem would arrive at an agreement allowing residents of both cities free passage between the two cities. Only those who wanted to settle or work on a permanent basis would require a special permit. This, again, was the norm in agreements between European countries. Thus, the city would continue to be an independent unit and its normal life, as currently organized, could persist in the future. It was proposed that, despite the fact that one could establish a customs post between the two cities that would effectively operate on the European model, both countries would reach agreements enabling the entire city – the Jewish region and the mandatory region – to operate as a single unit for customs purposes.[47] Although the two cities would maintain separate police units and courts, co-operation agreements between them would make it difficult for miscreants on one side of the boundary to perpetrate crimes on the other side and then escape back to the boundaries of their city. The treaties between Italy and the Vatican constituted an example of such agreements.[48]

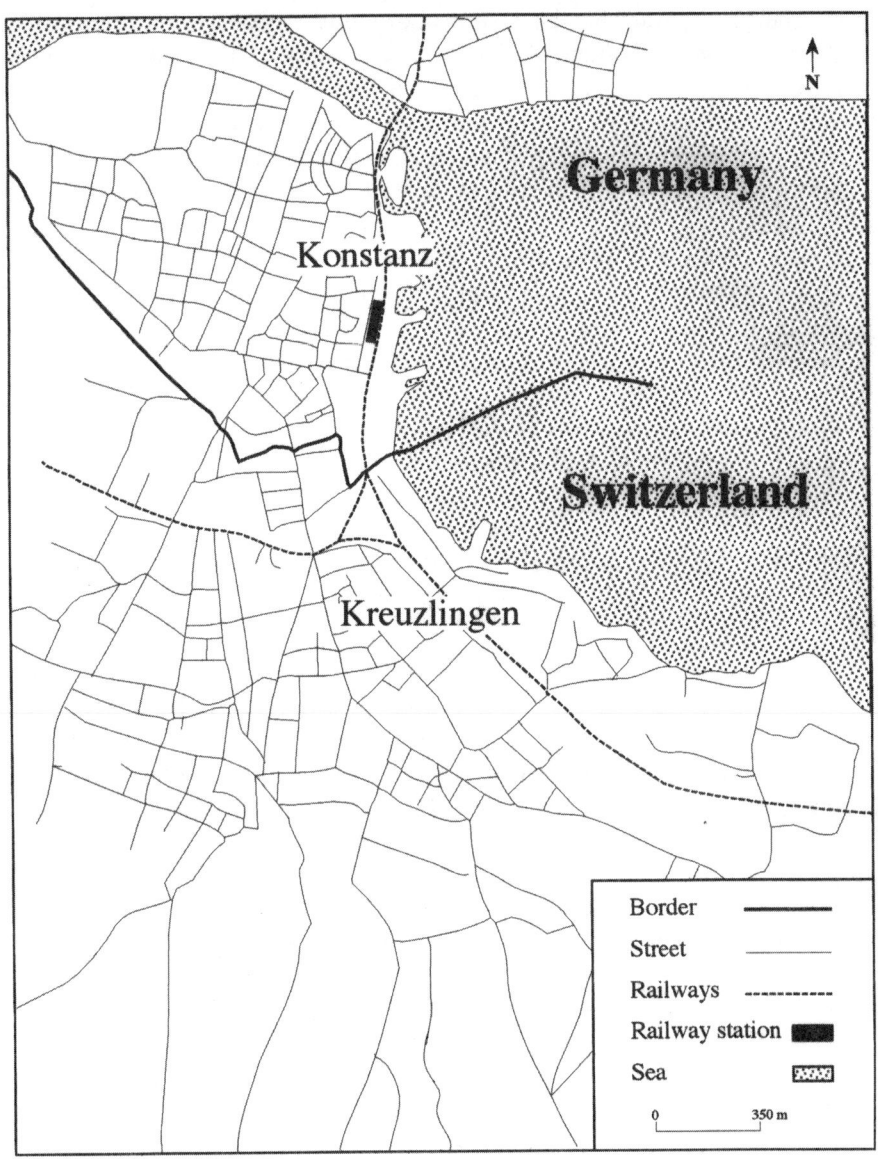

Map 9: Border Between Konstanz, Germany and Kreuzlingen, Switzerland

Another example that the Jerusalem Committee cited, concerning a city divided by political boundary lines into administrative units with different legal systems, was furnished by Shanghai. This city was divided into three administrative regions under separate and independent authorities, with a separate legal framework for each region. The 'Foreign Settlement' was managed by an elected municipal council, which included foreign and Chinese representatives; the French Legation was managed by the French Consul-General, and the Chinese region was managed by a Chinese mayor appointed by the Nationalist central government. Co-operation between the three administrative units led to the establishment of joint services between the three parts of Shanghai and free transit between the various areas. The city in its entirety functioned as an independent unit, and produced a situation whereby the boundaries between the various regions were generally only lines on a map.[49]

SUMMARY OF THE EXECUTIVE'S PROPOSAL FOR PARTITIONING JERUSALEM

The boundaries of the map that the Jewish Agency Executive presented for partitioning Jerusalem were induced by a number of considerations. New Jerusalem was demographically important to the Jewish state and its loss would have serious economic and political repercussions. The city occupied a prominent place in Jewish national consciousness and its loss could adversely influence the Zionist Congress's vote on ratifying a partition plan acceptable to the Executive. While the Executive displayed political realism on the Old City, it nevertheless realized the necessity of retaining a symbol (Mount Scopus).

It is hard to assume that the Jerusalem Committee, and the Jewish Agency Executive in general, were unaware of the political and technical difficulties besetting the city's partition. However, if these difficulties were presented in all their true asperity it would have harmed any chance that the British would accept the plan. On the other hand, they could not totally be ignored. Therefore, in the memoranda that it presented to the Partition Commission, the Executive emphasized those examples in various global locations where problems deriving from a boundary that cut across urban areas had actually been solved. Nonetheless, the case of Jerusalem was essentially different from the other places cited as examples, and indeed the British Partition Commission dwelt on this particular point among its reasons for rejecting the Executive's proposal.[50]

NOTES

1. CZA, Protocol of the Jewish Agency Executive's Meeting on 23 May 1938.
2. CZA, file S25/5172, letter from Shertok to Neumann on 2 December 1937. See also CZA, The Executive's Memorandum to the Partition Commission; PPCR (1938), p. 73; Ben-Gurion (1937), p. 359; Sharett (1937), p. 258; CZA, file S25/10109, letter from Neumann to Shertok on 28 November 1937; CZA, Protocol of the Jewish Agency Executive's Meeting on 23 May 1938 – Ben-Gurion's speech is taken from there.
3. PRO, file CO 733/348, letter from Weizmann to Ormsby-Gore on 15 June 1937.
4. CZA, Memorandum of the Executive to the Partition Commission.
5. Cohen, G. (1973), pp. 366–9.
6. Ibid., p. 378.
7. CZA, Protocol of the Jewish Agency Executive's Meeting on 18 December 1936. See also Shertok's statement, CZA, Protocol of the Jewish Agency Executive's Meeting on 17 June 1937 as well as Shertok's statement, CZA, Protocol of The Inner Zionist General Council's Meeting on 21 June 1937. See also CZA, Protocol of the Jewish Agency Executive's Meeting on 29 May 1938, from which it emerges that, in response to the Zionist demand for the new city alone, the Partition Commission raised the apprehension that the Arabs would also demand part of the city outside the wall. See ibid., the criticism voiced by members of the Inner Zionist General Council (in Protocols of the Inner Zionist General Council's Meetings on 20 June 1938 and 11 July 1938) that, even from a tactical point, the Executive had even forfeited the possibility of haggling over the Old City. One member of the Inner Zionist General Council hinted in his criticism that the Executive attached greater importance to retaining Degania in the Jordan Valley (the first kibbutz established in Palestine – a product of the Labor Movement and one of the pet symbols of a movement, which included Ben-Gurion and Shertok among its members) within the areas of the Jewish State (according to the Royal Commission's proposal, Degania was not included within the area of the Jewish State), than it did to the retention of the Old City within the Jewish State's borders. On this, see CZA, Protocol of the Inner Zionist General Council's Meeting on 11 July 1938, statement by R. Gafni.
8. CZA, The Executive's Memorandum to the Partition Commission; PPCR (1938), p. 73; CZA, file S25/5145, letter from Katznelson to Weizmann on 27 April 1937; Sharett (1937), pp. 242, 258, 315–16; Ben-Gurion (1937), pp. 254, 277, 359; the twentieth Zionist Congress, stenographic report, 1937, p. 71 – Statement by Weizmann; Klieman (1987), pp. 341–3, which cites Weizmann's letter to Ormsby-Gore on 14 July 1937; CZA, file S25/10.050, memorandum of P. Naphtali: 'The Budget of the Jewish State in Case of Partition', July 1937; PRO, file CO 733/348, letter from Weizmann to Ormsby-Gore on 15 June 1937; ibid., file CO 733/348, letter from P. Rutenberg to Sir John Maffey on 5 June 1937; CZA, Protocol of the Jewish Agency Executive's Meeting on 4 July 1937.
9. CZA, file S25/9239, memorandum of Dr. A. Bonne: 'The Jewish Share in the Economic Development of Jerusalem'.
10. CZA, file S25/5145, letter from Katznelson to Weizmann on 27 April 1937.
11. Ibid.; CZA, Protocol of the Jewish Agency Executive's Meeting on 4 July 1937 – statement by Rabbi Fishman.
12. Ibid.
13. See CZA, file S25/5145, letter from Katznelson to Weizmann; CZA, The Executive's Memorandum to the Partition Commission; CZA, file S25/9239, memorandum of B. Z. Dinaburg, 'The Historical Connection of the Jewish People with Jerusalem', provided to the Partition Commission by the Jewish Agency Executive on 1 July 1938; Ben-Gurion (1937), pp. 358–60.
14. Ben-Gurion (1937), p. 254.
15. Ben-Gurion (1937), pp. 237 (the source of the quotation), 277, 284, 358–60. See also Golani (1990). It should be noted that Ben-Gurion was initially prepared to yield Jerusalem in its entirety, but modified his position in the face of the vigorous opposition displayed by both

opponents and proponents of partition. On this, see Ben-Gurion (1937), p. 457; Golani (1990), pp. 229–300.

16. See the twentieth Zionist Congress, stenographic report, 1937, pp. 77–8. See also Heller (1984), p. 97. In his testimony before the Partition Commission, Rabbi Herzog, the Chief Rabbi of Palestine, contended that 'Jerusalem for the Jewish people is more than simply a country's capital city … Jerusalem is a special unit for the Jewish people as expressed in their oath: "If I forget thee Jerusalem, may my right hand lose its cunning" and in any event the Jewish people could not conceive of its country without Jerusalem.' On this, see CZA, Protocol of the Inner Zionist General Council's Meeting on 20 June 1938. See also PRO, file CO 733/348, letter from P. Rutenberg to Sir John Maffey on 5 June 1937. Regarding the position of Jerusalem in the arguments of those opposing the partition scheme within the Zionist Movement and within the Jewish people as a whole, see Eliash (1971), pp. 59–61.

17. See, for example, CZA, Protocols of the Jewish Agency Executive's Meetings on 8 July 1937, 25 May 1938; CZA, Protocol of the Inner Zionist General Council's Meeting on 20 June 1938.

18. CZA, Protocol of the Zionist Executive's Meeting on 8 July 1937 – statement by Kaplan. Ussishkin, who totally rejected the partition plan as proposed and demanded Jerusalem in its entirety (save for the sites holy to Christians and Moslems, which would remain under the supervision of the mandatory government), contended that there was no ethical–symbolic value to modern Jerusalem if one detached old Jerusalem from it. He added that: 'Tel Aviv, our master creation during the last 30 years, this great and holy esteemed if it constitutes a continuation of Jerusalem but it has no value if it is detached from it and becomes a colony of Jews in some place whatsoever. The Bronx in New York has 300,000 Jews which is double the population of Tel Aviv …'. On this, see CZA, Protocol of the Inner Zionist General Council's Meeting on 11 January 1938. See also Protocol of the Inner Zionist General Council's Meeting on 20 June 1938; Sharett (1937), pp. 315–16. See also the vigorous protests voiced by Ben-Gurion against Ussishkin's statement, and his contention that Ussishkin was in effect dividing the Old City, in Protocols of the Inner Zionist General Council's Meetings on 11 January 1938 and 20 June 1938.

19. CZA, The Executive's Memorandum to the Partition Commission; PPCR (1938), pp. 73–5; Ben-Gurion (1937), pp. 254, 359.

20. Ben-Gurion (1937), pp. 277–89; Sharett (1937), pp. 229, 258, 315–16; CZA, file S25/943, letter from Weizmann to Bernard Joseph on 22 July 1937.

21. Ben-Gurion (1937), p. 289.

22. CZA, Protocol of the Jewish Agency Executive's Meeting on 8 July 1937; CZA, Protocols of the Inner Zionist General Council's Meetings on 20 June 1938 and 11 October 1938, statement of Ussishkin; CZA, The Executive's Memorandum to the Partition Commission. See also Ben-Gurion (1937), pp. 323, 333, 358–60; Sharett (1937), p. 308. Weizmann even reported at the end of 1937 during a meeting of the Jewish Agency Executive that: 'On all the discussions regarding this issue, he has encountered complete understanding and has not encountered any opposition to the actual proposal of incorporating New Jerusalem within the Jewish State …'. On this, see CZA, Protocol of the Jewish Agency Executive's Meeting on 12 December 1937. See also the statement by the Archbishop of Canterbury in the House of Lords, and the words of the British Colonial Secretary, Ormsby-Gore, in the British Parliament in Klieman (1987), pp. 1–77.

23. CZA, file S25/9939, memorandum: 'The Goals of the Jerusalem Committee' (undated). See also, CZA, Protocol of the First Session of the Jerusalem Committee on 7 November 1937 which also includes the list of the committee's members. Owing to their fundamental opposition to partition, Professors Yellin and Klein left the committee at the start of its work. On this, see CZA, Protocol of the Jewish Agency Executive's Meeting on 8 May 1938.

24. The main subjects dealt with are included in the Protocols of the Jerusalem Committee Plenum's Meetings and the Sub-committee's Meetings, as well as in the correspondence and reports connected with the work of the Jerusalem Committee, which are located in CZA, files S25/9239, S25/8930, S25/5109.

25. See CZA, file S25/9239, Protocol of the Jerusalem Committee's Meeting, 7 November 1937.
26. CZA, file S25/9239, Protocol of the Jerusalem Committee's Meeting on 7 November 1937. Other experts were subsequently added to the sub-committees in each and every area. See also CZA, file S25/10109, memorandum of the Political Department's 'Jerusalem Committee' (undated); CZA, file S25/10109, letter from Simon to Dr. Bernard Joseph on 5 January 1938; CZA, list of memoranda regarding Jerusalem and the Jerusalem Committee, which were prepared and amassed in the Political Department (undated); CZA, file S25/10109, memorandum: 'Jerusalem', summarizing a number of experts' memoranda that were prepared regarding the partition of Jerusalem (undated).
27. Regarding the principles, see Paz (1994). See also note 26. CZA, file S25/5119, Protocol of the Jerusalem Committee's Meeting on 25 November 1937; CZA, file S25/5119, Protocol of the Geographic Sub-committee's Meeting on 24 December 1937; CZA, file S25/5119, memorandum of Dr. E. Loewenthal: 'Topographical and Juridical Questions Arising in Case Jewish Jerusalem is Included in the Future Jewish State', January 1938.
28. See memorandum of M. Hecker in CZA, file S25/9239, 'Suggestions for the Establishment of a Jewish Jerusalem' (undated). A discussion of Hecker's proposal was conducted at the meeting of the Jerusalem Committee on 25 November 1937 in CZA, file S25/5119 and in ibid. the second session of the Geographic Sub-committee on 24 December 1937. For a verbal description of the boundary and the considerations behind this demarcation, see, CZA, file S25/9239.
29. Regarding the plan for 'Rehavia Morhevet', see, for example, CZA, files A402/32 and L18/804.
30. There was talk of closing off Jaffa Road on both sides and building elevated walkways. There was also talk about a road that would by-pass the Jewish city from the north and reach the Damascus Gate.
31. See, for example, Katz (1995); Ussishkin (1933), pp. 238–9; at the laying of the cornerstone for the establishment of the Hebrew University on Mount Scopus, which took place on 24 July 1918, Weizmann said, *inter alia*: 'In the shadow of the walls of this university, the spirit of divine prophecy which previously resided in us will be revived. The university will be the focal point of our restored past glory. Our national soul will both soar and find refuge in this temple of ours. This is our belief ...'. See Weizmann's address in the Handwritten Manuscript Archives of the National Library in Jerusalem, file L 239.
32. CZA, Protocol of the Jewish Agency Executive's Meeting on 1 August 1937.
33. See Dr. M. Eliash's memorandum: 'Jerusalem and the Partition Question', in CZA, file S25/5107.
34. See also the opinions of Ben Zvi and Pach, who outspokenly demanded the annexation of Jerusalem's southern neighborhoods for security reasons, in CZA, their letters of 23 December 1937 and 26 December 1937. See also Hecker's memorandum in CZA, file S25/9239.
35. See, for example, the words of Bernard Joseph at the opening session of the Jerusalem Committee in CZA, file S25/10109. See also CZA, file S25/6654, which includes alternative maps to the corridor proposal.
36. See the memoranda of Hecker and Loewenthal in notes 27 and 28.
37. CZA, file S25/5119, Protocol of the Jerusalem Committee's Meeting on 25 November 1937.
38. Ibid.
39. See Hecker's memorandum in CZA, file S25/9239.
40. Nevertheless, Shertok intended to accompany Hecker on a survey in order to examine the possibilities outside the wall. On this see CZA, file S25/5109, letter from Shertok to Hecker on 12 December 1937. See also CZA, Protocol of the Jewish Agency Executive's Meeting on 8 May 1938.
41. The map was presented to the Partition Commission and appended to its reports. See Map 6. See also the original map prepared by the Jewish Agency in CZA, Map Collection. On

this map, the Jewish real-estate holdings in Jerusalem were marked. See also CZA, file S25/9239, memorandum: 'Jerusalem Under Partition', which was presented by the Jewish Agency Executive to the Partition Commission on 16 August 1938. See also CZA, Protocol of the Jewish Agency Executive's Meeting on 25 July 1938 where the Executive authorized the partition map of Jerusalem, presented to the Partition Commission. See also CZA, Protocol of the Jewish Agency Executive's Meeting on 23 May 1938.

42. See note 13.
43. See note 28, and see appendix 1: 'Boundary Line of the Area of New Jerusalem to be Included in the Jewish State' in the Jewish Agency Executive's memorandum: 'Jerusalem under Partition', in CZA, file S25/9239.
44. CZA, file S25/5100, letter from Bernard Joseph to Zalman Lifshitz on 29 April 1938; PPCR (1938), pp. 73–5.
45. See the memorandum: 'Jerusalem under Partition' in note 41, pp. 11–13. regarding the co-operation among the four cities on both sides of the Canadian–American border see in detail the work by Davis (1974), pp. 289–311.
46. See the memorandum: 'Jerusalem under Partition' in note 41, pp. 3–7, 18–20. See also PRO, file FO371/21863, letter from the British Foreign Office to the British Legation in Berne on 26 August 1938.
47. See the memorandum: 'Jerusalem under Partition' in note 41, pp. 6–7. For a discussion on the question of possible agreements, see also the memorandum of Dr. M. Eliash in CZA, file S25/5107.
48. See the memorandum: 'Jerusalem under Partition', CZA, file S25/9239, pp. 7–9. See also CZA, file S25/245, letter from A. Lourie to Leo Kohn of the Jewish Agency from 13 January 1938, to which is appended the 'Conciliation Treaty between the Holy See and the Kingdom of Italy', 11 February 1929. See also CZA, Protocol of the Jewish Agency Executive's Meeting on 8 May 1938.
49. See the memorandum: 'Jerusalem under Partition', in note 41, pp. 20–2. See also CZA, file S25/9239, the memorandum: 'Further Note on Shanghai' from 17 June 1938. Regarding the partition of Shanghai, see, in detail, Johnstone (1937). See also Katz (1993).
50. See PPCR (1938), pp. 34–9; 73–80; statement of the British Colonial Secretary Ormsby-Gore in the League of Nations (1937b), pp. 23, 38. See also PRO, file CO 733/354 regarding British analyses of the Jewish Agency proposal for partitioning Jerusalem and the arguments that they raised for rejecting this proposal.

4

Attempts to Formulate a Plan for Transferring the Arab Population Within the Framework of Partition

FROM INCREDULITY TO FULL SUPPORT FOR THE RECOMMENDATIONS

The partition boundaries drawn by the Jewish Agency Executive would leave the Jewish State with a quite sizeable total Arab population. Even if New Jerusalem were included within the Jewish State's boundaries, the Arab population, according to the data available to the Executive, would total nearly 45 per cent of the Jewish State's population (297,000 out of 666,000).[1] The Royal Commission, as aforesaid, was aware that leaving such a sizeable Arab minority within the areas of the Jewish State was problematic and that population exchanges – even compulsory ones – were a necessary part of the partition process, and a precondition for obtaining the yearned-for peace. It would appear that the Royal Commission's recommendation regarding the transfer of populations – even if necessary by force – took even the Executive by surprise. During the course of 1936 and on until the first months of 1937, the idea of transferring Arabs from Palestine arose during the deliberations of the Executive in various contexts, including preparations for the appearance before the Royal Commission. However, the plan was quickly dropped, because it was deemed impractical and because if it was raised as a Zionist initiative it could provoke anti-Zionist responses.

Thus, for example, in May 1936, Arthur Ruppin lashed out at Menahem Ussishkin:

> I also entertained the same dreams as you. I once said that Iraq would absorb the Arabs of Palestine and all the nations of the world would recognize the morality of our just demands. I stopped hallucinating and dreaming. How could you imagine that the Arabs would leave Palestine and go to Baghdad? What would they gain from it? What do they lack in Palestine? Their material conditions are good ... Why should he go to Iraq – simply because it is an Arab country? In his opinion Palestine today is still an Arab country as well and he intends to wage battle to preserve its Arabic nature. And Palestine possesses

an additional advantage over Iraq: A number of Europe's advantages have penetrated into this country. He can wander through the city's streets and ogle at the young girls with bare faces which he cannot do in the outskirts of Baghdad ...

Ruppin added that Britain, for whom the Arab world was more important from a political standpoint than the Jewish one, would not take part in implementing such a plan.[2]

Ben-Gurion emphasized as well that 'England [sic] won't do this for us and won't eject the Arabs from Palestine', and 'if we were to tell them [the Royal Commission] that the Arabs should go to Iraq or Iran, this would simply strengthen the anti-Zionist innuendo and members of the Commission would return to Britain convinced that the Jews are seeking to expel the Arabs from Palestine'.[3] Nonetheless, at the same time Ben-Gurion believed that one should create a large territorial reserve for areas of concentrated Jewish settlement, and that Arab land-sellers should be encouraged to transfer to the east bank of the Jordan. All this should be done out of the totally free will of those transferring, however, and after they had received full assistance from the Zionist bodies. Ben-Gurion wished to receive the Royal Commission's agreement for this policy.[4] A few months prior to the publication of the Royal Commission's report, Shertok also contended that '... it is necessary to put out of our mind the possibility of population exchanges in the immediate years. I am not talking about a vision for the future. In the next ten years the thing is simply impractical ... At this stage one should not toy with parallels regarding the population exchanges between Turkey and Greece'.[5]

The Royal Commission's recommendation, namely the transfer of the Arab population from the Jewish State, even by force, as part of the partition process, was therefore much more than the Executive could have expected. After a first reaction of shock and incredulity that this recommendation could be implemented, and 'these are only mere words',[6] the Executive began to consider the issue soberly. It expressed its agreement with the recommendation and observed its great importance for implementing the partition idea.[7] Ben-Gurion was in favor of picking up the gauntlet:

> In my notes on the report immediately after a first reading, I ignored a central point whose importance surpasses all the other positive elements and outweighs all the deficiencies and faults in the report ... and if it will not remain a dead letter it can give us something which we never ever had even when we were independent, even during the First Temple and the Second Commonwealth: *forced transfer* [emphasis in the original] of Arabs from the

valleys which are offered to the Jewish State. I ignored this fundamental point out of *prejudice* [emphasis in the original] that this thing was simply impossible and these were only mere words. However, when I perused the Commission's findings a bit further, and the gigantic importance of this proposal became clear, I arrived at the conclusion that the primary obstacle to the implementation of this proposal is our lack of preparedness and our being captives of opinions and modes of thought that flourished in our midst under other circumstances and we must first of all liberate ourselves from flaccid thinking and the prejudice that this transfer would not be possible. I see, as previously, the tremendous difficulty of uprooting by a foreign force 100,000 Arabs from the villages in which they resided for hundreds of years. Will England [sic] dare to do it? She will definitely not do it if we don't want it and if we don't push her to it ... But if because of our flaccidness ... nothing will be done, we are going by our own fault to forfeit a chance that we never had and who knows if it will ever recur. And before we ask ourselves will Britain do it, we must uproot from our own hearts ... the assumption that this is impossible. It is altogether possible ... and we are not those who proposed it. The Royal Commission which the British Government has confided in ... it was the Commission which imposed the matter on the British Government and we must take hold of this conclusion as we clung to the Balfour Declaration, further just as we clung to Zionism itself ... with our full force, will and faith – that of all the Commission's findings this is the one thing that represents compensation for the severance of other parts of the country and offers *a large measure of raison d'etre from an Arab standpoint* [emphasis in the original]. For Trans-Jordan needs settlements and increased population, development and money and the British government, the wealthiest of all governments, is summoned by its own Royal Commission to supply the necessary money, and in the implementation of this transfer there is a great latent blessing to the Arab State whereas for us, it is a question of life, existence, security, culture, increased freedom and independence ... The transfer clause in my opinion is more important than all our demands for increased territory. This is the greatest and most important and most vital territorial increment. If we do not succeed in ejecting the Arabs from our midst and transfer them to an Arab area, when a British Royal Commission proposes this to England [sic], we will not so easily succeed in doing so (if we are to succeed at all) after the state has arise ... this has to be done *Now* and the first step and perhaps the *decisive one is to prepare ourselves* for implementing it ...[8]

Since the Royal Commission spoke of principles alone, the Executive had to examine in depth the possibilities of implementing transfer and to formulate a practical and detailed plan of transfer, which it intended to present before the British Partition Commission. Similar to the way it handled the boundaries question and the issue of Jerusalem, the Political

Department entrusted the bulk of handling the transfer issue to an Experts Commission, which it appointed and which received the sobriquet of the 'Committee for Population Transfer'. As was the case with the Royal Commission, the Greco–Turkish precedent served as a model for this committee as well. For political–information reasons it was important for the Zionist Committee to make use of the Balkan precedent owing to the use which the Royal Commission had made of it. It would therefore be proper to clarify the Balkan precedent before examining the deliberation and work of the Committee for Population Transfer.

TRANSFER OF POPULATIONS FROM GREECE AND TURKEY, AND THE RESETTLEMENT OF THE GREEK REFUGEES

The population exchanges between Greece and Turkey in 1923 were a direct result of a series of wars fought between the two countries following the conquest of Smyrna (which Greece obtained in the peace agreements) by Greece in 1919. In June 1921, the Greeks advanced until the river Skaria, not far from Ankara. However, about a year later, during the months of August and September 1922, the Turkish Army launched a counter-attack that defeated the Greek Army, which then retreated back to Greece. This defeat had far-reaching repercusssions for the sizeable Greek population in Asia Minor and in Eastern Thrace: the entry of the Turks into Izmir was accompanied by the massacre of many Greeks in reprisal for the suppression of the Turkish population by the Greeks during the years 1919–22. This was another link in the chain of violence between Greeks and Turks, which stretched back to the fifteenth century.

In September 1922, the Greeks were requested to vacate the area of Thrace in very short order.[9] Between that period and January 1923 – when the Lausanne Conference convened to establish the boundary between Greece and Turkey and the two countries signed the treaty calling for the compulsory population transfer of Orthodox Greeks and Moslem Turks – 1,150,000 Greeks were expelled. The agreement calling for compulsory population transfer merely ratified what had already been perpetrated upon the Greek population. The unilateral emigration of the Greek population, already at an advanced stage, was transformed into a population exchange backed by international legal guarantees.[10] In the words of Ladas, in his detailed study of 1932: 'in practical terms, the emigration of the Greek population in Turkey had already been completed when the agreement referring to exchanges and which determined the procedures of exchanges and compensations was signed in Lausanne ...'.[11]

Only 150,000 Greeks out of a total of 1,300,000 Greek refugees emigrated and were resettled in an organized fashion. Unlike the Greek minority, the 450,000-strong Turkish minority emigrated almost entirely in the wake of the agreement and did so in an organized fashion.

An additional agreement, signed at the same time, determined that compulsory population exchanges would occur between Greece and Bulgaria. In contrast to the Greco–Turkish case, this accord was preceded by a prior understanding between the two countries that they would be best advised to obtain an exchange of populations. The transfer was free and accompanied by the right to take objects and movable property, and was far removed from the emigration from Asia Minor to Greece. In the wake of the agreement, some 50,000 people emigrated from Bulgaria to Greece, and about 100,000 people emigrated from Greece to Bulgaria. The entire process of population exchanges between Greece, Turkey and Bulgaria was completed in the course of one year.[12]

While the emigration of the Greek population from Turkey was a tragic process, replete with suffering, the resettlement of the Greeks was a success story. The various contemporary sources are most loquacious about this fact. Since the Greek government could not bear the burden of the rehabilitation of the refugees and their resettlement, the task was imposed on a Committee appointed by the League of Nations. Monies for the rehabilitation were extended to Greece as a loan by the United States and Britain in return for guarantees pledging Greek income from custom duties and taxes.[13] There was no shortage of land. The Committee had at its disposal lands that were abandoned by the Turks (and they were the majority), lands which the Greek government had leased or expropriated,[14] and additional lands that had been vacated when the agricultural-reform law had been put into effect.[15] Most of the land was located in Macedonia and Thrace, where the refugees resided and where most of the development projects were launched. Elementary means of subsistence were extended to the refugees by the Committee, and it was the Committee that engaged in building the villages and developing an infrastructure, paving roads, draining swamps and establishing infirmaries and schools.[16]

Some of the immigrants turned to the cities and were housed in buildings that had been abandoned by the Turks and Bulgarians and in temporary housing that survived for many years hence. Merchants and professionals did not generally encounter absorption problems in Greece, as they had resources, ability and economic initiative, which greatly contributed to the development of the Greek economy. It was necessary to build residential neighborhoods for members of the middle class and for the workers, and to provide them with sources of income.[17] The urban development that resulted from the activity of entrepreneurs among the refugees who were industrialists, merchants and shipping magnates helped industry and ship-building to flourish. The building, development and industrial projects provided work for the entire urban population, both for refugees and for long-time residents. In general, about 700,000 of the 1.3 million emigrants were settled in the cities.[18]

The results of the population exchanges with reference to Greece were therefore positive. Greece gained a population that had know-how, initiative and skills in industry, fishing and agriculture. The malaria-stricken areas in Macedonia and Thessaly became flourishing agricultural areas as a result of the development projects and the established residents also benefitted from the agricultural reforms. This was also true for the cities, which were rehabilitated from the devastation of the First World War thanks to the refugees.[19] However, it should be emphasized that failures also occurred in the process of resettling the Greeks; but the general assessments recorded during the 1930s spoke of a major success. For example, the agronomist Akiva Ettinger, one of the senior operatives of the Jewish Agency, who visited Greece in the early 1930s, wrote:

> I talked with settlers and those in charge of resettlement and received tables and diagrams from the settlement offices. The impression of success and failures, the ups and downs, and back again, all these reinforced my esteem for this gargantuan project which proved unusually successful, even though many victims succumbed due to malaria and other diseases and as a result of interminable suffering and tortures. Thus, Greek settlement was a vast success even if one takes into account the important factors which contributed to this success, the active assistance rendered by the League of Nations during the project's initial years until it was on its feet and flourishing, the provision of land by the Greek Government, the devotion displayed by this government and its capable organization of the activity ...[20]

The political results, which constituted the acid test of whether such a drastic action was truly justified and whether the end justified the means, also proved positive. Since the close of the first decade of the century, the region had been an arena of national conflict, and a maelstrom of imperialist influence and global political rivalries. The result had been suffering and bloodshed, and a situation that appeared unbridgeable. However, in the course of a number of years following the exchange agreement, far-reaching changes occurred. The homogenization of the population promoted internal stability within the states, and the rivalry and enmity gave way to co-operation and genuine amity. These new attitudes found expression in agreements and conventions on co-operation in various spheres such as trade and economy; a declaration by Greece's leaders that their country was content with its present boundaries and desired to live at peace with its neighbors; the waning of old nationalist sentiments, and the formation of feelings of amicability and mutual sympathy between the two countries. In sum, to cite Ladas: 'it is certain, however, that the political and religious jealousies of the past are giving way before new economic forces, now more than ever before essential to the life and happiness of the Balkan Peoples'.[21]

CENTRALITY OF THE BALKAN PRECEDENT FOR THE COMMITTEE FOR POPULATION TRANSFER

The Jewish Agency's Committee for Population Transfer was composed of specialists in the areas of land purchases, settlement, economics and law, and experts familiar with the Arab village, Arab affairs and the neighboring Arab countries. The central figures were the chairman, Dr. Yaakov Thon, at that time the director of a Zionist Company for land purchases – the Palestine Land Development Company (PLDC), Dr. Kurt Mendelsohn, an adviser in the Jewish Agency's Institute for the Study of the Economy, Joseph Weitz, head of the JNF's Lands Department, Dr. Avraham Bonne, a member of the Institute for the Study of the Economy, and Eliyahu Epstein, who was in charge of the Political Department's relations with the neighboring countries. In autumn 1937, Thon and Mendelsohn made a special trip to Greece in order to observe at close range the experience of population transfer that had occurred there.[22] Upon returning from their visit to Greece, Thon and Mendelsohn contended that first one should create a extensive information infrastructure to proselytize on behalf of a transfer based on the Greek precedent. They believed that such an information policy was a precondition for any transfer program, especially since the Royal Commission had based its own recommendations on the Greek precedent. Furthermore, they believed that the Jewish Agency's operative programs should adopt the central facets of the transfer and resettlement programs as they had been accomplished in the Balkans, including the element of coercion. This was both a matter of political utility and because the Balkan experience had proven a success.

By November 1937, Mendelsohn had completed a draft of an exhaustive survey on the Greek precedent entitled 'The Balance of Resettlements', which summarized his joint research with Thon.[23] On that subject, in

December 1937 Yona Silman completed a research proposal (written at Thon's invitation) with the title of 'Greco–Turkish Exchange of Populations and Resettlement Schemes'.[24] At the end of December 1937, Thon wrote to the Political Department of the Jewish Agency stressing the urgency of disseminating Mendelsohn's work widely, and, *inter alia*, emphasized that:

> the idea of transferring the Arab populations as an act of legal compulsion encounters reluctance in many circles. A description of the experiment that occurred in Greece will demonstrate that in that region the exchange of population conferred only benefits to all parties. They put an end to the war of extermination fought for over 200 years by two people who were mortal enemies, and created relations of friendship and good neighborliness between them. In our country, as well, similar action could put a stop to the attacks of the Arab people on the Jews and bring about peace and good neighborly relations between them. The study of Greece informs us that those Greek exiles bestowed a great blessing on their Greek homeland and greatly invigorated it, after the defeat which it had sustained at the hand of the Turks. The additional manpower which they furnished far outweighed victories and territorial conquests. It is important for the Arab world to recognize this fact. Then perhaps it will be possible to find leaders of vision who will agree out of a sense of national conviction to the partition plan which involves the transfer of an Arab population amidst a belief that this will only strengthen and invigorate the new Arab state ...[25]

Thon proposed publishing the research in various languages including Arabic.[26] Subsequently, at the start of 1939, the work was published. A central place in the aforementioned information policy was to be occupied by the testimony of Greek settlers, directors of the project, officials, etc., who all voiced the same response: 'this was a glorious chapter in Greek History ...'.[27] Together with the aforesaid, it should be noted that, notwithstanding the attempts of Thon and Mendelsohn to demonstrate the resemblance between the Balkan case and the Palestinian case, despite the differences, in the end the propaganda line they urged was political and tendentious, and its scientific basis far from unassailable.

In pursuit of the aforementioned policy line, Thon and Mendelsohn believed that one should adopt, amidst the policy of transferring the Arabs from the boundaries of the Jewish State, those central elements that had been put into practice in the Balkans and especially in those cases where the transfers were implemented following the signature of treaties. In their opinion, the necessary first step, similar to the Balkan precedent, was to put into effect agrarian reform:

The major transfers that were implemented in the Balkan States could be put into effect only via an extreme agrarian reform in Greece by the expropriation with low indemnification of the large estates, whose owners were in the majority Turks. In the absence of a vigorous agrarian reform (the right of expropriating the large estate owners *musha* land etc. [parentheses in the original; *musha* were lands commonly owned by members of the village]) it will prove impossible to obtain the necessary land areas for the resettlement of the Arabs and this will encumber, slow-up and increase the cost of transferring territorial property to Jewish hands ... Experience teaches us that the transfer of population is tied to an agrarian reform which can place entire nations on a new path ...

In conjunction with the agrarian reform, they recommended adoption of supplementary measures similar to the practice undertaken in the Balkans:

amongst these, one should include the various easements such as debit arrangements, tax abatements and free transfer from place to place, etc., which had been awarded to the Greek and Bulgarian emigrants. The Greco-Bulgarian transfer project was exemplary in that the candidates for transfer were to be awarded various privileges on condition that they would obligate themselves to move within two years ... In order to promote a voluntary transfer process, in the case of Palestine, one should determine a series of easements, such as purchasing land from the emigrants on the basis of an estimate of the land and its structures, equalization of debts, exemption from taxes and fines, the right of resettlement and the receipt of working capital ...[28]

Mendelsohn and Thon argued that the desirable rate of transfer could also be deduced from the Balkan precedent:

A transfer which was organized on a contractual basis and under the supervision of an international court, was implemented in a very short time. The transfer of the Turks from Greece to Asia Minor and of the remnants of the Greek community in Bulgaria to Greece, a total of more than 300,000 people was accomplished in the space of 12 months. In any event, we must see to it that the transfer of the Arab population in the first stage should be performed in a short period and should not last more than 10 years, otherwise, we face the danger of sabotage and added population because of natural increase ...[29]

It was for this reason that Mendelsohn rejected the policy of a gradual transfer, which had been practiced by the Zionist institutions up to this juncture. Under this policy, lands had been purchased by Zionist bodies and the tenant farmers had been transferred to other areas, at a ratio of 2,000–3,000 people per annum: 'This method is ill-suited to the goal of population transfers on a large scale and does not accord with the proposed recommendation of the Royal Commission. The transfer movement in the Balkan countries was an extreme one and took place in one shot. Only over the course of time were settlement plans eventually formulated.' Nonetheless, the transfer of Arabs and their settlement had to be done on a more gradual and variegated basis, 'according to the following order: tenant farmers, agricultural workers of the large estates, laborers performing the brute labors of development work, artisans in the building trades and finally the peasant farmers'. Thon and Mendelsohn insisted on the necessity of making provision in the settlement plans for the transferees, because 'as opposed to the Balkan countries, a greater feeling of moral responsibility for the fate of the transferees must prevail amongst us'. The two did not linger on any type of preference regarding the preferred region of origin of the transferees. They envisaged the target areas to be Trans-Jordan and Syria.[30]

The impact of the Balkan precedent on Thon and Mendelsohn was so immense that they agreed to coerced transfer, although they were aware of its inherent moral defect, and, as Thon wrote: 'It is not only the technical difficulty [in the transfer] that could prove burdensome to us but the moral value can exasperate us as well. We must not forget that we were once strangers in Egypt and likewise we cannot forget that we have wandered through every place and one cannot produce a situation where people who have been living in a certain place for hundreds of years will be forcibly ejected from it.'[31] The possibility of obtaining a total peace as a result of the transfer, as demonstrated by the Balkan precedent, was viewed by Thon as of a more lofty value than the moral defect. Mendelsohn also contended, on the basis of the Balkan precedent, that the fate of the general population took precedence over the harm inflicted upon individuals as a result of the transfer.[32]

ATTEMPTS TO FILL IN THE DETAILS

A detailed plan for transferring the Arab population from the confines of the Jewish State was proposed by one member of the Commission, Joseph Weitz. His plan was based on two basic postulates, and his recommendation incorporated both of these. First of all, the importance of transferring the Arab population from the Jewish State did not derive solely from political and security considerations but was also required to make the land they retained available for Jewish settlement. Secondly, as opposed to Thon and Mendelsohn and contrary to the Greco–Turkish precedent,

Weitz did not believe in the possibility that anybody whatsoever could coerce this transfer. The only possibility lay in voluntary transfer. Prior political agreements would constitute a precondition for this and would help create a conducive atmosphere. However, these would not suffice. In Weitz's opinion, one had to create in the region earmarked for the absorption of the transferred population conditions that would encourage people to emigrate there.

To borrow a concept from the realm of immigration theory, Weitz believed that, in order for an immigration movement to begin, it was necessary significantly to encourage those factors of economic attraction in the target area. In the light of these basic assumptions, he also determined that although one should aspire for a maximum transfer, the preferred candidate population for initial transfer, in his opinion, would be the rural population, defined as those lacking land or retaining a small amount of land but who cultivated vast amounts of land belonging to other owners. This population comprised tenant farmers, villagers who worked as hired hands in agriculture, and owners of small areas (up to 3 dunams per capita). The size of this population was estimated as 87,300 people (to whom one could add about 10,000–15,000 persons from the Bedouin population), i.e. one-third of the Moslem population in the Jewish region, which was then cultivating about 680,000 dunams out of the 3.7 million dunams in the Jewish State that were not Jewish owned. In Weitz's opinion, after the lands had been vacated by their Arab cultivators, the Zionist bodies would have to purchase them from their owners.[33]

In order to encourage the forces of attraction to the target areas, Weitz recommended the adoption of the following measures. Firstly, the selection of target areas similar in their soil and climatic conditions to the areas of origin, and which had enough land to settle the transferees. Therefore, a population that sprang from the coastal plain (18,000 people) should be transferred to the Gaza District; the population of the Beisan Valley (3,400) should be transferred to the eastern side of the Jordan Valley; the population of the Lake Hule plain and the mountains of the Upper Galilee (13,000) should be transferred to Syria; the population in the mountains of the Galilee, as well as the populations of Tiberias, Haifa, Acre and Nazareth, should be transferred to a mountainous region and the slope of Trans-Jordan. Aside from the Gaza District, Weitz believed that there was insufficient space in the western side of Palestine, within the confines of the Arab State, to resettle the transferees. He added that sending the bulk of the transferees to Trans-Jordan would contribute to the development of that region, which would constitute an element central to the success of the transfer program in general. An additional focus of activity recommended by Weitz for adoption was to have the Jewish Agency purchase all the necessary lands in the target areas on behalf of the transferees, so that each transferee would have enough land as determined by the conditions of each region. As Weitz writes: 'the entire transfer project will thus encounter a resonant echo in the world of politics and practice if our plan will demonstrate that it intends to transform people bereft of land into farm owners, property holders, something which can stimulate a desire amongst this element to transfer to a new area'. Weitz estimated the total amount of lands that had to be purchased at 1,150,000 dunams, of which 850,000 were located in Trans-Jordan. Additionally, Weitz contended that the Jewish Agency had to prepare detailed settlement plans for the transferees and finance through its own resources the entire burden of settling the transferred population. In Weitz's opinion, the cost of the entire transfer project under this plan (including the purchase of the vacated lands, the purchase of lands for the settlement of the transferees, and the financing of the settlement project) would total £8,276,000.[34]

Dr. Bonne, who in general believed in cleaving to the Royal Commission's proposal on transfer (save for the element of forced transfer) for utilitarian and political reasons,[35] added operative components to Weitz's plan. He estimated that financing the transfer and the resettlement of those involved would pose no difficulty, because the Royal Commission had already recommended imposing the burden upon the British people. He did not believe that the Jewish people would be capable of raising the requisite capital for implementing the plan. Indeed, Bonne believed that one should not easily give up on forced transfer, since this proposal was 'suggested not by Jews but by the British'; however, fearing that the Zionists and diaspora Jewry would be sharply attacked in the event of their participation in the forced transfer plan, he proposed yielding on the principle of compulsion.[36] In order to obtain voluntary transfer, they should camouflage Zionist aims in the guise of a broad agrarian reform program in the states that bordered on the proposed Jewish State. Those actually implementing the program would be, as in the Balkan precedent, neutral committees nominated by various bodies headed by the League of Nations. The committees would formulate a range of goals, such as developing water resources, swamp drainage, distribution of *musha* land, etc. The transfer of population would thus not appear as a goal in its own right, but would be swallowed up by the other objectives. Bonne believed that the exhibition of far-reaching development plans in the areas of the proposed Arab State in Palestine, in Trans-Jordan and Syria would constitute a force of attraction for the Arabs within the areas of the Jewish State, obviating the need for coercion.[37] As for the future, Bonne believed that with a change in the political conditions, and once both sides agreed to partition, 'the question of transfer would be transformed into a state objective which would be fulfilled even if the assent of every single Arab in the villages were not forthcoming'.[38]

The recommendations of Thon and Mendelsohn, as well as those of Weitz and Bonne, stimulated discussions in the Committee for Population Transfer and in the Political Department of the Jewish Agency – both on fundamental issues (voluntary or even forced transfer) and on operative details: the number of those to be transferred, their attributes, the target areas, etc. Shertok challenged a number of Weitz's recommendations. He contended that a population bereft of land in the villages was precisely the population that the village requires, since it engaged in specific and vital non-agricultural professions that provided services to the agricultural population. Therefore, if the landless were transferred, the void that they left would be filled in short order by a population of similarly meager means, which would immigrate from the Arab State, thus vitiating the entire purpose of transfer. Shertok raised an additional contention: the territorial legacy of the migrating population 'was dispersed over the entire country and strewn over small plots and it is highly doubtful that we can concentrate it into blocs', since, under Weitz's plan, the entire population of the village would not be transferred in toto but only certain elements in each village.[39] Bernard Joseph also argued that Weitz's plan was only a partial solution and it was necessary to prepare a transfer plan covering other segments of the Arab population.[40] The principle of adhering to the recommendations of the Royal Commission was also criticized by Shertok. The Royal Commission dealt with population exchanges similar to the Balkan precedent, whereas the Zionist proposals spoke of a unilateral transfer of the Arab population.[41] Bonne, relying on the historical sources, replied that the Balkan precedent was in practice more a transfer than an exchange: the departure of the Greeks from Turkey was already a *fait accompli* by the time that the exchange agreement was signed. Furthermore, it had not been critical to transfer the Moslem population from Greece to Turkey, as this minority had displayed loyalty to Greece and had lived in peace and harmony with the Greek population.[42]

Another member of the Committee for Population Transfer, Avraham Granovsky, the Managing Director of the JNF (Jewish National Fund), also opposed any transfer by coercion for reasons similar to those raised by Bonne: 'It is hard to describe a greater danger to the position of Jews in the Diaspora countries which is everywhere the position of a minority, and this applies also to the status of the Jews in Oriental countries.'[43] On the other hand, Granovsky did not believe that Arabs would transfer voluntarily and suggested limiting the discussions of transfer exclusively to the Jewish State's need for lands.[44] Those Arab-owned lands in the Jewish State could, in Granovsky's opinion, be transferred only within the framework of agrarian legislation, whereby the state would essentially expropriate lands that were unsettled or uncultivated. This redistribution of lands suitable for intensive cultivation would vacate an area that could accommodate many Jews. He added that in the event that the transfer of Arabs proved unfeasible, the need for agrarian legislation would be all the greater.[45] He proposed moving the transferees, as far away as possible from the boundaries of the Jewish State even as far as Iraq, because the areas adjacent to the boundaries of the Jewish State, including Trans-Jordan, were to serve as a territorial reserve for Jewish settlement.[46] Others in the committee joined Weitz in arguing that, in determining the target areas for transfer, they should consider the living conditions and the economy of those being transferred for 'it would be easier to transfer Arabs from this side of the Jordan to the other side to a place where conditions were not appreciably different than those of Palestine than it would be to transfer them to distant and totally different countries'.[47] Eliyahu Epstein suggested the Djezireh district in Syria as a target area for emigration, 'one of the most fertile and unsettled areas of Syria's districts which could afford mass settlement'. He believed that the Syrian Government would be interested in such large scale Arab settlement in Djezireh.[48]

THE FAILURE OF THE COMMITTEE'S EFFORTS TO FORMULATE AN
AGREED AND DETAILED PLAN FOR TRANFERRING THE ARABS

As the deliberations within the Committee for Population Transfer delved more deeply into the issue, the disagreements between committee members both with regards to principles and with regards to details began to surface in greater number. There was a lack of clarity as a result of missing details, which also encumbered efforts to formulate a clear and detailed transfer proposal. In the deliberations until the end of July 1937, the members of the committee succeeded in reaching a formulation, which was accepted unanimously only with regards to the very need to conduct a transfer within the framework of partition.[49] In the words of the committee:

> the Jewish State which was slated to arise in the future, will not be able to survive as long as a large Arab minority remains there. The transfer of Arab population on a large scale is a pre-condition to the establishment of the State for the presence of such a minority would constitute a perpetual danger of

movements which would try to subvert the new Jewish State. Aside from questions of security, it would prove necessary, considering the limited area of the Jewish State, to vacate lands presently cultivated by Arabs employing outmoded methods. Far-reaching measures in the area of agrarian legislation together with the delegation of governmental power and prerogatives are necessary for implementing this sweeping program to secure the necessary lands ...[50]

Regarding coercive transfer, the committee again arrived at a unanimous conclusion, that if the Arabs opposed transfer while Britain and other international bodies proved unable to implement transfer, then it would prove impossible to implement any transfer plan whatsoever.[51]

In practice, at the end of July 1937 these same conclusions were already being mentioned by Weizmann in his discussions with Ormsby-Gore.[52] In any event, these conclusions did not reject forced transfer but, rather, imposed responsibility for its implementation on Britain and international bodies. However, these conclusions totally contradicted the British government's decision on the issue of coercion and the positions of international bodies, as explicitly expressed in the deliberations of the League's institutions in summer 1937. All these bodies rejected forced transfer.[53] It would appear therefore that the Committee for Population Transfer, as well as the Executive, did not view the decision of the British government as final, and believed that under certain conditions the British decision was subject to modification. Indeed, at the beginning of February 1938, Shertok approached Yaakov Thon, and advised the committee to focus 'on investigating the possibilities of locating vacant and arable land in the Arab portion of Palestine, in Trans-Jordan and Syria and elaborating a plan for the settlement of Arabs from the Jewish State on these lands. Such a plan is a pre-condition for any negotiation on our part regarding the issue of coercion.'[54] Shertok's approach induced the committee to decide that its work henceforth would concentrate on determining the target areas for implementing transfer, proposing agrarian reform and settlement programs for these areas – reforms that would attract the Arabs to settle there – and elaborating plans for agrarian reform in areas within the Jewish State, which would allow lands to be transferred to Jewish bodies. A series of exact studies in order to suggest proven or tested plans, was required in advance of all these measures. The committee was aided by the staff of the PLDC (Palestine Land Development Company) and the Jewish Agency's Institute for the Study of Economy, who used archival records from the PLDC the mandatory government, and especially from the offices of land registration and agricultural taxation.

The committee began gathering research, conducting surveys and amassing information on the following subjects: the occupational and economic demographic composition of the Arab population of the areas that were intended to be part of the Jewish State in both town and village; Arab possession and ownership of lands on the boundary of the Jewish State in both town and village; the economic structure of the villages, the size of the economic units and the characteristics of the cultivators in those areas. In the agricultural sphere alone, it was necessary to gather data on 400 villages, which had a total of 400,000 economic units. By mid-June 1938, the examination of 200 villages, especially in the Safad, Acre, Haifa and Nazareth subdistricts, was completed.[55] An analysis of the data regarding the Arab villages within the confines of the Jewish State produced the following findings: between 40 and 50 per cent of the population of the villages were totally landless or had small plots and could not derive an income from agriculture; in various areas, the land-owners had large areas of land, but they did not have the possibility of fully cultivating these by themselves. On the basis of these two findings, the members of the Committee attempted to infer that, firstly, 'we could perform something useful on behalf of the aforementioned landless people if we were to settle them in a different place on a territorial unit of 100 dunams'; and secondly, that the surplus land of the large estate-holders had to pass within the framework of agrarian reform to the new Jewish settlement. However, members of the committee were aware of the counter-argument to these findings, which had already been raised by the investigation of the British expert, John Hope-Simpson, who had been dispatched by his government in 1930: namely, that such a large number of landless Arab people precluded the new settlement of fresh Jewish immigrants and that the surplus land of large land holders was needed first of all for the settlement of landless Arabs. Given the impossibility of firming up Zionist contentions at this stage, a proposal was made to examine the conditions in the remaining 200 villages, an undertaking that would require both time and a great deal of money.[56]

In tandem, work began on data-gathering for the areas of the Jordan Valley and Trans-Jordan in the districts of Ajlun, Bulka, Karakh and Ma'an, primarily concerning the breakdown of local land ownership and the economic condition of the farmers. However, the data gathered was insufficient to support clear conclusions.[57] Additional research was conducted on the Djezireh district in Syria by Eliyahu Epstein, who even made a special journey there as the emissary of the committee.[58] The research showed that the Syrian government would have a great interest to settle this rich and under-populated district with an appreciable Arab-

Moslem population, since it bordered on Turkey and was perpetually menaced by the Kurds and Bedouins who resided there and flouted the authority of the Damascus government. The prevalent opinion was that if the present situation in Djezireh persisted, Syria would lose its grip on the area to Turkey, or it would become a French colony and the population there would serve by its very nature as a source of intrigues and political adventures against Syria. Syria did not possess the requisite human resources to alter the population balance in Djezireh, let alone the means to invest in the creation of a settlement project there. Epstein therefore believed that the Arabs in the proposed Jewish State, and especially the farmers there, would constitute the most suitable material from the vantage point of the Syrian government in order to increase its strength and influence in Djezireh:

> a vast settlement project in Djezireh would revive this fertile district, would increase the tax base of the residents to the coffers of the impoverished Syrian government and in the main it would guarantee that this area would remain in Syrian hands and would not slip out of its hands as a result of the continuation of the present situation. The last factor could under given circumstances prove decisive regarding the readiness of the Syrian government to discuss the population transfer of Arabs from the Jewish State to Djezireh and to justify this project from a national Arab standpoint ...[59]

However, Epstein's memorandum lacked many essential details: it did not address the question of land ownership in Djezireh; the quality of the soil in the various areas; the condition of agriculture there; whether improvement works were needed in order to ready the land for intensive agriculture; the possibilities for irrigation; or the status of local transport and health care. The absence of these details precluded the prompt preparation of a program for transfer and resettlement in Djezireh.[60]

It was agreed in the Committee for Population Transfer that the areas of western Palestine, which lay within the areas of the proposed Arab State, were almost certainly ruled out for resettling the transferees from the areas of the Jewish State. Given the absence of sufficient areas for settlement, especially since the Agency executive believed in the framework of partition, the Negev should be included in the areas of the mandatory enclave and not in the areas of the Arab State. As may be recalled, the hidden ultimate intention of the Agency Executive was to turn the Negev into a target for Jewish settlement. In contradistinction, as has already been noted, members of the committee found it difficult to formulate an agreed-upon position regarding the areas to which they should channel the transferees. Some believed that the areas to be considered were Trans-Jordan and Syria, because they abutted Palestine and offered conditions similar to those obtaining in the transferees' areas of origin and could provide free areas for settlement.[61] Others believed that 'one should attempt to transfer the Arabs as far away as possible to areas remote from our boundary – and if it could be done to Iraq …'[62] because Trans-Jordan should be left as a reserve for future Jewish agricultural settlement.[63] A third group of members believed that they should lump Trans-Jordan, Syria and Iraq together as targets for transfer.[64] Indeed, their inability to formulate an agreed-upon opinion regarding the target areas induced the committee to drop the decision in the lap of the Political Department.[65]

The committee's decision to inform the Political Department that it should decide for itself the target areas to which transferees would be directed symbolized to a large extent the beginning of the end for the Committee for Population Transfer. Beyond the disagreement on this subject, the members of the committee became increasingly aware of the fact that the formulation of a clearly reasoned transfer proposal, which could withstand criticism, was an impossible objective in the light of the insufficient data in their possession. The procurement of the additional data necessitated a great deal of investigation, requiring in turn vast amounts of time and capital. Even if these data could be obtained, the composition of a proposal would encounter many structural difficulties. In addition, the members became conscious of the impossibility that any body, either in Palestine or in the international arena, would impose a coerced transfer, which was a necessary condition for implementing any transfer whatsoever, given the Palestinian reality of that period. It therefore seemed impossible to translate theoretical discussion into practicality. In June 1938, the last meeting of the committee took place, and, even though its dissolution was not formally announced, it never met again. Indeed, no memorandum regarding the transfer proposal was ever presented to the British Partition Commission.[66]

Nonetheless, upon the request of the Partition Commission to the Jewish Agency, members of the Committee for Population Transfer participated in writing reports on the possibility of agricultural settlement in Syria, Iraq and Trans-Jordan. These reports provided a general survey on extensive settlement prospects in these areas, but contained no components of a transfer plan. The Jewish Agency was not even requested by the Partition Commission to prepare such a plan, although it was clear that the plan and its components were tied to the possibilities of the voluntary transfer of the Jewish State's Arabs to specific target areas.[67] In a report on Syria, emphasis was laid on the feasibility of extensive settlement in the Djezireh district, 'one of the most fertile areas in Syria and most conducive to new settlements', and that large-scale Moslem settlement was vital to Syria's own needs.[68] In a report on Trans-Jordan, attention was drawn to the area's paucity of settlement there and its immense agricultural potential, especially in the Jordan Valley, where innumerable families could be settled. The cheap price of these lands was also noted, together with the fact of their being privately owned, and therefore could be purchased relatively easily. The Arabs, according to the study, felt an equal affinity for Trans-Jordan as for the western side of the Jordan.[69]

It would appear that, in addition to the aforementioned reasons for the dissolution of the Committee, its members themselves had become aware – following a year of deliberations – of the fissures in the essential pillars of the transfer proposal that they had submitted. The initial feverishness seemingly gave way to soul-searching and a thorough examination, which revealed the flaws in a number of their basic assumptions. First of all, as mentioned, the Balkan precedent had been employed not only to demonstrate that the transfer method could be used to provide a solution; it had also served as a device for justifying the employment of this method despite its inherent moral flaws, which did not escape the members of the Committee. However, one cannot say that the committee had even managed partially to demonstrate the moral validity of the transfer. Furthermore, a penetrating examination revealed that the Greco–Turkish precedent was quite far removed from the Palestinian case. It became ever more clear that forced transfer with the agreement of the two relevant states (the Jewish and the Arab) and carried out under international supervision, as occurred in the Greco–Turkish precedent, could not be implemented in the Palestine case. Likewise, there seemed to be no prospects for economic reparations to the transferees, and, in particular, there was no chance that the international system would engage in the resettlement of the transferees after both the British government and the League of Nations had spurned the idea of forcible transfer.

Voluntary transfer also did not appear feasible. Thus, for example, encouraging the forces of economic attraction to those places where it was proposed to transfer the Arab population constituted an essential pillar in the deliberations of the committee, because this was a necessary condition for voluntary transfer. However, it appeared that members of the Committee estimated at the beginning that this would be a sufficient condition for voluntary transfer, and this was not the case. It is amazing that the committee ignored the opposing, non-economic forces, such as nationalism, sentiments, religion, etc., whose weight had not been proven smaller than the economic factor and strengthened the tie to the place of origin.

In the condition that prevailed in Palestine in the latter half of the 1930s, these forces had exerted especially great weight. The Permanent Mandates Commission of the League of Nations in its session of summer 1937, raised these contentions to demonstrate the problematic nature of the implementation of voluntary transfer.[70]

Likewise, the implementation of agrarian reforms for transferring lands both in the areas intended to be evacuated and in the areas scheduled to absorb the transferees, which constituted an additional basic factor in the deliberations of the committee, could not withstand critical scrutiny; for no attention was given to the question of the population's consent to these reforms or to the possibility and the feasibility of implementing these reforms in the absence of the population's consent. It seems that when members of the committee became aware of these fissures, which compounded the other difficulties inherent in the formulation of the transfer program, the committee seemed to have no grounds to deal with the subject for whose purpose it had been established, and the committee died of its own accord.

THE EXECUTIVE WISES UP: THE RETREAT FROM THE TRANSFER POLICY

The dead end at which the Committee for Population Transfer arrived was of course perceived by the Executive; but this was not the only fact that pushed the Executive into sobriety on the subject of transferring the Arab population from the areas of the Jewish State. By mid-1938, it was clear to the Executive that the British government was firmly against implementing forced transfer.[71] Although the British government had already begun to clarify this position in summer 1937, the Executive, as we have learned, apparently believed during those very same months that under certain conditions this British decision was subject to modifications and that perhaps they could implement a forced transfer within the framework of an inter-governmental agreement.[72] From the Partition Commission's investigations in spring 1938, the Executive could have drawn the conclusion that coercive transfer was irrelevant,[73] and the same from a letter which Coupland sent to Weizmann in mid-April 1938.[74] Ben-Gurion, who had from the publication of the Royal Commission's Report enthusiastically endorsed forced transfer and continued to support it ('I support forced transfer and I don't see anything immoral about it')[75] now believed that, given the British position, they should no longer speak of forced transfer because its implementation was only possible if the British would carry it out. He believed that if the subject was even raised at the Zionist initiative it could greatly imperil both world Jewry and Zionism in Palestine. The only thing that remained was to talk of an extremely qualified voluntary transfer, limited in scope and from the standpoint of lands to be vacated for Jewish settlement.[76]

The Executive adopted Weitz's plan of voluntary transfer in principle, and decided that

> the Jewish State would enter into discussion with the neighboring Arab countries regarding the voluntary transfer of tenant farmers, workers and Arab fellahin from the Jewish State to neighboring states. For this purpose, the Jewish State or a special company which would be recognized as a company for public benefit, will purchase lands in the neighboring countries for the settlement of those fellahin and tenant farmers who would desire to leave the Jewish State ...

To the extent that the Arab State would assist in the receipt of the transferees, the Executive would not only pay for the cost of the land but would also assist in the settlement of the transferees. The content of this decision was conveyed to the attention of the Partition Commission, which in turn asked the Executive to prepare a memorandum on the prospects for settlement in Trans-Jordan and Syria.[77] Nonetheless, it was clear to the Executive that voluntary transfer would not necessarily be implemented. Among other things, it required the assent of the neighboring countries, and, even if it were implemented, its scope would be very limited.[78] The land problem therefore demanded another solution. There was talk of expropriation and the declaration of a development regime.[79] Now, however, the Executive would have to grapple with a key issue, which to a large extent resulted from the fact that the transfer idea had become largely irrelevant: the question of the status and rights to be enjoyed by the large Arab minority that would remain within the Jewish State.

NOTES

1. CZA, file S25/10109, quantitative data on the total population of the Jewish and Arab States and the ethnic breakdown for both of them.
2. CZA, Protocol of the Jewish Agency Executive's Meeting on 22 May 1936.
3. CZA, Protocol of the Jewish Agency Executive's Meeting on 21 October 1936 (afternoon).
4. CZA, Protocols of the Jewish Agency Executive's Meetings on 21 October 1936 (afternoon), and 1 November 1936.
5. Sharett (1937), p. 109.
6. Ben-Gurion (1937), pp. 297–8.

7. See Weizmann's letter to Ormsby-Gore on 14 July 1937, cited in Klieman (1987), pp. 341–2; CZA, file S25/993, Weizmann's letter to Bernard Joseph with addenda, on 22 July 1937; CZA, Protocol of the Jewish Agency Executive's Meeting on 4 July 1937 – statement by Kaplan.

8. Ben-Gurion (1937), pp. 297–9. See also ibid., pp. 296, 331; Ben-Gurion (1938), pp. 214–15. The question of transfer also arose in the deliberations of the twentieth Zionist Congress. Ben-Gurion and others reiterated their support and, *inter alia*, raised the contention that historically the Jewish settlement process in Palestine was frequently accompanied by the transfer of tenant farmers from place to place, most of whom transferred voluntarily, and only a minority having to be coerced. The transfer of Arabs from the areas of the Jewish State would not involve deprivation. Others in the congress contended that transfer, especially forced, was not practical. Those who rejected the idea also emphasized the immorality of forced transfer and the considerable damage that it would inflict on Zionism. Similarly, they did not view voluntary transfer as realistic. On this, see the twentieth Zionist Congress, stenographic report, 1937. See also Eliash (1971), pp. 67–8, 125, 130, as well as CZA, Protocol of the Jewish Agency Executive's Meeting on 1 August 1937 – statement by Ruppin.

9. On the imposed agreement for population transfer between Turkey and Greece (as well as between Greece and Bulgaria), the background to the agreement, the settlement of the Greek refugees, and the results of the process, see Ladas (1932); Eddy (1931); Hope-Simpson (1931); Morgenthau (1929); Blanchard (1925); Mendelsohn (1939), Ettinger (1937a); Ettinger (1937b); Ettinger (1937c); Ettinger (1937d); Ettinger (1938); The Lausanne Conference (1923); Pentzopoulos (1962).

10. Mendelsohn (1939), p. 149.

11. Ladas (1932), p. 721.

12. Ibid.

13. Eddy (1931), pp. 58–60.

14. Ladas (1932), pp. 623–41.

15. Eddy (1931), p. 154.

16. Ibid., p. 88.

17. Ibid., p. 45.

18. Ibid., pp. 102–4.

19. Ettinger (1937b); Ettinger (1937c); Ettinger (1937d); Ettinger (1938).

20. Ettinger (1938).

21. Ladas (1932), p. 736. See also Mendelsohn (1939), pp. 12–13; PRCR (1937), pp. 390–1.

22. Mendelsohn (1939), pp. 3–7; CZA, PLDC Archives, file 7, 1936, Research and Opinions, section 9 – Population Exchanges, address by Dr Yaakov Thon, which took place on 20 October 1937 in Jerusalem, on the subject of population exchanges between Turkey and Greece.

23. Mendelsohn (1939).

24. See CZA, file S25/5103.

25. CZA, PLDC Archives, file 7, 1936, Research and Opinions, section 9 – Population Exchanges, letter from Thon to the Political Department on 30 November 1937.

26. Ibid.

27. CZA, PLDC Archives, file 7, 1936, Research and Opinions, section 9 – Population Exchanges; CZA, PLDC Archives, file 34, 1938–1940, Researches and Opinions, section 9, letter from Thon to the 'Palcor' Company.

28. CZA, PLDC Archives, Protocol of the Committee for Population Transfer's Meeting on 29 November 1937.

29. Ibid.

30. Ibid.

31. CZA, PLDC Archives, file 7, 1936, Research and Opinions, section 9 – Population Exchanges.

32. Mendelsohn (1939), pp. 27–30.

33. According to the data available to the Committee on Population Transfer, in accordance with the plan of the Royal Commission, the total population in the Jewish State was 591,356, of whom 294,671 were Jews and 296,685 non-Jews (of the latter 243,000 were Moslems, 42,000 Christians and 11,000 Druse and others). The territory of the Jewish State totaled about 4.85 million dunams, of which 1.15 million were Jewish owned and 3.7 million non-Jewish owned. On this see CZA, file S25/10109, from the Report on the Activities of the Committee for Population Transfer.

34. Regarding Weitz's plan, see CZA, Weitz's manuscript, 'General Contours of a Plan for Population Transfer' (undated); CZA, PLDC Archives, file 34, 1938–1940, Research and Opinions, section 9, Protocol of the Committee for Population Transfer, 21 November 1937.

35. CZA, file S25/5103, Bonne's statement on 'Operative Plans Regarding the Transfer of Arabs to the Arab State' delivered on 22 November 1937. See also CZA, PLDC Archives, file 7, 1936, Protocol of the Committee for Population Transfer's Meeting on 22 November 1937; Ibid., letter from Bonne to Thon on 26 July 1937 and the appended memorandum.

36. CZA, file S25/5103, Dr. Bonne's statement on 'Operative Plans Regarding the Transfer of Arabs to the Arab State', delivered on 22 November 1937.

37. CZA, PLDC Archives, letter from Bonne to Thon on 26 July 1937 and the appended memorandum; CZA, file S25/10109, Report of the Political Department on the activities of the Committee for Population Transfer (undated).

38. CZA, PLDC Archives, Protocols of the Procedural Sub-committee of the Committee for Population Transfer's Meetings on 1 December 1937 and 5 December 1937.

39. CZA, PLDC Archives, letter from Shertok to Bernard Joseph on 13 December 1937; CZA, file S25/5103, letter from Simon to Weitz on 8 May 1938. Shertok's comments came to Weitz's attention, and he responded only on the question of concentrations of vacated land. On this see CZA, letter from Weitz to Simon on 11 May 1938.

40. CZA, PLDC Archives, file 7, 1936, Protocol of the Committee for Population Transfer's Meeting on 21 November 1937.

41. CZA, file S25/5l03, Shertok's comments, on April 1938.

42. Ibid., letter from Bonne to the Political Department on 11 May 1938; Bonne notes that he relied on Ladas's book (1932).

43. See CZA, PLDC Archives, file 7, 1936, Protocols of the Procedural Sub-committee of the Committee for Population Transfer's Meetings, and compare Nedava (1978), p. 157.

44. Ibid.

45. CZA, PLDC Archives, Protocols of the Committee for Population Transfer's Meetings of 29 November 1937 and 19 December 1937.

46. CZA, PLDC Archives, file 34, 1938–1940, Research and Opinions, section 9, Protocols of the Committee for Population Transfer's Meetings on 22 May 1938 and 27 May 1938.

47. Ibid., Protocol of the Committee for Population Transfer's Meeting on 22 May 1938.

48. CZA, PLDC Archives, Protocol of the Committee for Population Transfer's Meeting on 29 November 1937. An additional proposal was brought to the Committee for Population Transfer by Yehoshua Hankin. This was a general proposal and was not awarded real discussion. According to Hankin's proposal, the Zionist institutions would purchase lands in Syria, Trans-Jordan and even in Egypt, and thus establish the essential conditions for transferring the population there. On this see CZA, Protocol of the Jewish Agency Executive's Meeting on 8 May 1938.

49. See CZA, PLDC Archives, letter from Shertok to Joseph.

50. CZA, PLDC Archives, Protocols of the Committee for Population Transfer's Meeting on 19 December 1937.

51. Ibid.

52. Jeffries (1939), pp. 666–8.

53. See above, pp. 12–14, regarding the British government's retreat from the idea of forced transfer, and see also League of Nations (1937b); Jeffries (1939), pp. 664–6; PPCR (1938), p. 52.

54. CZA, file S25/5103, letter from Simon to Thon of 3 February 1938. See also file S25/5123,

letter from Simon to Shertok on 27 January 1938; see also Sharett (1937), pp. 15, 70, 109, 450. It would appear that Shertok did not believe that voluntary transfer could be implemented, and if transfer was to be implemented by force an international body would have to carry it out. One should take care that 'the people won't be thrown into the street while their property was expropriated without compensation and without concern for their condition in the new location'. See the quotation in Sharett (1937), p. 450. See also CZA, file S25/10109, letter from Neuman to Shertok on 28 November 1937; ibid., letter from Shertok to Neumann on 2 December 1937.

55. See the data gathered in CZA, files S25/5103, S25/247, S25/10109, S25/10061; CZA, file S25/5103, letter from Simon to Granovsky on 23 February 1938; CZA, PLDC Archives, file 34, 1938–40, Research and Opinions, section 9, Protocol of the Committee for Population Transfer's Meeting on 12 June 1938.

56. CZA, PLDC Archives, file 34, 1938–40, Research and Opinions, section 9, Protocol of the Committee for Population Transfer's Meeting on 12 June 1938; CZA, file S25/10109, Memorandum of the Political Department on the summary of quantitative findings gathered by the Committee for Population Transfer, (undated); CZA, file S25/6889, Memorandum of the Political Department: 'Exchange of Population: The Religious and Ethnical Minorities – A Statistical Survey'.

57. PLDC Archives, file 34, 1938–40, Research and Opinions, section 9, Memorandum of 10 June 1938; ibid., Protocol of the Committee for Population Transfer's Meeting on 22 May 1938.

58. CZA, PLDC Archives, file 34, 1938–40, Research and Opinions, section 9, Epstein's report of April 1938. The same report but differently edited appears without the chapter on conclusions and recommendations in Epstein (Elath) (1954), pp. 160–75.

59. Elath (1954); see also Epstein's statement in CZA, PLDC Archives, file 7, 1936, Protocol of the Committee for Population Transfer's Meeting on 29 November 1937; CZA, PLDC Archives, file 34, Protocol of the Committee for Population Transfer's Meeting on 23 March 1938.

60. CZA, PLDC Archives, file 34, letter from Lifshitz to Thon on 1 May 1938. Even Epstein admitted this. On this see ibid., Protocol of the Committee for Population Transfer's Meeting on 23 March 1938.

61. CZA, PLDC Archives, file 34, Protocols of the Committee for Population Transfer's Meetings on 22 March 1938 and 23 May 1938.

62. The quotation is taken from a statement by Granovsky in CZA, PLDC Archives, file 34, Protocol of the Committee for Population Transfer's Meeting on 23 May 1938. Regarding Iraq, a special memorandum was prepared by Engineer Hecker (who opposed a transfer to Djezireh). He recommended the transfer of 40,000–50,000 Arab families 'to this land which requires an additional Sunni Arab settlement'. Hecker estimated that the transfer would cost £25 million – £5 million for purchasing the land of those to be transferred. He believed that one could obtain this sum as a loan in the British financial market for 60 years, guaranteed by the British government. On this, see CZA, PLDC Archives, file 34, Protocol of the Committee for Population Transfer's Meeting on 22 May 1938; CZA, file S25/5103, letter from Simon to Epstein appended to which is Hecker's Memorandum on 3 March 1938; CZA, file S25/10109, letter from Hecker to Thon on 26 May 1938.

63. CZA, PLDC Archives, file 7, Protocol of the Committee for Population Transfer's Meeting on 5 December 1937; CZA, PLDC Archives, file 34, 1938–40, Protocol of the Committee for Population Transfer's Meeting of 22 May 1938.

64. CZA, PLDC Archives, file 34, 1938–40, Protocol of the Committee for Population Transfer's Meeting on 23 March 1938.

65. Ibid., Protocol of the Committee for Population Transfer's Meeting on 22 May 1938.

66. Eliyahu Elath (Epstein), oral testimony to the author, Jerusalem, 27 September 1987; Granovsky's statement in CZA, PLDC Archives, file 34, Protocol of the Committee for Population Transfer's Meeting on 27 May 1938. Ben Ami contended at the committee's meeting on 5 December 1937, in CZA, PLDC Archives, file 7, that he believed that transfer

was impossible, for practical considerations. See also CZA, Protocol of the Jewish Agency Executive's Meeting on 8 May 1938, Shertok's statement regarding the Committee for Population Transfer.

67. CZA, file S25/5118, 'Memorandum on Possibilities of Agricultural Settlement in Syria Accompanied by Two Articles Written by Dr. Bonne, Indicating Such Possibilities in Iraq', presented to the Partition Commission on 14 June 1938; CZA, S25/10060, letter from Dr. Bonne to the Political Department on 31 May 1938; CZA, S25/5118, 'Memorandum on Trans-Jordan' presented by the Jewish Agency Executive to the Partition Commission on 8 June 1938. See also CZA, Protocol of the Jewish Agency Executive's Meeting on 29 May 1938. As may be recalled, the directive given to the Partition Commission in its terms of reference was to examine the possibility of exchanges of lands and populations and the prospects for locating places to settle those about to be transferred. On this, see PPCR (1938), pp. 7–8.

68. CZA, file S25/5118, 'Memorandum on Possibilities of Agricultural ...'.

69. CZA, file S25/5118, 'Memorandum on Trans-Jordan'.

70. League of Nations (1937b).

71. CZA, Protocol of the Jewish Agency Executive's Meeting in Conjunction with the Political Committee of the Inner Zionist General Council on 12 June 1938, p. 6030; Ben-Gurion (1938), pp. 212–17.

72. See also Sharett (1937), p. 450.

73. CZA, Protocol of the Jewish Agency Executive's meeting in Conjunction with the Political Committee of the Inner Zionist General Council on 12 June 1938.

74. CZA, file S25/10058, secret letter sent by Coupland to Weizmann on 17 April 1938.

75. Ben-Gurion (1938), p. 216.

76. Ben-Gurion (1938), pp. 214–17.

77. CZA, Protocol of the Jewish Agency Executive's Meeting on 7 June 1938. Compare (above) Weitz's plan for voluntary transfer and see also CZA, Protocol of the Jewish Agency Executive's Meeting in Conjunction with the Political Committee of the Inner Zionist General Council on 12 June 1938 (where the matter of transfer was discussed in detail), statements on transfer by Shertok, Ben-Gurion, Senator, Ruppin, Kaplan, Katznelson. See also Ussishkin's statement, wherein he contended that he would agree to partition only with the proviso that the British would agree to implement transfer. Berl Katznelson contended that one should not give up the idea of reaching agreement with Britain and an Arab country on the matter of forced transfer. See also the statement of Ben Zvi. S. Zuchovitzky was the only person at the session who contended that the Jewish State, by itself, would have to implement forced transfer.

78. The Partition Commission reached the conclusion a few months later that the prospects for a voluntary transfer of the Arab population were minimal, while in addition the possibility of further agricultural settlement in the areas of the Arab state including Trans-Jordan was minute. On this see PPCR (1938), pp. 52–72.

79. See CZA, Protocol of the Jewish Agency Executive's Meeting on 12 June 1938, in note 73, especially the statement by Ben-Gurion.

5

The Status and Rights of the Arab Minority in the Future Jewish State

The question of the status and rights of the Arab minority in a future Jewish State began seriously to preoccupy the Jewish Agency Executive in mid-1938.[1] As opposed to the issues of boundaries and Jerusalem, where the Jewish Agency demanded modifications in the Royal Commission's Plan, the Agency Executive initially believed that it could sit back and rely on the Commission's recommendations regarding population transfer.[2] Once it finally became clear that there were no prospects that the British government would implement forced transfer, that voluntary transfer had no realistic chance, and that the Committee for Population Transfer had come to a dead end, the Executive was left with no recourse. It had to come to grips with formulating policy regarding the status and rights of the Arab minority that would remain in its area. Pursuant to the demands of the Partition Commission in mid-1938,[3] a demand originating in the Commission's terms of reference,[4] the Executive was also obligated to present its position regarding the status and rights of the sizeable Arab minority slated to remain within the area of the Jewish State. Given the assumption that New Jerusalem would be incorporated within the boundaries of the Jewish State, the size of the Arab minority approached nearly *half* the size of the future Jewish State's population.[5]

It comes as no surprise, therefore, that whereas the Jewish Agency had already begun handling the issues of boundaries, Jerusalem and transfer of population by 1937, the Agency only began dealing with the issue of the Arab minority's status in mid 1938 – this after the population transfer issue had ceased to be relevant and the Agency was forced to address the issue not at its own initiative but under external prodding. Not only did the Agency find itself without prepared contingency plans on the issue,[6] but it was compelled to formulate its policy in the brief time-frame represented by the Partition Commission's sojourn in Palestine. Let us add that the Royal Commission addressed in the margins of its report the need to provide suitable guarantees for the protection of the minorities who would remain in both countries.[7] However, it appears that, since the bulk of the minorities problem was to be solved in the context of population exchanges, the Jewish Agency Executive did not originally give much thought to the subject.

FUNDAMENTAL ZIONIST ASSUMPTIONS

The inherent necessity of awarding rights to the Arab minority (as well as to the other minorities of the Jewish State, although their total population was minuscule) in the future Jewish State was obvious to the Jewish Agency, and particularly so once the forcible transfer proposal mooted by the Royal Commission was ruled out. This appreciation derived first and foremost from pragmatic considerations. Firstly, the Zionist Movement considered itself bound by the declaration of British Foreign Minister, Arthur Balfour, in 1917, which had supported Zionist aspirations and determined that Britain would assist the establishment of a national home for the Jewish People in Palestine but also contained the explicit proviso: 'It being clearly understood that nothing shall be done which may prejudice the civil and religious rights of existing non-Jewish communities in Palestine.'[8] Secondly, when the League of Nations certified the British mandate over Palestine in 1922 the writ of certification also spelled out that the rights of non-Jews in Palestine would be safeguarded in the Jewish national home.[9] It was equally clear to the Jewish Agency Executive that the League of Nations would condition its assent to the establishment of a Jewish State upon a pledge by the latter to award rights to its minorities. These rights were laid down in the various minority treaties adopted in the course of the post-First World War peace treaties and in various regulations adopted subsequently.[10] The Zionists further assumed that if the Jewish Agency were to guarantee rights to a non-Jewish minority this would enhance the prospects for British assent to modifications in the boundaries proposed by the Royal Commission and enlarge the territory of the future Jewish State – an enlargement that, of course, implied a further increase in the total Arab population of the Jewish State.[11]

A further consideration necessitating the award of rights was raised by David Ben-Gurion. He contended that, for a number of reasons, the Jewish State must fundamentally aspire to relations of understanding with the Arabs. Firstly:

> The Arab problem within the Jewish state is not merely a minority question. The question of the relations of the Jewish state with the Arab world is a central

political issue. The question of the Arab minority does not resemble the question of Germans in Czechoslovakia. In theory, Czechoslovakia can forego good relations with Germany if she enjoys a secure alliance with other great powers such as Britain, France, and Russia. For a Jewish state, the question of relations with the neighboring Arab states is a cardinal and central issue in the entire foreign policy of the Jewish state and the question of the Arab minority constitutes an organic part of this immediate problem ...[12]

If they could somehow prevent the Arab population from adopting a hostile attitude towards the Jewish State and attain relations of understanding with the Arab minority, this would not only facilitate the possibility of establishing a Jewish State within the partition boundaries but would open possibilities for its further expansion beyond those boundaries.[13] In the words of Ben-Gurion, uttered during the deliberations of the Zionist Executive regarding the status of the Arab minority in the future Jewish State: 'in his opinion the point of departure for solving the Arab problem in the Jewish state, is the need to create conditions for an Arab–Jewish agreement. He is in favor of the Jewish state not because he is content with part of the country, but because he assumes that once we have become a strong power, by virtue of the establishment of the state, we will annul the partition and expand throughout Palestine.'[14]

The fact that the Jewish people constituted a minority in many countries the world over also played a role in the essential recognition that rights had to be awarded to the Arab minority.[15] The relatively large percentage of the Arab minority within the Jewish State also militated on behalf of awarding rights. Given the high Arab birth-rate and natural population increase, it would be difficult to reduce drastically the percentage represented by the Arab minority, even if the rate of Jewish immigration to Palestine were accelerated.[16] All these considerations, however, did not stir the Zionists from their basic conviction that the status and rights that the Jewish State would award its minorities were those stipulated in the demands of the League of Nations, but no more. As Moshe Shertok, head of the Political Department of the Jewish Agency, noted: 'in practice we must give them only those rights which we are obliged to grant the minorities in accordance with the accepted practice of the League of Nations'.[17]

This concept, as well as the assumption that international precedents would furnish Britain and the League of Nations with the basis for fulfilling their demands upon the Jewish State regarding minorities, compelled the Jewish Agency to start with a thorough study of international precedents concerning minority rights. Such a study would form the basis for formulating the Zionist position on the minority issue, a position which the Jewish Agency had to submit to the British Partition Commission.[18] The authorities consulted, including experts in international law affiliated with the Jewish Agency, were requested to examine international precedents and address these in the context of the status of the Arab minority in the future Jewish State.

THE RIGHTS AND PROTECTION OF MINORITIES IN INTERNATIONAL PRECEDENTS

The regime extending international protection to minorities applied at the close of the 1930s to 14 states. It was instituted in the special treaties that were concluded in the peace conference of 1919 and 1920, and thereafter. At the peace conference the following countries committed themselves to awarding minority rights: Czechoslovakia, Albania, Greece, Yugoslavia, Austria, Hungary, Bulgaria and Turkey. The treaties signed with these countries were similar in content to the original minority treaty, signed in June 1919, with Poland. The treaties established that a country could not discriminate against a minority in any form whatsoever, and had to grant equal civil and political rights as well as prerogatives in the spheres of language, culture and social affairs.[19] Only a few minorities were guaranteed special and quite extensive rights: the Ruthenians were to enjoy territorial autonomy in Czechoslovakia; the Szeklars and the Saxons would have local autonomy in Rumania's Transylvania; and the Wallachs would possess the same in the Pindus area of Greece.[20]

The first paragraph of each of these minority treaties obligated the states to recognize the instructions incorporated in the other paragraphs – to the extent that they applied to people belonging to a racial, linguistic or religious minority – as part of the country's basic laws. The treaty further determined that each member of the League Council reserved the right to bring to the Council's attention any violation of one of the treaty's passages, and that the Council could take measures against a country that violated the rights of a minority. Since the minority treaties established only general procedural basic principles, the League Council over the course of the years found it necessary to decide on a series of detailed procedural ordinances that would govern its conduct as it constantly monitored the observance of minority rights.[21]

It emerged that the states that signed the minorities treaties did include the treaties in their constitutions, but did not scrupulously observe minority rights. Minority rights were violated, especially in those states where the ruling nationality possessed a strong majority and a well-developed national culture. In such places, even the civil equality guaranteed by the minorities treaty was circumscribed. In those states where the ruling nationality had come to power only following the war and lacked the time to consolidate their power, or where they constituted only a relative majority (as in Czechoslovakia), minority rights were generally realized. However, even in these countries minority rights diminished over time and were honored only in the cultural sphere and in the schools. Additionally, although the minorities treaties dealt with the civil and cultural rights of minorities, they failed to display adequate concern for their economic rights. The treaties apparently assumed that civil equalities sufficed to ensure that the livelihood and rights of minorities would not be jeopardized. However, over time the governments stepped up efforts to award economic control to the ruling nationality.[22]

One of the ordinances promulgated by the League of Nations in 1931 to increase protection of minority rights determined that a country that was freed from mandatory protection and obtained independence would be compelled to extend guarantees for the protection of minorities in its territory. The intent was to allow the League of Nations, via the Permanent Mandates Commission, to demand that a country about to achieve independence should consent to a more thorough protection regime than that which had been established in the treaties following the First World War.[23]

The first country to whom the ordinance of 1931 was to apply was Iraq, which secured its independence in 1932. In its request for membership in the League of Nations, Iraq committed itself to extending minority rights in its territory. In general, the Iraqi obligations were similar to those contained in the minorities treaties signed after the First World War: full protection of life and liberty for all residents of Iraq, irrespective of nationality, language, race or religion; freedom of activity for all religions; full political rights for minorities; an electoral system that would guarantee fair representation to minorities; guarantee that minorities would not suffer discrimination in obtaining work or public posts, etc.; and in certain districts, Turkish and Kurdish would serve as official languages, alongside Arabic. The officials in these districts would have to possess a knowledge of either Kurdish or Turkish. Likewise, Iraq committed itself to appointing in the districts officials from the local nationality, as far as possible. In other districts, citizens whose mother tongue was not Arabic could employ their language both orally or in writing before the courts. Minorities would enjoy the right to establish and manage funds, charitable, religious and social institutions, as well as schools and other educational institutions, and they would have the right of religious worship. They could employ their language in such cases, and their laws governing marital issues would also be recognized. In areas containing an appreciable minority concentration, the government would allow the minority language to be the language of instruction in the schools, and in any event it would not impose the Arabic language by force. Additionally, in those areas minorities would enjoy budgetary support from the state to maintain educational, religious and charitable institutions. Iraq committed herself to recognize these ordinances as basic laws of the country, thus barring any possibility that an alternative law contravening these ordinances could be promulgated either in the present or in the future. As in the case of previous minority treaties, members of the League of Nations Council could bring to the Council's attention any violation of minority rights, and if necessary the Council could take measures against Iraq.[24]

During the course of deliberations, which took place in the Permanent Mandates Commission pursuant to the Iraqi request, the members were not persuaded that the aforementioned obligations undertaken by Iraq (which did not go beyond the obligations subscribed to by the other minority states in the treaties they signed following the peace agreement) sufficed. These members were acutely aware that countries that had previously signed minorities treaties failed to honor their obligations, that the enforcement power of the League of Nations was limited, and that the Iraqis had harshly treated the Bahai community that year. Members of the Permanent Mandates Commission therefore recommended the adoption of enforcement measures to increase the protection of minorities and establish a realistic and efficient procedure for guaranteeing such protection. Measures proposed included: the dispatch of an observer acting on behalf of the League of Nations to Iraq; assigning the task of observer to the British representative in Iraq; the establishment of a special tribunal in Iraq composed of two British citizens and an Iraqi citizen, which would consider the complaints of minorities; granting minorities the right to submit petitions and enter into discussions with the 'Minorities Committee' of the League of Nations, which would be appointed *ad hoc* to evaluate all petitions as well as the right to approach the Permanent International Court of Justice in the Hague.

These proposals and others were all rejected by Iraq and by the representative of the British government (which exercised the mandate over Iraq) in the Permanent Mandates Commission. The commission declared that, even after the liquidation of the mandate, it would continue to bear responsibility, from an ethical standpoint, for the conduct of affairs in Iraq. Faced with these objections, it became evident to the Permanent

Mandates Commission that it would not easily obtain assent to the most desirable method for enhancing the protection of minorities in Iraq. The Commission therefore elected not to formulate any concrete proposal but to content itself with the inclusion of a remark in its findings that directed the attention of the League Council to the various proposals for strengthening international supervision, which were entered in the protocols of the meetings. The declaration on minorities submitted by Iraq, therefore, did not include any special rule regarding minorities and the regular procedures would apply to Iraq as well.[25]

In contrast to the case of Iraq, the members of the Permanent Mandates Commission were not willing to waive the issue of enhanced international protection for minorities when the issue surfaced during the 1930s in discussions concerning the recognition of independence for Syria and Lebanon. In light of the Iraqi experience, especially in view of the atrocities that Iraq committed against the Assyrians, members of the Permanent Mandates Commission felt guilty for not having imposed stringent demands upon the Iraqis in order to guarantee more effective protection for the minorities. One of the members of the commission even announced that it would be better for the committee to resign than to agree in the Syrian case to the same minorities solution that had been approved at the time for Iraq. Nonetheless, it was difficult to foretell if the Permanent Mandates Commission would succeed in persuading the League Council to impose upon Syria a procedure that would be more realistic than what had been customary for all the countries, including Iraq, who had previously signed a minorities treaty. It was clear that opposition could be expected from the Syrian and French quarters, as well as from other countries subject to the international minorities regime who feared that they too would be subjected to intensified supervision.[26]

ZIONIST DILEMMAS

The international precedents concerning minorities' affairs until the second half of the 1930s, when taken alongside Zionist goals inherent in the establishment of a Jewish State in Palestine (for example, in the spheres of Jewish immigration and settlement) and the expectation that the international community would impose special requirements upon the Jewish State in terms of the rights to be awarded the Arab minority, posed a serious dilemma for the Jewish Agency Executive as it approached the task of formulating an official document. This document was to be presented to the Partition Commission and would summarize the proposed policy of the Jewish State regarding minorities residing within the state.

The Zionists had reasons for anticipating unique international demands. Ormsby-Gore, the British Colonial Secretary, had made certain declarations during a session of the Permanent Mandates Commission in Geneva in December 1937, which discussed the recommendation of the Royal Commission for partitioning Palestine. In contrast to the position that the British government had evinced regarding the expansion of the framework for minority protection in Iraq, Ormsby-Gore now expressed the opinion that if a Jewish State was established it would prove necessary to impose upon that state even more severe obligations than had been customary for the 'minorities' countries. In particular, the League would have to appoint an observer charged with exercising constant and strict supervision on behalf of the minorities. Additionally, Britain would sign a special treaty with the Jewish State that would guarantee minority rights.[27] It appeared that Ormsby-Gore's statement elicited comment from one member of the Jewish Agency Executive, who contended that 'we can say for an absolute certainty that Britain and the other nations will keep a vigilant watch over our obligations towards the Arab minority. There will be even be some who will attempt to use these obligations to our detriment and try to incite the Arab minority against us.'[28]

What were the dilemmas and problems that vexed the Jewish Agency Executive and its advisers in their deliberations concerning the rights of the Arab minority and its status? We will detail these below.

The immediate adoption of democratic principles following western practices and the establishment of an elected parliament, as was customary in the west, would have introduced a sizeable Arab element into the legislative bodies of the Jewish State. As already noted, the Arab population in the Jewish State totaled nearly half the population of the Jewish State. Although it was expected that this proportion would drop upon the establishment of the Jewish State, which would expend prodigious efforts to encourage Jewish immigration (and would not make any efforts to encourage Arab immigration),[29] the presence in any event of such a sizeable Arab representation in the Jewish State would obviously have impaired the interests of the Jewish State. On the other hand, any circumvention of democratic principles would have exposed the leadership of the Jewish State to the accusation that they were manipulating democratic institutions for their own benefit.

One of the advisers of the Jewish Agency Executive, and himself a deputy member of that body, L. Stein (of whom more below), believed that 'it should be carefully considered whether the Jewish State should really start with a Parliament at all, and whether it might not possibly be better to dispense for the time being with full-blown parliamentary institutions, and to devise some other constitutional machinery which will avoid these difficulties while at the same time providing ... for something that can fairly be represented as giving reasonable representation to Arab interests'.[30] Ben-Gurion suggested announcing that a democratic regime would follow after peace and order had been established in the country, but without fixing a specified date.[31] Shertok, in contradistinction, believed that such a formulation, which would leave the date unspecified, 'would arouse against us harsh accusations of hypocrisy', and he suggested the establishment of a provisional Jewish government in the transition period, which the Royal Commission recommended. This provisional government would enjoy exclusive powers in various areas, including the area of Jewish immigration, and would do its utmost to promote immigration. An additional task of the provisional government would be to pave the way for a parliamentary regime, and thus the timetable for the establishment of democratic institutions would be postponed. By then 'it would become clear who among the Arabs had consented to remain a citizen of the Jewish state and the Arab total will probably be less than our current estimate. By reducing the number of Arab citizens on the one hand and stepping up Jewish immigration during the transition period on the other hand, we can guarantee an absolute Jewish majority in advance of instituting a parliamentary regime.'[32] There were Agency advisers who predicted that many Arabs would leave the Jewish State the moment they were convinced that a Jewish State was slated to arise,[33] while others expected the very opposite: they had ascertained, after talking with Arabs, that the latter expected a new era of prosperity and did not fear that the Jews would harm them.[34]

Another parliamentary issue which merited consideration was the right of universal suffrage. If one awarded universal suffrage to all residents of the Jewish State this would place the Arabs at a disadvantage, because, owing to cultural and religious reasons, Moslem women would apparently forgo the advantage of the franchise. In this manner, the Arab residents of the Jewish State would be represented in the legislative body by a delegation that was vastly under-representative in terms of their proportion within the population.[35]

The legal fate of Arabs residing within the boundaries of the Jewish State who would not be prepared to accept citizenship of the Jewish State also posed dilemmas. To allow them to accept the citizenship of an Arab State contravened the interest of the Jewish State, which was interested in minimizing the number of citizens of the Arab State resident within its borders. Equally, the Arab state could not be compelled to award citizenship to the Arab residents of a Jewish State who were not interested in accepting citizenship of the Jewish State. Making citizenship in the Jewish State compulsory was also problematic. It appeared to the members of the Agency Executive and their advisers that the problem could be solved in the spirit of Paragraph No. 3 of the minorities treaty with Poland.[36] In this manner, all residents of the Jewish State would automatically receive the citizenship of the Jewish State, unless, within a set time limit, they decided not to accept citizenship. Then these people would be compelled to leave the territory of the Jewish State, provided that another state were prepared to accept them.[37]

The issue of appointing workers for the civil service also posed dilemmas. If objective criteria such as educational level, professional training and full command of Hebrew and Arabic were instituted to gauge the abilities of the various applicants, this would lead to the nearly total exclusion of Arabs from the civil service.[38] It was hard to imagine that more than a minuscule number of Arabs could successfully compete with Jewish candidates, even if one set aside the demand that they should have a perfect command of Hebrew. In addition it was an ostensive interest of the Jewish State to reduce the Arab presence in the civil service (especially in the senior civil service and officialdom engaged in sensitive duties such as the police); there were Agency advisers who believed that the Arabs should not be employed in any civil-service post.[39] This, however, would have been construed as discrimination. In addition, the Jewish State would in fact be interested in a modicum of Arab representation within the civil service (especially in the lower rungs), since the Arabs constituted an appreciable portion of the country's population.[40] One of the main proposals raised in the Jewish Agency Executive regarding the appointment of Arabs to senior positions and key posts was to test their loyalty to the Jewish State: 'Only under this principle can equality of rights exist ... He [Executive member Arthur Ruppin] does not believe that in the initial stage there will be many Arabs to whom one could entrust key posts. This could only come about gradually.'[41] Others contended that loyalty could be secured only if the Arab citizen felt that he could attain a civil-service position as an equal partner. A suggestion was therefore made to consider the establishment of Arab police units in those areas where the Arab population constituted an absolute majority.[42]

Within the context of the issue of appointing Arab civil servants, the question of Arab military service also arose. This question was inextricably tied to another problem: would the Jewish State's army be predicated on a compulsory draft or would it be a volunteer army? In any event, the possibility of Arabs acquiring arms aroused anxiety. On the other hand, to impose limits on Arabs either under a compulsory-service system or within a volunteer army would have been discriminatory.[43]

Another thorny question for the Executive was to what extent could the Jewish State provide equal services to the Arab population? On the one hand, such equality was mandatory if the Arabs were to feel at home in the Jewish State; if they felt otherwise, it would work to the detriment of the Jewish State.[44] On the other hand, the financial experts in the Agency Executive contended that the Jewish State could not carry such a burden, especially in light of the current disparity between the level of services that the two populations currently received, which disadvantaged the Arab population: 'We can talk about establishing a certain minimum [of budgeted services for the Arab population] but we must be aware that this minimum will be modest, especially in the initial years ...'. A member of the Agency Executive, Arthur Ruppin, estimated that at least 10–20 years would have to pass before the state could grant equality of services to the Arab population. One suggestion was to consider the British model in the realm of educational services. According to this model, the state granted budgetary allocations in proportion to the allocations that the local authorities made for these services. In any event, the general opinion within the Executive was that it would take quite a long time to provide equality of services, and this equality could be achieved only on a gradual basis.[45]

Let it be noted that educational services posed a special problem, since they were stipulated in the precedents contained in the international minorities treaties signed after the First World War. The public treasury would have to fund the Arab educational system in those areas where the Arabs constituted an appreciable percentage of the population.[46] Aside from the financial burden, it was unclear how much intervention by the state in the establishment of curricula and selection of teachers was desirable. On the one hand, allowing the Arab population free rein on these issues could prove prejudicial to the interests of the Jewish State (for example, if hostile propaganda were to be conducted against the Jewish State). On the other hand, intervention could provoke complaints from the Arab population. The experts whom the Agency Executive consulted on this issue were divided. Some advocated predicating the financing of Arab education primarily upon local taxation, to which the Jewish government, for its part, would provide incremental assistance. On the one hand, this assistance would demonstrate to the world and to the Arab population that the Jewish State was helping the Arabs. On the other hand, the aid would permit the state a degree of involvement in determining curricula and choosing teachers. In this fashion, the dangers of political incitement that could occur in the schools would be minimized.[47] Other experts were inclined 'not to exercise rigorous supervision but to do everything that can be done to gain the confidence of the Arabs themselves'.[48]

With regard to religious, cultural and linguistic affairs, and the management of religious property, agreement prevailed within the Agency Executive that total equality, and even autonomy if the need arose, would be awarded:[49]

> It shouldn't therefore prove difficult to secure a positive decision regarding the linguistic and cultural rights of the Arab minority in the Jewish State. No one would want to impose the Hebrew language by force. In Arab villages and towns the Arabic language can be employed for all the necessities of public life and this applies to government offices and the courts as well. A basic constitutional law would establish these rights and would require only that the Hebrew language be accorded recognition as the official language also in these areas ...[50]

Though it appeared that the Jewish State would have no difficulty in awarding full rights in the religious and cultural spheres, matters were different when it came to granting rights in the economic sphere. In this area the discrimination practiced by 'minority' countries such as Poland, Czechoslovakia and Rumania against the minorities within their borders, irrespective of the treaty they had signed after the First World War, was most flagrant.[51] The dilemma involved in the award of equal economic rights to the Arab minority upon the establishment of the Jewish State was eloquently expressed by Yitzhak Gruenbaum, a member of the Jewish Agency Executive:

> It will prove even more difficult to determine the rights of the Arab minority and preserve them in the economic sphere. It is patently clear that we cannot maintain the slogans of Jewish labor and Jewish products [i.e. deliberate Zionist exhortations to employ a Jewish worker whose salary was in many cases double that of the Arab[52] and to prefer Jewish-made goods]. These slogans were necessary for a population that was settling without government assistance, in a land whose residents supplied cheap workers and goods. They could not be utilized in a Jewish State unless it intended to follow the practice of the Polish Endeks or other uprooters of minorities. It was inconceivable that a Jewish State would uproot its minorities. Not only would Great Britain and the other countries which sanctioned the establishment of the Jewish State oppose such a policy but Diaspora Jews would also rebel against it because the consequences for them would be nefarious. But doing away with such slogans posed a danger

to Jews immigrating to Palestine. They would find that many jobs were already taken while Jewish goods in many branches and especially in agriculture, would not be able to meet Arab competition ...[53]

Gruenbaum believed that an attempt should be made to solve the dilemma via a minimum wage for labor. While this wage would be lower than the wage paid to the Jewish worker it would still much higher than the prevailing wage of the Arab worker: 'Possibly in this fashion we could establish a rough equality that would allow the Jewish worker to penetrate into unskilled branches without our having to resort to the slogan of Jewish labor. This slogan, if employed in a Jewish State would be tantamount to a boycott against the Arab worker launched by the nation that assumes responsibility for the state.'[54] Gruenbaum also recommended the establishment of a joint workers' confederation representing both Jewish and Arab workers, which every worker would have to join, as well as efforts by the Jewish State's government to raise the living standard of the Arab worker. Nonetheless, Gruenbaum believed that the living standard of the Arab worker undoubtedly could not equal that of the Jewish worker. As a result, the Arab worker would continue to dominate the low-paying branches of labor as opposed to those branches that required skilled and more highly paid workers.[55]

Just as the slogan of Jewish labor had to be abandoned on ideological and practical grounds, the Jewish State equally could not preach the preferment of Jewish goods, as Zionism had done prior to the establishment of the Jewish State: 'One could not persist in a campaign to merchandise the produce of the Land of Israel a term which denoted Jewish-made goods. Produce of the Land once a Jewish State had been established would now mean the produce of all citizens of the country irrespective of nationality.'[56] However, as a consequence, it was possible to anticipate the problem of stiff competition between (primarily) Arab agricultural produce and Jewish produce, which was appreciably dearer.[57] There were some within the Agency Executive and among the advisers who believed that matters should be best left to market forces. It was necessary, however, to strive for the establishment of a unified economic system for Jews and Arabs, and develop the Arab areas in order to achieve the end result of total equality between the two communities.[58] Gruenbaum and others, in contradistinction, did not talk about the need to attain equality or of unifying the economies, and they also did not have a clear answer to the question of economic competition, which would harm Jewish products. Nonetheless, Gruenbaum proposed considering government intervention via the establishment of government-sponsored marketing companies, which would market Arab and Jewish produce at a price that would represent the average of the two current prices in both sectors.[59] Another suggestion raised by one of the economic advisers to the Agency Executive was to impose identical labor practices on the two sectors and establish an equal rate of taxation, as well as a minimum wage; these measures would have limited the competitive advantage of the Arabs. Nonetheless, the policy should also encourage the establishment of joint Jewish–Arab factories, joint investments and mixed labor (i.e. the employment of Jewish workers alongside the Arab workers): 'The Jews would thus clearly manifest their earnest intention to treat the minorities in conformity with the principles of equality ... In any case it should be clear that only a very far-reaching economic collaboration with the Arab Permanent Minority is likely to prevent it from becoming a factor of constant strife and hostility to the Jewish State.'[60]

An additional problem raised in the economic context derived from plans to establish Saturday as the official day of rest in the Jewish State, and a day when work would be prohibited by law. Such a law would have injured the Arab population, especially the Christian elements, because, as opposed to the Jews, they would be forced to abstain from work on two days – a factor that would place them at a distinct disadvantage vis-a-vis their Jewish competitors.[61]

An additional issue that the Jewish Agency discussed was land, which also included a number of subsidiary issues. First of all, there was the problem of Arabs purchasing lands from Jews once equality was awarded to the Arabs in this sphere. There were some who viewed the issue as purely theoretical, because they did not believe that the Arabs would pay the high prices for land that would obtain in a Jewish State. Others raised the specter that certain effendis, inimical to the Jewish State, would attempt to purchase most of the country's land. Two solutions were offered to this problem: one was to impose limitations on Jews concerning the sale of land to Arabs;[62] the second was to declare an agrarian reform that would prevent the entire population from purchasing large tracts of land in order to speculate on them.[63]

No less weighty a problem was the issue of attaining a development regime and creating conditions for extensive Jewish settlement, which was a precondition for absorbing the maximum number of Jewish immigrants, without having to resort to expropriation.[64] In general, if the current laws affording protection to tenant farmers and actual cultivators of the soil remained in force, they would block free trade and the possibility that the Jewish State could purchase lands on a massive scale for the purpose of expanding the Jewish settlement map, one of the Jewish State's prime objectives. The experts whom the Agency Executive consulted were united in their opinion that the Jewish State could not forgo voluntary transfers of land, which meant the repeal of the British protection laws. Some of the advisers felt that there was no reason to hide from the British and the League of Nations the need for forcible transfer of lands in order to implement a policy of dense Jewish settlement.[65] Another solution raised sought, on the one hand, to provide a supply of land for Jewish settlement, while, on the other, extending protection to the Arab farmer against the threat of expropriation by land speculation. The proposal spoke of implementing an agrarian reform that would transfer the Arab farmer to intensive agriculture while diminishing his slice of the land. The Jewish State would determine the size of the agricultural unit, which would be identical for all the country's farmers, irrespective of nationality. Nonetheless, it was the obligation of the state to put all the farmers on a similar economic footing and treat them equally.[66]

The question of whether to offer guarantees to fulfill obligations regarding the rights and status of the Arab minority in a Jewish State was a pivotal problem taxing the minds of the Jewish Agency Executive. It was clear, given the sorry history of the minorities issue before the League of Nations, as detailed earlier, coupled with the declaration by Ormsby-Gore, that more stringent demands would be imposed on the Jewish State. This would induce both the League of Nations and Britain to demand genuine guarantees.[67] With this background in mind, a number of experts consulted by the Jewish Agency on this issue suggested that the Agency Executive should propose a scheme of guarantees that would satisfy the international authorities. It appeared that Britain and the League of Nations would not make do with less than an observer acting on behalf of the League of Nations, and resident in the Jewish State. The observer would receive complaints from minorities, verify them and report to the League Institutions: let it be emphasized that, prior to 1938, no country with a minorities regime was prepared to accept such a demand. Nonetheless, if the Zionists displayed a readiness to accept the notion of an observer, provided that his prerogatives were pre-defined and acceptable to the Jewish State, this would demonstrate the sincere intentions of the Jewish State. In addition, such an observer could help restrain false rumors, groundless complaints and political incitement in educational institutions.[68]

Other experts whom the Zionist Executive consulted objected to the idea of an observer, and viewed the arguments of the supporters as pure naïveté. They argued that the basic stance of the observer could not be essentially different from that of the present British officialdom in Palestine, which viewed the Zionist praxis as baleful to the Arabs:

What ground can we have for assuming that a League of Nations observer, responsible not to us but to the Council of the League, whose job will not be two fold like that of the British official under the Mandate but exclusively that of looking after the interests of the Arab minority ... I submit that there will be no measure in the field of our economic policy and colonization which will not be capable of being interpreted by an outside observer who is not interested in the growth of the state and in the Jewish problem in its totality as harmful to the existing Arab population. I don't think that we can afford a beau geste of this kind ...[69]

Additionally, if the observer were to express opinions favorable to the Jewish State, the neighboring Arab states could then contend that he was bribed by the Jewish State and should be replaced:

One need only be reminded of the virulent campaign conducted by Germany against Mr Lester, High Commissioner of the League of Nations at Danzig, which finally compelled this really fair-minded official to give up his position in which he has been replaced by a perfect nincompoop who tolerates everything the Germans are doing ... even to the extent of not raising any objection to the introduction of the Nuremberg laws in Danzig ...[70]

The fact that no minority state had agreed to the positioning of an observer in its boundaries also strengthened the position of the opponents:

Only in Danzig and Silesia were they positioned and their activity was of no avail when it came to protecting minorities and their rights. Once they came up against force, they immediately withdrew. But it is quite doubtful that they would encounter such force in our state in the initial stages of its development and therefore they would develop into a meddlesome and harmful factor.[71]

THE OFFICIAL ZIONIST POSITION BEFORE THE PARTITION COMMISSION

A study of the international precedents, the problems and various dilemmas voiced by members of the Agency Executive and the sundry experts whom they consulted shaped the content of the memorandum that the Jewish Agency presented to the Partition Commission at the close of July 1938 regarding the status and rights of the Arab minority.[72] The draft of the memorandum was prepared by Attorney L. Stein in accordance with the directives of the Jewish Agency's Political Department. Ben-Gurion's position on the minority issue – a position that he presented before the Agency Executive at the beginning of 1938 – also had a major impact on the content of the memorandum.[73] Stein resided in London, where he served as a deputy member of the Jewish Agency Executive, honorary legal counsel to the Jewish Agency, and as a member of the Political Committee of the Zionist General Council of the World Zionist Organization.[74] The draft was debated in the Jewish Agency Executive and the final memorandum was submitted to the British after a number of changes, decided upon by the Executive, had been introduced in the draft.[75]

The memorandum set forth principles and deliberately refrained from entering into clear and detailed commitments. This stance was adapted to by-pass obstacles and evade issues when the Agency was unsure how they would be tackled by the Jewish State and after they had given rise to various dilemmas in the preliminary discussions. Indeed, it appeared that in order to avoid the future entanglement of 'over-commitment', as a result of the memorandum's content, the Zionist Executive noted in its preface to the memorandum that

> It is assumed that what is at present required of the Jewish Agency is a general statement of its views and not a full discussion of every point which may eventually have to be dealt with. Accordingly, no attempt will be made in this memorandum to provide for every possible contingency, nor will legal precision be aimed at the choice of language ...[76]

The memorandum made clear that the Jewish State would in a general fashion adopt the pledges to protect minorities that Iraq had made in 1932.[77] In the draft that Stein prepared, it was stated that the advantages and disadvantages attendant on dispatching an observer on behalf of the League of Nations to guarantee the obligations towards the minorities would be weighed in the future.[78] The Jewish Agency Executive decided that in the final text submitted to the British the subject of the observer should not be mentioned.[79] This modification, which the Executive inserted into the draft that Stein prepared, was the only change of substance.

At the outset, the memorandum specifies that the Jewish State should enjoy full capacity of decision-making regarding Jewish immigration to Palestine and the creation of an infrastructure for absorbing this immigration. Zionism would not entertain any compromise on this issue. Zionism's very consent to partition, the memorandum explained, was to a large extent motivated by the desire to secure the advantage of absorbing the maximum number of Jews in Palestine upon the establishment of a Jewish State.[80] Concurrently, the memorandum also resolves that the

Jewish State considers itself committed not only to respect the religious and civil rights of its minorities but 'also to safeguard and to the best of its ability to improve their position'. Nonetheless, in keeping with the desire to preserve the positive tone of the memorandum and in order to attain its political objectives, the memorandum totally ignored the issue of possible Arab immigration to Jewish Palestine.[81]

The memorandum emphasizes that cardinal principles that would guide the Jewish State regarding the details of the rights and status of the minority: firstly, that the Jewish State adhered to the fundamental principle of non-discrimination against the Arab minority; secondly, that the Jewish State, acting on behalf of its own self-interest and on behalf of the Arab population's interests was obligated to do its utmost gradually to achieve a genuine equality in education and living standards between the two populations. This could only be a gradual process, since at that time the levels of both populations were appreciably different.

The Arab population (as well as other minorities) should enjoy the same right as the Jewish population to vote for the parliament of the Jewish State. In addition, the Jewish State would work 'for the introduction of some form of proportional representation designed to ensure that elections shall result in Arab voters being represented in the Legislature in proportion to their numbers'.

On the issue of citizenship, the memorandum declared that the Arab minority would not be compelled automatically and immediately to accept citizenship in the Jewish State, but would be granted a period of two years to consider the matter. If at the end of this period there were some who were unprepared to accept citizenship of the Jewish State, then the state would retain the option of requiring them to leave the territory of the Jewish State. Ostensibly, this position was intended to convey flexibility towards the minority in contrast with international precedents, where the minorities had automatically received citizenship of the state and those who had not accepted it had been requested to leave within 12 months (the memorandum actually notes this). However, it is possible that the main intention of the Zionist memorandum was to minimize the total number of Arab citizens in the Jewish State during the first crucial stages following the establishment of the state when the constitution or the fundamental basic laws would be formulated. In this (apparently) non-discriminatory manner, the impact of the Arab minority during the initial and crucial stages of the state's establishment would be minimized.[82]

In accordance with the principle of non-discrimination against minorities, the memorandum set forth that 'no citizen of the Jewish state shall be at a disadvantage as a candidate for public employment by reason of his race or religion'; therefore, the Jewish State had to guarantee the Arabs a fair share in public-service positions and in projects financed by the public treasury. Nonetheless: 'As to what is meant by a fair share, the Jewish Agency does not think that at this stage it would serve any useful purpose to lay down hard-and-fast rules … A solution must be sought, not in any rigid arithmetical formula, but in the application, in good faith, of a well understood principle.' In the chapter dealing with the official language of the Jewish State, the memorandum postulated that civil servants would have to know the Hebrew language.

Relying on various British reports from the 1930s that had compelled the British government to prepare a systematic plan for the agricultural development of Palestine that would guarantee the most efficient and beneficial utilization of lands,[83] the memorandum states that this would indeed be one of the most important goals for the government of the Jewish State. It was incumbent on such a government to find room to settle new Jewish settlers and ameliorate the conditions of existing settlers.[84] The Jewish State would not attempt to achieve these goals through arbitrary intervention, but would try to use persuasion, force of example, instruction and financial assistance to guarantee that settlers, Jews and Arabs alike, exploited the land in the most efficient manner. Nonetheless, the memorandum does not rule out the possibility of government intervention in implementing a reparceling of estates or a redistribution of water to secure these aforementioned goals of freeing up land for new settlers and ameliorating the situation of the present cultivators – Arabs and Jews alike – but adds: 'The policy will be to restrict such intervention to a minimum.' In addition, the Jewish State reserved the right to conduct an agrarian reform if in the future this reform were required by the majority of the country's population, 'after the stage has been reached at which the racial division between Jews and Arabs has ceased to possess its present significance'.

The Jewish State would encourage Arab farmers to shift to intensive agriculture and to sell off their surplus land, but only on a voluntary basis and not by means of coercion and expropriation. This would be the policy save for cases 'where land is bona fide required for the purposes of frontier defense or for other public purposes, and expropriation would be generally agreed to be reasonable and in conformity with the normal practice of civilized states'. The memorandum emphasizes that land transactions would not harm tenant farmers, Arab and Jew alike, and that these would continue to enjoy protection within the framework of the law, which would be promulgated and in a format similar to the existing law. As opposed to the position of Ben-Gurion and others, who favored the voluntary transfer of Arabs to neighboring countries in order to free lands in the Jewish State for additional Jewish settlement and suggested that the Jewish State would purchase land in other countries for this purpose,[85] the Jewish Agency Memorandum did not broach the subject of voluntary transfer. It would appear that although the Jewish Agency Executive had not abandoned the idea of voluntary transfer, there was no room to raise the issue in a memorandum calculated to create trust and sympathy for the manner in which the Jewish State would treat its Arab minority. The Agency's wariness was reinforced by the fact that the transfer idea (albeit forcible transfer) as proposed by the Royal Commission had aroused opposition at both the League of Nations and within the British government.[86]

According to the memorandum, the Jewish State would take steps to reduce the gap between the wages of the Jewish and Arab worker. However, the memorandum refrained from noting in a clear fashion how this was to be achieved, aside for the fact that the state as an employer would implement this policy in the public sector. Thus, on the one hand, the memorandum noted that the state would employ legislation to obtain the objective; on the other hand, 'the Jewish Agency is not unaware of the difficulties of minimum wage legislation and recognizes that any such legislation would have to be cautiously framed'. Nonetheless, the state would act to impose forcibly minimum standards for work conditions, which constituted the norm in civilized countries.

To what standards would the Arab worker's labor conditions be elevated? On this issue, the memorandum poses a dilemma in which the Jewish State could find itself: if the state expended no efforts to improve the conditions of the Arab workers, it would be accused of neglecting them and exploiting cheap Arab labor; on the other hand, to the extent that it did improve conditions, it would face the accusation that it was denying Arab workers the competitive advantage conferred upon them by their cheap labor. The memorandum believed that a solution could be found in the gradual equalization of wages and the conditions, which

> in the long run create much healthier conditions than those prevailing at present in the labor market. A situation in which Jews and Arabs exercise their combined bargaining power in a labor organization which makes no distinction between them will clearly be preferable to one in which the Jews are undersold by the Arabs and Jews employ Arab labor, so far as they do employ it, solely because it is cheap ...

As already stated, the award of full rights in the religious and cultural sphere, such as the use of the Arab language, did not arouse any dilemmas in the deliberations of the Agency Executive and the opinion of its advisers. It is also striking that the Zionist memorandum presented to the Partition Commission attempts to emphasize the granting of full rights in these areas to the Arab minority. The memorandum notes that the Jewish State would not only adopt all the religious and cultural rights that Iraq had pledged to award its minorities, but that it would also award additional privileges not explicitly mentioned in the Iraqi declaration. Thus the memorandum pledges that there will no impairment in the status and authority of the Moslem religious courts and the courts of the Christian communities: 'The Jewish State would be ready to undertake that no change of any kind should be made in the jurisdiction presently exercised by any Moslem or Christian Religious Court.'

As regards language, the memorandum embraced in principle the relevant passages of the minorities treaties signed after the First World War. The Hebrew language would be the official language of the Jewish State, but Arabic would be recognized as the language of the Arab minority and there would be no attempt to impose the Hebrew language upon the Arab public. In definitively Arab regions, official documents would be issued in Arabic, which would also be the language of instruction in the Arab schools. Likewise, the Arab population would be entitled to address the government in Arabic and would also receive official replies in this language. Nonetheless, as noted earlier, knowledge of Hebrew would be compulsory for civil-service personnel.[87]

SUMMARY

The positive attitude evinced by the Jewish Agency on the issue of the Arab minority's status was calculated to maintain the prospects for implementing partition and establishing a Jewish State.[88] Likewise, this attitude departed from the assumption that the award of equal rights to the Arabs was in the interest of the Jewish State itself. It was also clear to the Jewish Agency that, in contrast to other countries hosting minorities, the international authorities would exercise the 'vigilance of Argus' over the Jewish State's handling of the minorities issue.[89] Some members predicated their positive approach on ethical considerations, but these considerations were probably not decisive and it is difficult to evaluate if they were ever more than declarative.[90] The exhaustive study of international precedents was also a direct outcome of practical considerations – 'to give the minorities what was customary under the League of Nations'. In any case, the more discussions veered from the theoretical level to the level of practical implementation of principles, the numerous difficulties that the Jewish State would face if it sought to implement these principles became clear. These difficulties were rooted in the goals that Zionism prescribed for the Jewish State (such as immigration and settlement), the planned character of the Jewish State, and the nature of the Arab minority. The discussions in the Executive, the positions taken by experts consulted by the Agency, as well as the final memorandum submitted to the Partition Commission, demonstrate that the Agency was not prepared to make concessions on its supreme goals and on the character of a Jewish State. Difficulties surfaced, especially in the economic sphere (in its broader context this included the issues of employment and land ownership), whereas in the social and religious spheres real difficulties did not present themselves. It appeared that difficulties surrounding the political realm, and attendant upon the establishment of a government, could be overcome provided that the Jewish population increased appreciably while the reverse held true for the Arab population.

The Jewish Agency also intended to exploit the transition period in order to overcome political difficulties. In the memorandum submitted to the Partition Commission, that elaborated the official Zionist position on minorities, the Jewish Agency embraced the Iraqi model in principle. The memorandum could have set forth in detail the obligations pertaining to those subjects that the Agency felt it could implement. However, the Agency contented itself with setting forth principles and circumventing obstacles on those issues where difficulties in implementation could be anticipated. It appeared that, although the memorandum displays a marked trend towards generosity in awarding rights, equalizing conditions and expending efforts towards ameliorating the condition of the Arab minority, the Zionist position could not speak of full equality of rights for the Arab minority. Such an equality could not dovetail with the goals of Zionism, which were inherent in the very establishment of the Jewish State.[91]

NOTES

1. CZA, Protocol of the Inner Zionist General Council meeting on 20 June 1938.
2. See Weizmann's statement in his letter to the British Colonial Secretary, Ormsby-Gore, on 14 July 1937, in Klieman (1987) pp. 341–3, see also above pp. 86–7.
3. CZA, file S25/246, Protocol of the Minorities Committee's meeting (chaired by Ben-Gurion) on 23 June 1938 (the committee convened only once); CZA, Protocol of the Jewish Agency Executive's meeting on 29 May 1938.
4. PPCR (1938), pp. 7–8.
5. See above, p. 85 as well as CZA, file S25/10058, memorandum of Dr. H. Oppenheimer: 'The Economic Position of the Arab Minority in the Proposed Jewish State', July 1937; see also Ben-Gurion (1937), p. 451.

6. See also Reches (1990).
7. PPCR (1938), pp. 381–2.
8. Ibid., p. 22.
9. Ibid., pp. 35, 39; CZA, file S25/4098, memorandum compiled by L. Stein: 'Minority Questions', on 8 July 1938; see also Ben-Gurion (1938), p. 218.
10. CZA, file S25/10058, Dr. Nathan Feinberg: 'Memorandum on International Protection of Minorities in the Event that a Jewish State will be Created', 11 May 1938; the memorandum appears also in Feinberg (1963), pp. 127–40.
11. CZA, file S25/246, Protocol of the Minorities Committee on 23 June 1938; CZA, Protocol of the Jewish Agency Executive's meeting on 7 June 1938.
12. CZA, Protocol of the Jewish Agency Executive's meeting on 9 June 1938; Ben-Gurion (1937), pp. 426–7.
13. Ben-Gurion (1938), pp. 5–6.
14. CZA, Protocol of the Jewish Agency Executive's meeting on 7 June 1938; Ben-Gurion (1937), pp. 426–7.
15. CZA, Protocol of the Jewish Agency Executive's meeting on 7 June 1938; Ben-Gurion (1936), pp. 528–9; Ben-Gurion (1937), pp. 398, 427; CZA, file S25/5102, memorandum: 'The Position of the Arabs in the Jewish State', on 21 June 1938.
16. CZA, file S25/5102, memorandum by L. Stein: 'Note on Minority Policy', on 23 June 1938.
17. CZA, file S25/246, Protocol of the Minorities Committee's meeting on 23 June 1938. A short time after the publication of the Royal Commission's Partition Plan, Ben-Gurion raised an ethical consideration for awarding equal rights to the Arab minority:

    The Jewish people who have returned to their country and will multiply in their state cannot forget the lesson of a thousands years residence in the Diaspora and the fate of their sons in foreign lands. No Jewish State, large or small, in part of the country or in the entire land is to be established save if in the birthplace of the prophets the lofty and eternal ethical objectives which we bore in our hearts and our souls for all generations: *There shall be one law for the stranger and the citizen* [emphasis in the original]. A just regime, love of one's fellow man, true equality are to be implemented. The Jewish State will be an example for the world to follow in its conduct towards minorities and to people of a different nation.

    On this see Ben-Gurion (1937), p. 398. However, the primary sources reveal that these were declarative statements and that ethical considerations did not underpin the need to award rights to the Arab minority. Compare with Ben-Gurion (1937), p. 388, and his statement at the Jewish Agency Executive's meeting on 7 June 1938.
18. CZA, file S25/246, Protocol of the Minorities Committee's meeting on 23 June 1938; CZA, Protocol of the Jewish Agency Executive's meeting on 9 June 1938; CZA, file S25/10058, Feinberg's memorandum.
19. League of Nations (1927); Treaty of Peace (1919), pp. 41–5; Grenville (1987).
20. Feinberg (1963), pp. 128–9.
21. See notes 19 and 20.
22. CZA, file S44/481, memorandum of Y. Gruenbaum to the Political Department regarding the rights of the Arab minority, on 13 July 1938; CZA, file S25/8929, memorandum of B. E. Dugdale, 'Notes for Guidance in Forming a Minority Policy for a Jewish State', undated; CZA, file S25/10058, memorandum of H. Oppenheimer: 'The Economic Position of the Arab Minority in the Proposed Jewish State', July 1937; Feinberg (1963), pp. 128–9.
23. Feinberg (1963), p. 129.
24. CZA, file S25/10058, Feinberg's 'Memorandum on International Protection of Minorities in the Event that a Jewish State will be Created'. For the complete text of the Iraqi declaration, see League of Nations (1932), pp. 1347–9.
25. Feinberg (1963), pp. 127–34; League of Nations (1930), p. 212; League of Nations (1931), pp. 128–40.
26. Feinberg (1963), pp. 127–34; League of Nations (1931), pp. 62–8, 91–2, 110–15, 121, 140, 156–8, 177–81.

27. Feinberg (1963), p. 137; League of Nations (1937b), pp. 37–8.
28. CZA, file S44/481, memorandum by Y. Gruenbaum to the Political Department regarding the rights of the Arab Minority, 13 July 1938.
29. CZA, Protocol of the Jewish Agency Executive's meetings on 25 May 1938 and 29 May 1938.
30. CZA, memorandum by L. Stein: 'Note on Minority Policy', 23 June 1938.
31. CZA, Protocol of the Jewish Agency Executive's meeting of 7 June 1938.
32. CZA, Protocol of the Jewish Agency Executive's meeting on 9 June 1938; see also Gruenbaum's memorandum in note 22. At the meeting of the Jewish Agency Executive on 29 May 1938, Ben-Gurion estimated that during this transition period the Jewish provisional government could promote the immigration of 100,000 Jews. On this, see CZA, Protocol of the Jewish Agency Executive's meeting on 29 May 1938. See also CZA, Protocol of the Jewish Agency Executive's meeting together with the Political Department of the Inner Zionist General Council on 12 June 1938, and CZA, Protocol of the Inner Zionist General Council's meeting on 20 June 1938.
33. CZA, file S25/8929, memorandum by Professor L. B. Namier, 'Treatment of Minorities', undated.
34. CZA, file S25/10058, comments on the memoranda of Mrs. Dugdale and Professor L. B. Namier on 23 June 1938.
35. CZA, memorandum by L. Stein: 'Note on Minority Policy', 23 June 1938.
36. The relevant passage stipulated that minorities automatically received Polish citizenship, but that they enjoyed the right to waive it and opt for the citizenship of another country. In such an event, they would have to move within a year to take up residence in the country whose citizenship they had adopted. For this passage see the sources cited in note 19.
37. CZA, file S25/5102, memorandum by L. Stein: 'Note on Minority Policy', 23 June 1938; CZA, file S25/5114, 'Analysis of Jewish Agency's Evidence before the Technical Commission', 12 July 1938; CZA, Protocol of the Jewish Agency Executive's meetings on 29 May 1938 and 9 June 1938. A proposal was raised in the Jewish Agency Executive to rely also on the precedents concerning Cyprus. There, the British government, upon receiving control of the island, had declared that anyone was entitled to receive British citizenship, but whoever did not do so during a given period would have to leave. Nonetheless, not everyone in the Executive was content with this proposal, because some members felt that compelling the Arabs to leave would arouse bitter disputes. See on this matter Kaplan's statement at the Jewish Agency Executive's meeting on 9 June 1938.
38. As proposed by L. B. Namier, one of the experts consulted by the Jewish Agency Executive. On this, see CZA, file S25/8929, memorandum by Professor L. B. Namier, 'Treatment of Minorities', undated.
39. See CZA, file S25/10058, comments on memoranda of Mrs. Dugdale and Professor Namier, 23 June 1938; CZA, file S25/42, Protocol of the Security Committee's meeting on 21 November 1937; CZA, file S25/8119, memorandum by the Security Committee: 'A Proposal for the Organization of Security Forces in a Jewish State' on 15 May 1938. See also the section on Security Forces in Chapter 6 (pp. 155–9).
40. See note 35; CZA, Protocol of the Jewish Agency Executive's meeting on 29 May 1938.
41. CZA, Protocol of the Jewish Agency Executive's meeting on 6 September 1938; CZA, file S44/481, memorandum by Gruenbaum in note 22.
42. CZA, file S25/5102, memorandum by Senator: 'The Position of the Arabs in the Jewish State' on 21 June 1938.
43. See note 35; CZA, Protocol of the Jewish Agency Executive's meeting on 29 May 1938; CZA, file S25/1519, Protocol of the Security Committee's meeting on 7 December 1937. See also below the sub-chapter on security forces in Chapter 6, pp. 155–9.
44. See CZA, file S25/5102, memorandum by Senator: 'The Position of the Arabs in the Jewish State', 21 June 1938.
45. CZA, Protocol of the Jewish Agency Executive's meeting on 9 June 1938.
46. CZA, Protocol of the Jewish Agency Executive's meeting on 7 June 1938.

47. See CZA, file S25/8929, memorandum by Professor Namier, 'Treatment of Minorities', undated.
48. See Stein's memorandum: 'Note on Minority Policy', 23 June 1938.
49. CZA, Protocol of the Jewish Agency Executive's meeting on 9 June 1938; see notes 34 and 42.
50. See Gruenbaum's memorandum, CZA, file S44/481.
51. See Oppenheimer's memorandum in 'The Economic Position of the Arab Minority in the Jewish State', July 1937, CZA, file S25/10058.
52. Ibid.
53. See Gruenbaum's memorandum, CZA, file S44/481.
54. Ibid. Other members of the Jewish Agency Executive and some of its advisers shared Gruenbaum's opinion. One of them expressed himself as follows: 'It is obvious that the present style of campaign against Arab labor and Arab production cannot and should not be continued in a Jewish State where Arab producers and Arab workmen are citizens with equal rights. Otherwise from the beginning, racial discrimination would be established with all the destructive consequences we have seen in Europe'. On this issue, see CZA, file S25/5102, memorandum by Senator: 'The Position of the Arabs in the Jewish State', 21 June 1938. There were others who believed that, in principle, one should not proclaim a policy of government intervention via setting a minimum wage and instead make do with a general declaration to the effect that the Jewish State favored improving the pay and working conditions of the Arab worker in order to close quickly the existing gaps between Jewish and Arab workers. On this see CZA, file S25/4098, memorandum by L. Stein: 'Minority Questions', on 8 July 1937.
55. See Gruenbaum's memorandum, CZA, file S44/481.
56. Ibid.
57. Ibid.
58. See note 42, and also CZA, Protocol of the Jewish Agency Executive's meetings on 7 June 1938 and 9 June 1938.
59. See note 22.
60. See note 5.
61. See notes 16 and 22.
62. CZA, Protocol of the Jewish Agency Executive's meeting on 9 June 1938.
63. CZA, Protocol of the Jewish Agency Executive's meeting on 12 June 1938.
64. Ibid.
65. See notes 33 and 34.
66. See note 22.
67. See note 33.
68. CZA, memorandum by L. Stein in note 16; Dugdale's memorandum, CZA, file S25/10058, 'Notes for Guidance in Forming a Minority Policy for a Jewish State', undated.
69. See note 34.
70. Ibid.
71. See Gruenbaum's memorandum, CZA, file S44/481.
72. CZA, file S25/8929, 'Memorandum on the Treatment of Minorities', submitted by the Jewish Agency Executive to the Partition Commission on 31 July 1938.
73. Compare the memorandum in the previous note with Ben-Gurion's statement at the meeting of the Jewish Agency Executive on 7 June 1938, in CZA. Ben-Gurion's statement also appears in Ben-Gurion (1938), pp. 206–10.
74. Report of the Executive (1939), pp. 10, 211; CZA, Protocol of the Jewish Agency Executive's meeting of 19 June 1938; CZA, Protocol of the Inner Zionist General Council's meeting on 20 June 1938, p. 734.
75. CZA, Protocol of the Jewish Agency Executive's meeting on 25 July 1938.
76. See note 72.
77. Ibid.
78. See the draft in CZA, file S25/10058, 'Draft – Memorandum on the Treatment of

Minorities', dated 16 July 1938.

79. CZA, Protocol of the Jewish Agency Executive's meeting on 25 July 1938.

80. Compare with Ben-Gurion's statement at the Jewish Agency Executive's meeting on 7 June 1938 in CZA, which states, *inter alia*:

> The principal goal of the proposed Jewish State is to absorb the maximum number of Jews and thus help solve the Jewish problem throughout the world. This goal will determine the entire nature, regime and modus operandi of the Jewish State ... The regime of the Jewish State assigns itself, as a task of the first echelon, the job of expanding the country's absorptive capacity to accommodate the masses of Jewish immigrants and settle an appropriate portion of these immigrants on the land ...

> See also Ben-Gurion's words in his diary on 26 August 1937, which appear in Ben-Gurion (1937), pp. 425–6, where he states, *inter alia*:

> The state that will arise will be Jewish in the sense that its function, goal and purpose will be Jewish. It won't be a state of Jews who simply reside in the country but a state for the Jews, for the Jewish people. A state designed to absorb Jewish immigration and provide a solution to the growth and expansion of the Jewish problem. The structure of the state, its constitution, its government, its external and internal relations will all be directed to a single goal: the absorption of the masses in Palestine ...

81. It is possible that the solution to the question of 'Arab immigration' is provided in the continuation of Ben-Gurion's (1937) words, as noted in the latter part of note 80: 'The Jewish State will prohibit all Arab "Aliyah" [quotation in original], and will piteously expel any foreign immigrants ...'

82. Compare with Ben-Gurion's statement in CZA, Protocol of the Jewish Agency Executive's meeting on 7 June 1938 and the decisions that were adopted at the meeting of the Jewish Agency Executive, Protocol of 25 July 1938.

83. Hope-Simpson (1930), pp. 143–4; Strickland (1930), p. 39.

84. Compare with Ben-Gurion's statement in CZA, Protocol of the Jewish Agency Executive's meeting on 7 June 1938, where Ben-Gurion stated, *inter alia*:

> The state will promote with all the means at its disposal the intensive cultivation of land and the increased productivity of the agricultural economy. It will sustain the planting of fruit trees in all the suitable mountainous regions; it will institute irrigation facilities in the valleys ... it will variegate the seed cycle; it will establish model fields and experimental stations in all parts of the country to provide expertise and upgrading ...

85. Compare with Ben-Gurion's statement in CZA, Protocol of the Jewish Agency Executive's meeting, on 7 June 1938.

86. Katz (1992b); PPCR (1938), p. 235, from where it emerges that the Partition Commission rejected the idea of voluntary transfer.

87. See note 72.

88. A similar tendency emerges in the Jewish Agency Executive's position on the partition boundaries, the issue of Jerusalem and in rejecting the issue of transfer.

89. See also the twentieth Zionist Congress, 1937, pp. 152, 188–9.

90. See note 17.

91. Compare with Sofer (1993), Reches (1990), and see note 45. See also Katz (1997).

6
The Demand for Full Sovereignty and Early Studies on the Issue of Forming a Jewish State

THE PRINCIPLE OF FULL SOVEREIGNTY

The Jewish Agency Executive demanded full sovereignty for the Jewish State. It was not prepared to make peace with the Royal Commission's recommendations, which implied a tangible infringement on the sovereignty and independence of the Jewish State and all that entailed. These recommendations included the following: the cities of Haifa, Tiberias, Safad and Acre were to be removed from the areas of the Jewish State and placed for a certain unspecified period under a British mandate; the Port of Tel Aviv, in conjunction with the Port of Jaffa, would be placed under the supervision of a joint port authority to be headed by an official appointed by the mandatory government; receipts from port duties levied in the ports of the Jewish State would be transferred, for a time unspecified in advance, to the mandatory government; duties between the Jewish and Arab State would be equalized; and finally, the Royal Commission recommended obligating the Jewish State to support the Arab State financially.[1]

The full inclusion of Safad, Haifa, Tiberias and Acre within the areas of the Jewish State

Aside from its tangible infringement on the sovereignty of the Jewish State, the exclusion of the four cities ('the sole city left to us was Tel Aviv')[2] from the areas of the Jewish State would necessarily have caused grave economic damage to the Jewish State. The total Jewish population of these cities represented 17 per cent of the entire Jewish population in the Jewish State (according to boundaries proposed by the Royal Commission) and 28 per cent of its Jewish urban population. The general population of the four cities constituted 20 per cent of the residents of the Jewish State and 46 per cent of its urban population. The exclusion of such a large percentage of taxpayers would have exerted a baleful influence on the income of the Jewish State, and would substantially increase the financial burden imposed upon the residents of the Jewish State if the state wished to preserve the same level of public services as it currently provided. The Jewish Agency's economic experts believed that under such circumstances the Jewish State could not balance its budget.[3] In addition, there was the problem posed by the geographic fragmentation of the four cities and their estrangement from the permanent mandatory enclave – with all the difficult repercussions which would ensue, such as different rates of duty and consequentially the severe economic damage which would befall both the cities themselves and the Jewish State.[4]

The Jewish Agency Executive was particularly opposed to the imposition of a temporary mandate on Haifa, where, according to the Royal Commission's report, 50,000 Jews and 48,000 Arabs resided. On the eve of the publication of the Royal Commission's report, Weizmann took pains to clarify to the British Colonial Secretary Ormsby-Gore that the Jewish State would agree to supply all the British Army's necessities in the city of Haifa, but 'apart from this the harbor and the commercial, industrial and residential area should be in the Jewish State'[5] In its memorandum to the Partition Commission the Executive emphasized that

> The importance of Haifa to the Jews lies not merely in the fact that the town has already today a Jewish majority, but even more in that it holds a key position as the strategic and the economic outpost of northern Palestine. It has the only deep water harbor in the country ... Communications by land, water and air with Europe and with the east converge in Haifa. The city of Haifa, and during the last ten years, the area of Haifa Bay have become thriving centers of Jewish industrial and commercial enterprise. Jewish building in the city has proceeded apace and in Haifa Bay a chain of Jewish suburban settlements has sprung up ... The exclusion of this town, with the widely ramified Jewish economic activities centered in and around it, would so seriously cripple the Jewish State at its very inception as to make its position untenable ...[6]

Prior to this, while comparing the importance of Haifa with that of Jerusalem, Ben-Gurion emphasized the political and economic importance of Haifa to the Jewish State:

> The Jewish community in Haifa is presently smaller than Jerusalem's but it has been growing more rapidly. Only a few years back we were still a minority in the city. Now we have reached the stage where we are a majority. However, as in Jerusalem, it is not the number of Jews alone that determines the value of Haifa, This city is the economic and strategic key to the country. It is the only natural port on the Palestine coast, and it is not by chance that the first top-drawer port in the country was built here. Haifa also has international

importance. This is the sole coastal city in the British Empire that has oil pipe lines. In the Eastern Mediterranean Haifa can be the chief city and there is no reason why it will not surpass Egypt's Alexandria. In Haifa our embryonic 'heavy industry' in the country already clusters. By sea, by land and by air, Haifa is linked to all parts of the world. Haifa Bay and the Carmel Mountain are in their vast portion Jewish-owned land and most of this is nationally owned land. More than any other city, Haifa is adorned with Jewish worker settlements. The possibility for expanding the city in valley and mountain are almost unlimited ...[7]

On the basis of a long list of quantitative – primarily economic – data that was assembled and refined by an Experts Committee on Haifa's affairs appointed by the Political Department, the Jewish Agency Executive sought to demonstrate that there was no justification for separating the city of Haifa and the Jewish settlements in the Bay from the Jewish State, even on a temporary basis. The statistics demonstrated that the decisive character of the city was Jewish. Jewish initiative was filling a decisive role in developing the city and promoting its economic growth and this trend was perpetually on the upswing. Separating Haifa from the Jewish State would harm both the economic life of the city as well as the economic life of other parts of the country: 'The exclusion of Haifa, even its temporary exclusion, could not fail to have a depressing effect on the economic life of other parts of the Jewish State by interposing barriers between the rest of the State and one of its principal markets and sources of supply.'[8] Echoing Weizmann's words, uttered in 1937, the Executive did not ignore Britain's special strategic interests in Haifa. It was clear to the Executive that the sole and exclusive reason for imposing a temporary mandate on this city was a desire to protect British interests (i.e. the port and the oil pipe line). Therefore, the Executive proposed to the Partition Commission that the two sides should reach a permanent arrangement on this manner via a military treaty that would form part of an inclusive treaty between the Jewish State and the British Empire. In the framework of such a treaty, the Executive considered allowing the British a foothold along the coast between Zikhron Ya'akov and Ras en Naqura for the purposes of protecting the port and the oil pipe line.[9]

With regards to Tiberias, whose Jewish population was twice the size of the Arab population, the Executive noted its historical role as the capital of Jewish Galilee and its present role as the center of the Jewish community in the Jordan Valley and the Lower Galilee. With regards to Safad, the Executive had to resort to the contention that it was a holy city and for hundreds of years had served as an important impetus to Jewish spiritual life. The Executive did not accept the contention of the Royal Commission that the imposition of a temporary mandate over Haifa, Acre, Tiberias and Safad was necessary in order to guarantee the fulfillment of treaty guarantees regarding the protection of minorities in these cities, since 'One cannot lash us with two whips. For the treaty between the World Zionist Organization and the British Government is to contain an article regarding the protection of the national minorities and this guarantee should suffice.'[10] Nonetheless, it appears that under certain conditions the Executive was willing to forgo Acre, whose population did not exceed 9,000 and whose Jewish population was minuscule. It would appear that the essential opposition was to the infringement upon sovereignty and the fear of a precedent-setting concession, and this stiffened opposition to imposing a temporary mandate on Acre as well.[11]

The independence of the port of Tel Aviv

The recommendation of the Royal Commission to unite the ports of Jaffa and Tel Aviv under the supervision of a Joint Port Authority would of necessity mean that the Jews would lose control over the port of Tel Aviv. The Executive did not need to enumerate the many reasons for its opposition before the Partition Commission, since by July 1937 the British Colonial Secretary had already expressed his opposition to this recommendation, given its infringement on sovereignty. He conceded that such co-operation would be possible only if both the Arab and the Jewish State gave their consent.[12]

Independence in determining customs rates and their collection

The Royal Commission's recommendation to entrust the collection of port duties to the hands of the mandatory government for a certain period stemmed from its perception that collection in the three separate political and fiscal regimes that were to be established in Palestine was bound to be exceedingly complicated. The Executive was alert to this logic, but contended that these problems were soluble only within the framework of an agreement between the three states as opposed to infringing upon sovereignty by expropriating the collection prerogative from the hands of the Jewish State. The Executive also found the Royal Commission's recommendation (even though this was not clear-cut) to equalize customs duties of the Jewish and Arab State unacceptable. This too the Executive viewed as an infringement of sovereignty, and something that went still further:

> The economic development of the Jewish State is liable to be seriously hampered unless it enjoys full tariff autonomy. Whatever the size of the State,

it is obvious that the need to enlarge its capacity of absorption would call for intensive industrial development, which requires a very elastic tariff policy, determined in full accordance with the internal needs of the country. If the tariff policy of the Jewish State were to depend in any measure on that of the Arab State, the latter would be in a position to obstruct the industrial development of the former ... Another consideration bearing on the subject is that the Jewish State would have a much more extensive foreign trade than the Arab, and that by far the greater part of Palestine's present exports would, presumably, have their origin in the Jewish area. In its foreign trade policy, therefore, the Jewish State would have to adopt a maximum degree of reciprocity in trade relations, and would have to conform to the modern system of bilateral trade agreements. This implies the purchase of the country's supplies from countries providing an outlet for its exports ... maximum reciprocity and bilateral trade agreements would have to be among the main features of the elastic trade policy which the Jewish State would probably find it desirable to adopt. A policy of this nature, however, would be made impossible by a compulsory commercial convention with the Arab State ...[13]

Opposition to supporting an Arab State

The Jewish Agency Executive viewed the Royal Commission's recommendation that the Jewish State should underwrite an Arab State financially as not only an infringement but as an immoral demand. The recommendation, in their view, insinuated that 'it is considered to be incumbent upon the Jews, first to pay a fee, as it were, to the Arabs in order to qualify for independence and, secondly, to justify their presence in Palestine by shouldering the responsibility for the welfare of the Arab population. Both these implications must be emphatically rejected, since the Jews consider themselves to be in Palestine "as of right".'[14] Additionally, the Executive added that this recommendation was totally impractical. With its limited budget, the Jewish State had first to concern itself with financing the security burden and other public needs including those of the Arab population within its borders, funding the financial obligations of the mandatory government and investing in development projects requisite for absorbing Jewish immigrants. It would therefore have no surplus in order to assist its Arab neighbor.[15] Let it be emphasized that the Jewish Agency Executive was aware of the severe economic problems that would confront the Arab State, whose income would be meager and which would find it difficult to cut the public services that the Palestine population had been accustomed to receive from the mandatory government. Senior bodies in the mandatory government also emphasized to the Executive that without significant financial support from the Jewish State, the Arab State would not be able to arise – a fact that cast a grave doubt on the implementation of any partition plan whatsoever.[16] Despite these facts, the Executive did not retreat from its principled stand, and it appears that it believed that the British had to bear the economic burdens as the Royal Commission had recommended in principle.[17] Nonetheless, in the deliberations of the Executive, as well as in its testimony before the Partition Commission, a possibility was raised regarding Jewish assistance to the Arab State in the framework of an agreement between the two countries on voluntary transfer.[18]

FROM MANDATE TO STATE: A PRELIMINARY ANALYSIS OF ISSUES REGARDING THE FORMATION OF THE STATE AND ITS PRACTICES

In the framework of its overall response to the Royal Commission's plan which resulted in the shaping of a Zionist Partition Plan, the Jewish Agency Executive addressed and formulated a position during the years 1937–38 on a series of major issues of boundaries, Jerusalem, the transfer of populations, the status accorded the Arab minority, and the demand for full sovereignty. The Zionist Executive and the special committees that it established tackled a number of additional issues, predominantly concerned with the transition from mandate to state and the fundamental procedures of that state once it was established. These issues were hashed over in position papers and internal deliberations, although one could hardly state that the deliberations on the issues proved conclusive or that a definitive position was formulated. These issues included the transition period and the stages leading to the establishment of the Jewish State; the fundamental norms of the regime; the relations between the Jewish State and Britain, and the bases of the former's foreign policy; immigration and development; the essentials of the budget; church and state; the military and security. The section that follows examines the tendencies of the Executive on these issues.[19]

The transition period and the stages leading to the establishment
of a Jewish State
Both the Royal Commission's Report[20] as well as the British Colonial Secretary's letter to the High Commissioner towards the close of December 1937, which announced the formation of the Partition Commission and enumerated its prerogatives, accorded a modicum of attention towards the stages bridging the termination of the mandate until the formation of two independent states in Palestine. The Colonial Secretary's letter noted the

following stages: the British government would authorize the partition plan; the League of Nations Council would ratify it; under the aegis of the mandate new governmental systems would be established for a limited period in the two areas where the two states were slated to arise; agreements with the British government would be reached concerning the formation of two independent states; and the League of Nations Council would approve Britain's request to terminate the mandate.[21] The British left the substance of the transition stage, during which the new systems of government would be erected under the mandatory government's protection, undetermined.

The Jewish Agency not only consented in principle to the transition stage because it assumed that neither the British nor the League of Nations would be prepared to forgo the stage where the Jews (as well as the Arabs) were expected to ready themselves in governmental procedure before power passed formally into their hands;[22] a more fundamental consideration was to get the most out of the transition stage to benefit the Jewish State. The pivotal factor was to guarantee an absolute Jewish majority once the State was established by taking control over immigration affairs during the transition period. The Executive also believed that it would not be possible to change power in a single day and this should be done gradually.[23] The Political Department was assigned to draft a plan for the transition period and the stages leading to the establishment of a Jewish State.[24] The Department presented a staged plan for the transition period, which would comprise three stages: the preparatory stage, the intermediary stage, and the final stage.

In the preparatory stage, overall control would still reside in the hands of the mandatory government, but this control would be tempered first and foremost by an agreement with the Jewish Agency that would guarantee a liberal policy of Jewish immigration and assistance towards its absorption. In consultation with the Jewish Agency Executive, a Deputy Director of the Immigration Department would be appointed in the Palestine mandatory government. In this stage, preparations would be made towards transferring certain prerogatives from the mandatory government to an appointed Jewish government. Provisions would be made for establishing a Jewish Army, and this would include delegating security for the Jewish settlements to a Jewish police, which would be subordinate to British authority. Legislative powers would remain in the hands of the High Commissioner. However, he would be required to consult with the Jewish Agency on all legislation bearing on areas of the Jewish State that might arise, and to consider requests for legislation submitted by the Jewish Agency to be promulgated in the areas of the future

Jewish State. The legal system would take on a fair number of new Jewish justices; the administration would absorb and instruct Jewish officials, who would be appointed by the Jewish Agency on the assumption that they would take over from the British officials. The postal services, the railways, the ports and customs would absorb and train additional Jewish manpower. The reorganization of the various government departments and the service networks would commence in order to adjust them to the new reality that would be created following partition and the establishment of two states. With regard to rail and postal services, the possibility that these services would ultimately be jointly operated by the three authorities sharing in the division of Palestine was admitted.

In the intermediary stage, the British government would appoint a provisional Jewish government, to which it would ultimately transfer the legislative and administrative prerogatives governing the territory that was decided to constitute the Jewish State. The members of this government and its leader would be appointed pursuant to the Jewish Agency's recommendations. Security affairs (except for the organization of the security forces of the Jewish State) and currency would remain under the supervision of the British mandate. Likewise postal, rail and port-custom services would remain under its control. The provisional government would be obligated to inform the High Commissioner regarding all legislative – administrative steps that were contemplated, and he would retain the authority to block their implementation if they could impair Britain's international obligations regarding the territories of Palestine, or if they contradicted the obligations assumed by the provisional government towards minorities. Nonetheless, an open-door policy would be practiced and the High Commissioner would have no authority to intervene in fixing the number of immigrants permitted to enter the area of the Jewish State in formation.

In the intermediary stage, the formation of an independent judicial system that would serve the future Jewish State would commence. Obviously, during the intermediary stage the appointed provisional government would prepare a plan for the establishment of a constitutional government on the basis of representative institutions, which would be submitted to the British government and the League Council for approval. The constitution would be a provisional constitution until it were replaced by a permanent constitution, which would be ratified at the conclusion of the transition period's final stage. The intention of the Political Department was to secure the replacement of an appointed government by a constitutional government only after a suitable Jewish majority had been ensured in the areas of the Jewish State in the making by Jewish immigration and perhaps also by voluntary transfer. Additionally, in order to grant voting rights even to immigrants who had recently arrived in Palestine, so they could help chose the elected institutions, the Political Department contended that one should award the right of franchise to all residents within the area of the Jewish State in formation even if they were not Palestinian citizens. To justify this demand, the Political Department relied among other things on the 1936 proposal of the British government itself to extend the franchise to residents of Palestine who were not yet citizens, so that they could help elect a legislative council.

In the final stage of the transition period, by force of a League of Nations ruling, the appointed provisional government would be replaced by a temporary constitutional government. The prerogatives of this government, as well as the prerogatives of the High Commissioner, would be identical to those which existed during the transition period. However, at this stage the Jewish government could establish an independent customs authority for the Jewish State in the making, which would enjoy independence in determining customs rates. Supervision over the ports would be transferred at this stage to the control of the Jewish government. In the event that prior to this stage of the transition period no agreement had been reached for joint operation of the postal and rail services by the three governments in control of Palestine, these services would be dissolved between the three regimes. Likewise, during the final stage, the final version of an agreement between the Jewish provisional government and the British mandatory government would be reached regarding the establishment of an independent Jewish State. The final stage of the transition period would come to an end with ratification by the League of Nations of Britain's request to terminate the mandate. Anticipating this last development, during the course of the final stage, voting for an elected assembly would take place in the area of the future Jewish State. This elected assembly would ratify the agreement with Britain and adopt a permanent constitution, which would enter into force upon the conclusion of the mandate and the nullification of the provisional constitution.[25]

Certain members of the Jewish Agency Executive voiced criticism of the Political Department's plan for the transition period. They demanded that the period be shortened, its stages simplified, and that the Jewish provisional government should be awarded broad prerogatives at the start of the transition period.[26] Leading the critics was Executive member Yitzhak Gruenbaum, who served in 1918–30 as a member of the Polish Sejm. Gruenbaum contended that the 'preparatory stage', when partition would already exist but the Jewish provisional regime would not yet have been established, was not only superfluous but also dangerous:

It is impossible to agree that an intermediary stage should be fixed within the transition period when all power will remain in the hands of the British government and we will only prepare ourselves and learn how to use power. All in all the Jews are not a people bereft of political culture and in Palestine there are many people who had acquired vast experience either in their work in Palestine or in various European countries and one should not make light of their experience ... one should be wary lest the first temporary period should turn into a protracted one leading to the creation of an abnormal and powerless situation. Partition will be implemented without proceeding to the establishment of a Jewish State. Such a situation would undermine the entire confidence which is bestowed upon us by the Jewish people in the Diaspora and in Palestine, and will furnish honed weapons in the hands of our internal and external enemies to be used against us; it will lead to the prolongation and intensification of Arab terror which in turn will provide major reinforcement to Jewish terror ... we must demand with all our might that our provisional government should be appointed immediately after partition is ratified by the League of Nations ...

It would appear that Gruenbaum also viewed the replacement of the appointed government by a provisional constitutional government during the transition period as superfluous, and preferred an appointed government proposed by the Zionist Executive and the Vaad Leumi.

Gruenbaum demanded the award of further prerogatives and executive power to the provisional government once it had been appointed. In his opinion, this meant first and foremost full control over handling the matters of immigration and absorption, while the British mandatory government would cease to handle this matter. The areas of education, local government (Jewish and Arab alike), justices of the peace, organization of the security forces, including the organization of a Jewish police and responsibility for internal security in the areas of the Jewish State, should pass in full to the hands of the provisional government upon its establishment. With regard to all other branches of power, the provisional government would receive the right to impose a veto on ordinances and laws proposed by the mandatory government. The provisional government would be permitted to introduce its officials into government departments that would be created to deal with matters pertaining to the area of the Jewish State. The total number of Jewish workers and officials in all branches of the political economy that would remain in the hands of the mandatory government would be increased gradually in the area of the Jewish State. Another major task to be imposed on the provisional government was the establishment of a Jewish army. This army would function under the authority of the British military command in Palestine, but in the future, when the Jewish State had full sovereignty, it would be able to act in its own capacity.

In contrast to the Political Department, which did not fix a time limit for the transition period, Gruenbaum placed a limit ranging from three to five years. At the end of this period, by force of a law to be promulgated by the provisional government in concurrence with the mandatory government, elections would be held for the Jewish State's constituent assembly, which would then assume authority in the state and appoint a provisional government. As in the recommendations of the Political Department, the constituent assembly would determine the state's constitution and ratify the treaty between the Jewish State and Britain.[27]

In view of Gruenbaum's critique of the Political Department's plan, as well as the criticism voiced by other members of the Executive regarding the excessive intervening period between the ratification of the partition and the establishment of the state, the Executive decided to postpone the adoption of a decision regarding the stages until an exhaustive deliberation on the topic had occurred. Prior to the publication of the Partition Commission's report no such discussion took place, and in the end the Partition Commission never received a memorandum explicitly enunciating the Executive's position on the stages leading to the establishment of a Jewish State.[28] Nonetheless, in a response to a question posed to him during his oral testimony before the Partition Commission, Ben-Gurion, in general terms, presented the plan of the Political Department but amalgamated the intermediate stage and the final stage into a single stage. He emphasized that the Jewish State and its parliamentary institutions would begin operations under conditions of an absolute majority of Jewish citizens.[29]

Foundations of the regime

In the conviction of the Jewish Agency Executive, the country's regime had to be a democratic parliamentary regime, and the government and its ministers were to be responsible to parliament. The full right of franchise would be awarded to adults, irrespective of sex, class and without distinction between Jews, Arabs and other minorities. The constitution would enter into force with the conclusion of the mandate, but the parliamentary institutions did not necessarily have to arise together with the ratification of the constitution. As we discovered in Chapter 4, the Executive hoped that during the transition period the proportions of the Arab population and the Jewish population within the areas of the Jewish State in the making would change in a substantial fashion, and thus the weight of the Arab factor in the elections would diminish. It would appear that, for this same reason, the Jewish Agency Executive left itself freedom of action in determining the date that parliamentary institutions were to be established.[30] In this fashion, a sort of compromise was reached between Ben-Gurion and Shertok regarding the date on which the democratic regime would be activated.[31]

Special ties with Britain and the foundations of foreign policy

The Jewish Agency Executive believed that the agreement to be signed between the Jewish State and Britain (which was essentially similar to the agreement between Iraq and Britain in 1930, and the Franco–Syrian Agreement in 1936, when Iraq and Syria made their way towards independence) would guarantee the internal and external sovereignty of the Jewish State, while concomitantly the Jewish State would award the British Army certain privileges in its territory and especially on the coasts, the ports and land-transportation arteries. Likewise, the agreement would guarantee that Britain would assist the Jewish State to gain admission to the League of Nations. The Jewish State would seek to have the agreement include a military treaty obligating Britain to assist in the defense of the Jewish State in the event that it confronted external attack. In recompense, the Jewish State would be obligated to conduct its foreign policy in consultation with the British government. Nonetheless, the Jewish State would preserve full independence for itself in two areas of foreign policy: '… an active and systematic policy to enter into relations of amity good neighborliness and economic cultural and political cooperation with the neighboring Arab states; b. without intervening in the internal affairs of any other country, to render assistance, protection and defense to Jews who required such help in other countries'.[32] Let us add that, within the framework of the efforts of the Jewish State to create relations of good neighborliness with its neighbors, the Executive believed that the Jewish State would have to adopt a special customs policy towards the Arab states.[33]

Immigration and development

The absorption of the maximum number of Jewish immigrants, thereby facilitating a solution to the Jewish problem the world over, was the Executive believed 'the primary goal of the proposed Jewish State'. Therefore, 'the regime of the Jewish State will be deployed in its first echelon towards expanding the absorptive capacity of the country to accommodate the multitudes of Jewish immigrants in order to settle a suitable number of immigrants on the land'. As we have been apprised in the previous chapters, this policy necessarily required extensive land and agricultural development, intensification, full and efficient use of all the lands in the

Jewish State, and the adoption of various measures to implement this policy, including the possibility of voluntary transfer. The Jewish State planned to absorb two-thirds of the immigrants in urban settlement. For this purpose it intended to adopt a policy of development and expansion of industry and crafts, to nurture trade relations with other countries, to encourage the immigration to Palestine of capitalists and investment capital, and to institute a tariff policy that would encourage exports and prevent dumping and unfair competition from cheap labor.[34]

The budgetary foundations of the state's initial years

With the aid of Peretz Naphtali, one of the Jewish Agency's economic advisers, the Jewish Agency Executive mapped out in general terms the budgetary structure of the Jewish State during its preliminary years. The intention was to arrive at a balanced budget that took into account the practical possibilities of the tax burden levied upon the population of the Jewish State. The budget was to be based, in principle, on the current budget of the Palestine mandatory government, as supplemented by the special items deriving from the establishment of a Jewish State. Assuming that the partition plan of the Executive would be implemented, the budget totaled £4 million. This was a balanced budget with a slight surplus and the main expenditure item was devoted to security, which was allocated nearly a quarter of the total outlay. The expenditures for security were estimated as the minimum required for the needs of an independent state, whereas an increase would necessarily force a tax increase. Another budgetary principle posited that the Jewish State would not carry the burden for land purchases and settlement. The Jewish people would continue to carry this burden via the special Zionist funds which had already been active for a number of years. The JNF (Jewish National Fund) would purchase land and Keren Hayesod would finance the actual settlement activity. In Naphtali's picturesque phrase: 'It would be a dangerous illusion to believe that the Jewish lilliput State would be able to assume the task of becoming the "Mother-country" for the colonization of its dispersed sons that will remain the task of world Jewry'.[35]

The budget for public services, mainly health and education, could not fund a level of services approaching that of the advanced states. In any case, 'only bit by bit, would the country assume the additional burden of services and participation in settlement projects. It cannot do this during the first year of its existence … The Jewish State can in no way institute compulsory general education because it will lack the money, the apparatus and the teachers. Compulsory general education must be the goal of our country a goal which we will attain only gradually.'[36]

The state's income would be predicated on customs duties – the principal tax benefitting the mandatory government; other indirect taxes that existed during the mandatory era and the imposition new direct taxes (not including those levied by the municipalities) – a progressive income tax ranging from zero to ten per cent; a one-time immigration tax imposed on new immigrants with capital of at least £1,000; an appreciation tax on real-estate transactions, the principal goal of which was to dampen land-speculation; and an inheritance tax levied on a certain minimal sum. As the country developed and shaped its economic policy, it could consider various changes in the tax clauses. On the basis of his calculations, Peretz Naphtali estimated that the tax burden that would be imposed on the population of the Jewish State would be high in comparison with their standard of living and current income.[37]

Church and state

In the years 1937–38, the Jewish Agency Executive did not adopt a policy on the relationship between church and state in the future Jewish State on its own volition. A majority on the Executive viewed this issue as subsumed under the contents of the Jewish State's constitution, which the parliament of the Jewish State would be called upon to discuss and decide at the appropriate time.[38] Nonetheless, since the subject did surface on the Jewish Agency's agenda, despite its intentions, the positions of the Executive and its members on this thorny issue become somewhat, if only partially, clearer.

The demand that the ultra-Orthodox and non-Zionist movement, Agudath Israel, submitted to the Executive and the Partition Commission that it be permitted to live according to its tradition within the Jewish State was the reason why this issue reached the agenda. Agudath Israel sought to have the Jewish State arise entirely on religious foundations. However, confronted with the reality that the majority of the Jewish population was irreligious, it assumed that this would be impossible. Therefore, it demanded that the state should not pass 'any laws which would not allow ultra-Orthodox Jews to live according to the spirit of religion as they understood it' and that Agudath Israel would be allowed 'to live according to its tradition' and continue to enjoy the religious autonomy that it enjoyed at present. Shertok, to whom Agudath Israel's demand was presented before it was brought to the Partition Commission, expressed his confidence that this demand would elicit a positive response, since 'the Jewish State to be established will not intervene at all in religious matters'.[39] The Executive wanted to prevent Agudath Israel, which was not part of the World Zionist Organization and was not represented in the Jewish Agency, from conducting independent religious activity and hoped to achieve co-ordination with this movement regarding the content of Agudath Israel's testimony before the Partition Commission. Shertok and Ben-Gurion therefore also agreed to Agudath Israel's request to form a committee that would act on behalf of the Executive. Agudath Israel, religious-Zionist circles and non-religious elements would all participate in this committee, which would deal with religious issues in the Jewish State. However, the committee managed to convene but one time during the period under discussion, without achieving any tangible results.[40]

In its testimony before the Partition Commission Agudath Israel noted that whereas 'in other matters they support the position of the Jewish Agency ... on the issue of religion Agudath Israel demanded that the regime in the Jewish State should conduct itself entirely according to the laws of the Torah, and that religious foundations would determine the character of the Jewish State'.[41] The religious-Zionist Movement 'Hamizrahi', which was a constituent organization of the World Zionist Organization and was represented on the Jewish Agency Executive, posed a similar demand before the Partition Commission. However, Agudath Israel was willing to make do with a promise that the majority in the Jewish State would not prevent it from living according to Jewish customs in the affairs of education, ritual slaughter, burial, courts, etc. Additionally, Agudath Israel's full autonomy would be preserved in these areas and its followers would not be coerced if an official religion were adopted by the Jewish State.[42]

This was not the case with Hamizrahi, however, which adopted a line consistent with its long-standing religious-Zionist ideology concerning the nature of the Jewish State as conceived by Hamizrahi. The Jewish State's constitution should not separate church and state, and should be predicated in its entirety on the foundations of Jewish law. Hamizrahi hence specified the following demands: the appointment of a Chief Rabbinate and local religious courts financed by the government, who would decide on all religious matters; affairs of marriage and divorce to be entrusted exclusively to the rabbinical authorities; Jewish dietary laws to be observed in all bodies financed or supported by government funds; Sabbath and Jewish holidays would be official holidays of the Jewish State, save for areas where the non-Jewish population was concentrated; education in the Jewish institutions of the state would be in the spirit of the Torah and Jewish tradition; the Hebrew language would be the official language of the Jewish State, save for Arab regions where Arabic would serve as the second official language; and other religions with government sanction would enjoy total freedom in disposing their religious matters in accordance with their laws and practices. Hamizrahi emphasized that the aforestated demands constituted

> according to our organization, the foundations of Judaism and the essentials of the Torah ... We are fighting for these demands and we will continue to fight for them also in the period when the Jewish State takes shape and when it has already become established and organized. And even if we have to confront a majority hostile to these demands – a development which we cannot imagine – we will still insist on their fulfillment ...[43]

The Chief Rabbi of Palestine, Rabbi Yitzhak Halevi Herzog, also a member the Hamizrahi, voiced similar sentiments before the Partition Commission.[44]

Though the Executive sanctioned Hamizrahi's request to appear before the Partition Commission in order to dispel the impression that Agudath Israel was the exclusive representative of the religious population in Palestine, the content of Hamizrahi's testimony was not cleared in advance with the Executive. When the testimony was divulged, it aroused great resentment among a majority of Executive members – and it appears that this resentment did not derive from the fact that most members were non-religious.[45] Shertok's statement on the religious issue, in response to Agudath Israel's demand prior to its appearance before the Partition Commission, and Hamizrahi's declaration, which reflected the position of its representative on the Executive, were exceptions. Other members of the Executive, as well as the Executive as a whole, preferred to view the issue of religion as an issue that lay in the future purview of the Jewish State's parliament, when that body drafted a constitution.[46] It would appear that the sensitivity that both the Jews of Palestine and world Jewry displayed about this issue, and the lack of urgency to address the issue in the present, contributed to a policy of deferring treatment into the future. In particular, the Executive had not even been requested to present a position on the issue before the Partition Commission. However, the testimonies of Agudath Israel and Hamizrahi before the Partition Commission, and the Partition Commission's demand that the Executive (in the context of protecting minority rights) respond to the concerns of Agudath Israel, induced members of the Executive, as well as the Executive as a whole, to clarify their viewpoints. This in turn touched off a bitter confrontation between the Executive and Hamizrahi on the issue of religion.

It would appear that the position taken by certain members of the Executive reflected a memorandum on the religious issue authored by Yitzhak Gruenbaum, himself a member of the Executive, which he dispatched to the Political Department at the close of July 1938. Gruenbaum demanded that every citizen or group within the Jewish State should be guaranteed full freedom to live according to its conscience or religious customs, and totally rejected the forcible imposition of religious laws upon the state or any infringement on the freedom of conscience of beliefs and opinions. In his words,

> a law will not compel a Jew to live in a Jewish State according to religious law. The Jewish citizen cannot suffer discrimination as opposed to the remainder of the citizens on this issue. One cannot legally determine for example, that a Jew is prohibited from traveling on the Sabbath. It is inconceivable that the law should read that all citizens of the Jewish State would be prohibited from travelling on the Sabbath. The pressure of religious opinion will remain as it is but one cannot imagine a situation that such pressure would yield a similar prohibition as prescribed by law. Likewise, it is unimaginable that the law should decree that all restaurant owners should be Jewish or obligated to observe dietary laws. If they were to promulgate such laws, then these laws would circumscribe the rights of Jews in the Jewish State and impair their freedom of conscience ...

Therefore, Gruenbaum also believed that the Jewish State was barred from imposing any restrictions whatsoever on the right of the individual or a group to live its religious life according to their beliefs:

> It goes without saying that the Jewish citizen would not be limited in this right. One cannot describe a situation where a Christian or Moslem could live according to his belief ... but the Jew would be subject to one particular and fixed law. The aspiration for unity in religious institutions cannot be transformed into an impediment to the religious freedom of a Jew who does not accept the formal law and the accepted custom. Therefore, the Jewish State would grant Agudath Israel members total freedom to live according to their customs and laws and will not compel them to assent to the majority of the believing Jewish public [i.e. Hamizrahi]. The same thing hold true for members of Reform Judaism, if such were to be found in Palestine. There is no need to add that the Jewish State will not compel a Jew just as it will not compel any other citizen to observe religious law and custom ...

Gruenbaum accepted the fact that the Jewish religion would have an imprint upon the civic life of the Jewish State, because this was the religion of a majority of the future State's citizens. Likewise, he favored preserving the link between the spirit of the Torah and Jewish religious law and the law of the Jewish State, which would probably draw a great deal upon the Torah and Jewish religious law, but he would not be subordinated to this law in advance. The new law of the Jewish State would be a living law which would reflect day to day life, and the needs of the State's population rather than a book or a tradition … It would remain faithful to the achievements of humanity and modern science and first and foremost it would distance itself from any servitude or exploitation and from injustice and iniquity. Jews in their thousands years of Diaspora, made such demands in all the states where they resided and fought against states which were predicated on religion, and which emanated from the outlook that the state had a religion and it was the obligation of all citizens to adjust more or less to the demands of this religion. The Jews must remain faithful to this spirit in the State which they will establish in their Homeland and let them not transform it into a theocracy not in even in the smallest manner …[47]

The formal response of the Jewish Agency Executive to the Partition Commission regarding the apprehensions of Agudath Israel reflected to a large extent the spirit of Gruenbaum's memorandum. Again, the Executive refrained from entering into details and noted in the first paragraph of its response that the issue of religion in general was part of the constitution that the Jewish State would determine for itself in the future according to the needs and outlooks of the people. Simultaneously it emphasized that 'in the constitution, freedom of conscience and religion will be guaranteed and every group will be able to dispose of its religious needs independently within the framework of the constitution'. Likewise, the Executive added that the Sabbaths and the Jewish holidays would be the official days of rest of the Jewish State, and members of the other religions would be allowed to maintain their religious holidays in their places of residence.[48] Prior to this juncture, the Executive informed the Partition Commission that the status of the religious courts would be preserved in a Jewish State.[49]

The response of the Executive could have satisfied both the Partition Commission and the Agudath Israel itself.[50] However, it encountered vigorous opposition on the part of Hamizrahi and its representative on the Executive. Hamizrahi was angered by the fact that the Executive had refused to provide it with a pledge that the constitution of the Jewish State would be based on the law of Moses and the Jewish religion. Furthermore, the Executive also permitted the granting of equal status in the Jewish State to any religious group within Judaism – a fact that stood in public contradiction to the *Weltanschauung* of Hamizrahi, according to which 'the Jewish people is one and contains no sects and religious communities'.[51] As opposed to the isolationist sectarian approach of Agudath Israel, and its concern first and foremost for guaranteeing its own affairs, Hamizrahi represented an inclusive Jewish world outlook, and, from its perspective, it bore an overall responsibility to the Jewish State and its traditional Jewish character. The Executive's declaratory response regarding the Agudath Israel was viewed by Hamizrahi as hinting at a future separation of church and state: definitively granting religious status to Jewish groups who defined themselves as religious but were far removed from religious observance according to orthodox religious precepts (for example, Reform Jews); instituting civil marriage and divorce contrary to the laws of Moses; and in general marking 'the beginning of destruction and not construction. The demand of the Agudath Israel strikes not only at the Jewish religion but at the Jewish State'.[52]

In his irate response to the Executive's decision, the President of Hamizrahi, Rabbi Meir Berlin, added:

> In practice, the second paragraph [of the Executive's decision] embodies a de facto negation of religious Judaism. We always fought against the creation of special communities and congregations outside the official public framework and now by virtue of your decision there will not only be special communities but every single group of people can make provisions for its own Rabbinate, ritual slaughter, etc. They will not only enjoy such permission, but any group of people will view itself as obligated to create a special sect, because no recognized public authority will exist to handle all these vital affairs both on a public and on an individual basis ...[53]

> What is the meaning of the fact that there will be freedom for each and every one? Will there be no Jewish foundations even in the affairs of the dietary laws? Must there be an institution that will preserve ultra-Orthodox Judaism. This means that tomorrow Rabbi Wise [most probably the reference was to Rabbi Stephen Wise, a Reform Rabbi and a Zionist leader who served as the president of the American and World Jewish Congresses] will arrive to conduct marriage ceremonies according to his ritual. Similarly Rabbi Dushinsky [a Rabbi and leader of Agudath Israel] will arrange marriage ceremonies according to his views ...[54]

In any case the outcry of Hamizrahi did not succeed in modifying the official position of the Jewish Agency Executive regarding religion in the Jewish State.[55]

The security forces

At the beginning of November 1937, the Political Department appointed an Experts Committee, which was requested to formulate a proposal for the structure of the security forces of the Jewish State in the making. The committee was composed of experts in the security field – most of them affiliated with the Hagana organization. Eliyahu Golomb, who headed the Hagana organization, chaired the committee. A high degree of secrecy was maintained surrounding the deliberations of the committee, which stretched out for a number of months and touched on a number of central issues. These included the structure of the police and the army, as well as the division of labor between them, the goals of the army, the manpower levels for each of the security branches and requisite budgets; whether the army would be based on compulsory conscription or was to be a volunteer army; the formation of a militia alongside the army; the establishment of special border units (the border guard); the question of their subordination to the police or the army; and the status of Arabs in the security forces. Let us note that the committee did not always arrive at a position that was shared by all its members.[56]

The concluding memorandum that the committee presented to the Political Department was very detailed and based on the deliberations of the committee and a study of the current structure of the security forces in Palestine and in other small countries, while taking into consideration the special needs of the Jewish State in the making. The memorandum clarified from the very outset that despite the complex security problems that the Jewish State would encounter initially – which derived from the length of the country's borders, the appreciable size of the Arab minority, and the fact that the Jewish State was surrounded by Arab countries that constituted a menacing presence to its security – it would be impossible to establish 'permanent security forces of the power and quality that would ensure the state at a time of war', owing 'to both the vast sums which would be involved in such a solution and which the State could not raise at the time of its formation and to the paucity of the present Jewish population'. Given this background, the committee based its proposal for organizing the security forces on two objectives: 'To guarantee the State from its inception for a two or three year period against events and complications disruptive to security on the order of those which it presently confronted from the day that the revolt [Arab] erupted until now. The second objective – after a lengthier process – to create over time security forces whose power and quality could safeguard the State from larger complications of an international nature'. The security branches were to include internal security forces, frontier forces and defense forces.

The internal security forces were to be organized within the framework of an internal security department of the Jewish State's government. This department would comprise the police and the gendarmerie. The total force, of about 1,600 individuals, was calculated on the basis of the existing ratio between the country's population and the number of policemen. In addition, a reserve of 2,000 individuals engaged in police duties, primarily in the frontier settlements, would be at the disposal of the police force, and they would be drafted from members of the settlements for fixed periods as needs dictated.

The police would fulfill normal police functions (preserving public order, maintaining the law, investigating crimes, bringing people to trial, guarding prisons, etc.). Subordinate to them would be the investigations bureau, prisons, police training academy and the naval section, whose job would be to guard the coasts and assist the immigration department. The job of the gendarmerie, i.e. a mounted force of 600 people, would be to function first and foremost as a reinforcement to the police in imposing order and maintaining the guard in areas populated by a large Arab population, and to establish a demonstrative presence via periodic visits 'in order to drive home the point that "there is a government in the country", to demonstrate the power of the government and show that governmental authority reaches every single place. In other words, it would function as a mobile "garrison force" in places where disturbances against authority were likely to occur, simultaneously the force would fulfill normal police functions in its area of operation'.

The Security Committee recommended that the internal security forces be based on salaried personnel. Those serving in the mandatory police could not automatically transfer to the internal security forces of the Jewish State and would have to pass certain proficiency tests. These tests were intended to guarantee that the total number of Arabs serving in the security forces would be low. In principle, any citizen of the country, aged 20–30, could present their candidacy to the internal security forces. Following the recommendations, a delegation of 25 people would be dispatched abroad and would pursue studies for a year in all subjects related to internal security forces. Upon their return, members of the delegation would constitute the nucleus for the establishment of these forces and for the establishment of a Police Academy. In tandem, a delegation of experts would be invited from Britain to advise and train the principal departments of the internal security forces for a period of half a year.

The task of the frontier forces, numbering 1,428, would be primarily to protect the frontier regions from the infiltration of bands across the frontier and from the illegal immigration of an Arab population to the Jewish State. The force would be spread along the northern and eastern frontier of the Jewish State, and together with the natural obstacles and the frontier fence would constitute a barrier between the Arab population in the Jewish State and that across its frontiers. The Security Committee assumed that the job of the frontier force would be very important in the transition period and in the initial years following the establishment of the Jewish State. Subsequently, however, one would be able to cut back its size and frontier security would then be based on the Jewish settlements that would be established over time along the frontiers. The committee was divided over the issue of whether the frontier forces should be sub-ordinated to the defense forces or to the internal security forces, and did not manage to reach a decision on this issue.

The role of the defense forces was to protect the Jewish State in the event of a war initiated by its neighbors. Since, as already noted above, it would be impossible to maintain on a permanent basis the entire quantity of forces required in the event of war, the committee recommended building the defense forces around a small nucleus of permanent regular army forces and an additional large force – a militia – a national defense force. Both the army and the militia would be under the command of the general staff, and the commander-in-chief of the defense forces would head the general staff. The army would comprise 4,150 soldiers – including an air unit – and it would be based on compulsory service for all Jewish citizens of the country, aged 19–20. The period of service would be divided between a year of active service and annual reserve duty, until the age of 45. The process of establishing an army would be based on dispatching a delegation abroad to study for a period of one year and inviting a delega-tion of experts from abroad in order to assist in the organization of the army. Pursuantly, military academies, which were to prepare the command and administrative apparatus of the units in the various forces, would be established. The various preparations leading to the establishment of the army would take three years.

The main defense forces would be based on a militia of 30,000 soldiers, who would serve as a reserve for the permanent defense forces and would be drafted in times of emergency to reinforce the regular army and expand its framework. The structure of the force would be analogous to the structure of the army. Similar to the army, the militia service would be based on compulsory service, with every citizen aged 20–40 who was not already serving in one of the other military frameworks being obligated to serve. The period of service would stretch over five years, and would be composed of basic training lasting a month-and-a-half in the first year, training two weeks every year, and call-up once every second month. The units would double as a combat-ready force, which could immediately reinforce the regular forces in the event of war.[57]

The Security Committee was concerned over the large percentage of Arab soldiers who would serve in the army and militia units, given the recommendation that service would be compulsory. It was clear to the committee that Arab participation in the army could not be rescinded, but ways would have to be devised to lower their number. There was talk that 'educational, medical examinations etc. would disqualify many Arabs'.[58]

NOTES

1. See above, pp. 6–10.
2. CZA, Protocol of the Jewish Agency Executive's meeting on 8 July 1937 – statement by Shertok.
3. Ibid; CZA, file S25/5113, memorandum by David Horowitz, presented to the Political Department of the Jewish Agency in May 1938; CZA, file S25/10050, memorandum by P. Naphtali: 'The Budget of the Jewish State in Case of Partition', July 1937; CZA, The Executive's Memorandum to the Partition Commission.
4. CZA, The Executive's Memorandum to the Partition Commission; the twentieth Zionist Congress, stenographic report, 1937, p. 173 – Shertok's statement. CZA, Protocol of the Inner Zionist General Council on 18 May 1938 – Ben-Gurion's statement; CZA, Protocol of the Jewish Agency Executive's meeting on 23 May 1938.
5. PRO, file CO 733/348, letter from Weizmann to Ormsby-Gore on 15 June 1937; see also CZA, file S25/5119, Protocol of the first meeting of the Haifa Committee on 20 November 1937; CZA, file S25/993, letter from Weizmann to Bernard Joseph on 22 July 1937.
6. CZA, The Executive's Memorandum to the Partition Commission.
7. Ben-Gurion (1937), p. 360.
8. CZA, The Executive's Memorandum to the Partition Commission; see also CZA, file S25/5157, 'Memorandum on the Position of Haifa under Partition' submitted by the Jewish Agency Executive to the Partition Commission, August 1938; CZA, file S25/5119, in note 5; CZA, file S25/5113, in note 3; CZA, file S25/5119, letter from Meyerowitz to Simon on 19 June 1938, to which is appended the protocol of the Ports Committee Meeting of 9 June 1938; Ben-Gurion (1937), pp. 360–1; Ben-Gurion (1938), p. 120; the twentieth Zionist Congress, stenographic report, 1937, p. 85; CZA, file S25/10109, letter from Neuman to Shertok on 28 November 1937; Heller (1984), p. 191, which cites Katznelson's letter stating: 'I won't waste even one word in order to prove that removing Haifa from the boundaries of the "Jewish State" diminishes and endangers the industrial and commercial development of the country'. See also Granot (1951), pp. 251–8.
9. CZA, The Executive's Memorandum to the Partition Commission; CZA, file S25/5157, in note 8; CZA, file S25/5119, letter from Meyerowitz to Simon on 19 June 1938, to which is appended the Protocol of the meeting of the Ports Committee on 9 June 1938; CZA, Protocols of the Jewish Agency Executive's meetings on 8 May 1938, 23 May 1938, 12 June 1938, 6 December 1938; Ben-Gurion (1938), p. 120.
10. CZA, Protocol of the Jewish Agency Executive's meeting on 4 July 1937.
11. CZA, The Executive's Memorandum to the Partition Commission; the twentieth Zionist Congress, stenographic report, 1937, p. 85.
12. CZA, The Executive's Memorandum to the Partition Commission; see also Ben-Gurion (1937), p. 361; CZA, file S25/5113, in note 3; CZA, file S25/5119 in note 9.
13. CZA, The Executive's Memorandum to the Partition Commission (citation from there); CZA, file S25/5113 in note 3.
14. CZA, The Executive's Memorandum to the Partition Commission.
15. Ibid.; CZA, file S25/10050, in note 3; CZA, Protocol of the Jewish Agency Executive's meeting on 4 July 1937 – statement by Shertok; Eliash (1971), pp. 123–4; CZA, Protocol of the Jewish Agency Executive's meeting together with the Political Committee of the Inner Zionist General Council on 12 June 1938 – statement by Ben-Gurion.
16. CZA, file S25/6689, Shertok's letter to Ruppin on 10 January 1938.

17. PRCR (1937), pp. 386–7.
18. CZA, Protocol of the Jewish Agency Executive's meeting with the Political Committee of the Inner Zionist General Council on 12 June 1938; see also CZA, file S25/10110, summaries of the Political Department regarding the various recommendations of the Finance Committee appointed by the Political Department, undated.
19. See also Ben-Gurion's statement in CZA, Protocol of the Inner Zionist General Council on 3 November 1937.
20. See above, pp. 2–4.
21. Official declaration by the government, No. 1/38 on 4 January 1938; CZA, file S25/10109, The Terms of Reference of the Technical Commission.
22. CZA, file S25/5164, Gruenbaum's Memorandum: 'Stages in the Establishment of the Jewish State', undated.
23. See above, pp. 117–20; CZA, Protocol of the meetings of the Jewish Agency Executive in conjunction with the Political Committee of the Inner Zionist General Council on 12 June 1938 – statements by Shertok, Remez, Ben Zvi, Kaplan and Ben-Gurion; CZA, file S25/3786, Ben-Gurion's response to Ormsby-Gore's letter, undated (although it is clear that the words are from the beginning of 1938).
24. CZA, Protocol of the Jewish Agency Executive's meeting on 5 August 1938.
25. CZA, file S25/3751, draft – 'Stages by which the Establishment of a Jewish State might be Reached under a Scheme of Partition', 15 July 1938; CZA, Protocol of the Jewish Agency Executive's meeting on 5 August 1938, from which it emerges that the Political Department's plan for the transition stage was essentially prepared by Attorney L. Stein at the invitation of the Political Department.
26. CZA, Protocol of the Jewish Agency Executive's meeting together with the Political Committee of the Inner Zionist Committee on 12 June 1938; CZA, Protocol of the Jewish Agency Executive's meeting on 5 August 1938.
27. See Gruenbaum's memorandum: 'Stages in the Establishment of the Jewish State', CZA, file S25/5164; CZA, Protocol of the Jewish Agency Executive's meeting on 5 August 1938. See also Ben-Gurion's comments at the joint meeting of the Jewish Agency Executive with the Political Committee of the Inner Zionist General Council. Ben-Gurion felt that during the transition period the Jewish government should be appointed.
28. CZA, Protocol of the Jewish Agency Executive's meeting on 5 August 1938.
29. CZA, Protocol of the Jewish Agency Executive's meeting with the Political Committee of the Inner Zionist General Council on 12 June 1938 – statement by Shertok.
30. See the memorandum, 'Constituent Assembly', presented to Shertok on 26 July 1938 in CZA, file S25/5147; CZA, file S25/5147, memorandum by Ben-Gurion: 'On the Non-partisan Position of the Jewish State' on 6 June 1938. The words were delivered by Ben-Gurion at the Jewish Agency Executive's meeting on 7 June 1938.
31. See pp. 118–20 above.
32. CZA, Protocol of the Jewish Agency Executive's meeting on 7 June 1938 – statement by Ben-Gurion, and the quotation is from there. The memorandum 'Constituent Assembly' in CZA, file S25/5147; CZA, Protocol of the Jewish Agency Executive's meeting on 29 May 1938 – statement by Shertok.
33. CZA, Protocol of the Jewish Agency Executive's meeting with the Political Department of the Inner Zionist General Council on 12 June 1938 – statement by Shertok.
34. CZA, Protocol of the Jewish Agency Executive's meeting on 7 June 1938 – statement by Ben-Gurion and the citations are from there; CZA, Protocol of the Jewish Agency Executive's meeting with the Political Committee of the Inner Zionist General Council on 12 June 1938.
35. CZA, file S25/10050, memorandum of P. Naphtali: 'The Budget of the Jewish State in Case of Partition', July 1937.
36. CZA, Protocol of the Jewish Agency Executive's meeting on 9 June 1938, Shertok's statement, and the citation is from there; CZA, Protocol of the Jewish Agency Executive's meeting on 8 May 1938; CZA, file S25/10050, in note 35. A member of the Executive,

Werner Senator, opposed Shertok's position regarding education at the Executive's meeting on 9 June 1938, and demanded the institution of compulsory education for all children aged 6–12 immediately upon the establishment of the state. He believed that: 'The expenditure on this goal is as imperative as are expenditures for security matters'.

37. See CZA, file S25/10050, memorandum of P. Naphtali: 'The budget of the Jewish State in Case of Partition', July 1937.
38. See, for example, CZA, Protocol of the Jewish Agency Executive's meeting on 24 July 1938; CZA, file S25/5112, Protocol of the meeting between representatives of the Jewish Agency Executive and Rabbi Herzog, Rabbi Berlin and Mr Burstein, Chairman of the Hamizrahi, in England on 12 September 1938.
39. CZA, Protocol of the Jewish Agency Executive's meeting on 17 October 1937 – the citation is from there. See also CZA, Protocol of the Jewish Agency Executive's meeting on 21 November 1937; CZA, Protocol of the Jewish Agency Executive's meeting on 8 May 1938; memorandum submitted by the Agudath Israel Center to the Royal Commission, 1936.
40. CZA, file S25/5112, in note 38; CZA, Protocol of the Jewish Agency Executive's meeting on 29 May 1938 and 7 June 1938.
41. CZA, Protocol of the Jewish Agency Executive's meeting on 19 June 1938 – the citation is from there; CZA, Protocol of the Jewish Agency Executive's meeting on 24 July 1938.
42. CZA, file S25/5112, the demands of Agudath Israel, undated; CZA, file S44/160, part of the memorandum presented by Agudath Israel to the Partition Commission; CZA, Protocol of the Jewish Agency Executive's meeting on 28 August 1938.
43. CZA, file S25/5112, letter from Rabbi Meyer Berlin, President of the Hamizrahi to the Partition Commission in London on 28 August 1938. The letter gave written expression to what the Hamizrahi had orally informed the Partition Commission of during the latter's sojourn in Palestine. See also CZA, file S25/3817, letter of Rabbi Ostrovsky to the Jewish Agency Executive's meeting on 22 June 1938; CZA, file S25/5112, letter from Rabbi Ostrovsky to Shertok on 23 September 1938.
44. CZA, file S25/5112, in note 38; CZA, file S33/481, letter from Rabbi Ostrovsky to members of the Jewish Agency Executive on 13 July 1938, appended to the letter of David Horowitz to Ben-Gurion, on 13 July 1938.
45. CZA, file S25/5112, in note 38; CZA, Protocols of the Jewish Agency Executive's meetings on 10 October 1937 (comments by Rabbi Fishman), 24 July 1938, 4 September 1938.
46. CZA, see, for example, the Protocol of the Jewish Agency Executive's meeting on 24 July 1938.
47. CZA, file S25/5112, letter from Y. Gruenbaum to the Political Department, on 24 July 1938 – the citation is from there. See also CZA, Protocol of the Jewish Agency Executive's meeting on 24 July 1938.
48. CZA, Protocol of the Jewish Agency Executive's meeting on 28 August 1938.
49. CZA, Protocol of the Jewish Agency Executive's meeting in conjunction with the Political Committee of the Inner Zionist General Council on 12 June 1938.
50. CZA, Protocol of the Jewish Agency Executive's meeting on 28 August 1938; CZA, file S25/5112, in note 38.
51. CZA, Protocol of the Jewish Agency Executive's meeting on 28 August 1938 – statement by Rabbi Fishman.
52. Ibid., statements by Rabbi Fishman and Shapiro – citation is from Shapiro's statement; see also CZA, file S25/5112, in note 38 – statements by Rabbi Herzog and Rabbi Berlin; PPCR (1938), pp. 163–4.
53. CZA, file S25/5112, letter from Rabbi Berlin to the Jewish Agency Executive in London on 2 September 1938.
54. CZA, file S25/5112, in note 38. See also CZA, file S25/5112, Gruenbaum and Shertok's telegram to Luria in London, undated; CZA, Protocol of the Jewish Agency Executive's meeting on 4 September 1938.
55. CZA, Protocol of the Jewish Agency Executive's meeting on 4 September 1938; see also Eliash (1984), pp. 55–74.
56. CZA, files S25/42, S25/5119, Protocols of the Security Committee's meetings on 10

November 1937, 21 November 1937, 28 November 1937, 7 December 1937, 12 December 1937, 6 February 1937. See also CZA, file S25/5120, notes of the members of the Security Committee; CZA, file S25/5152, letter from Simon to members of the Security Committee on 31 January 1938; Ibid., letter from Simon to Golomb on 31 March 1938; Ibid., letter from the Association of Jewish Officers in Palestine to the Jewish Agency Executive on 24 January 1938.

57. See the Concluding memorandum in CZA, file S25/8119, 'A Proposal for Organizing the Security Forces of the Jewish State', dated 15 May 1938. See also the memorandum: 'A Summary of the Arguments in Favor of Including the Frontier Force within the Framework of the Army' from 21 December 1937; see also Avidar (1984).
58. CZA, file S25/5119, Protocol of the Security Committee's meeting on 7 December 1937.

7

Land Purchases and Settlement as Tools for Attaining the Partition Boundaries Conforming to the Plan of the Jewish Agency Executive

AGRICULTURAL SETTLEMENT

In its efforts to implement the plans for the partition boundaries that it had formulated, the Jewish Agency Executive did not content itself with political activities (i.e. efforts targeted at the various British authorities and the international community). During the years 1937–38, the Jewish Agency Executive together with the JNF (Jewish National Fund) directed their land-purchase and settlement activity towards securing in the final outcome those partition boundaries coveted by the Jewish Agency Executive, which were detailed extensively in Chapter 2 of this book. The land-purchases and the settlement activity therefore concentrated on the one hand, on those areas that were not incorporated into the Jewish State according to the original recommendations of the Royal Commission, but which the Zionist Executive sought to include within the final boundaries of the Jewish State; on the other hand, efforts were lavished on the Galilee region, which was included in the areas of the Jewish State according to the Royal Commission Plan but where the Jews had only a sparse territorial foothold in terms of settlements. Alert to this weakness, and aware of the protests voiced in British governing circles against the Royal Commission's recommendation regarding the Galilee, the Executive feared that the recommendation of the Royal Commission regarding the Galilee would ultimately be rejected. The Executive assumed that Jewish-owned lands and especially Jewish settlements would play a decisive role in the recommendations of the Partition Commission and the decisions of the British government regarding the final boundaries of partition.[1] They could adduce evidence for this assumption from the Royal Commission's Report itself, which included the majority of the Jewish settlements within the boundaries of the Jewish State. As Dr Avraham Granovsky, the Managing Director of the JNF, emphasized in November 1937:

> in the same fashion that the land which we previously settled influenced the demarcation of boundaries by the Royal Commission similarly the current

enlargement of our territorial capital can prove decisive in defining the final boundaries. Therefore we must make haste and purchase lands in the Arab region [that is in the area of the region that was allocated to the Arab State according to the Royal Commission] ... we have reached the final moment for these activities. Who knows if a year later it will not be too late ...[2]

The conquest of the Beisan Valley and settlement activity until the close of 1937

In practice, in the last months preceding the publication of the Royal Commission Report, when the drift of the report became clear to the Executive, a distinctive settlement policy began to crystallize. Juxtaposed with the Executive's political activity directed towards influencing both the recommendations of the Royal Commission and the contents of the British government's decision, a settlement policy was adopted to attain that very same purpose. Priority at that time was accorded to the Beisan Valley, which, as mentioned above, was included in the boundaries of the Arab State under the Royal Commission's plan but within the boundaries of the Jewish State in the Jewish Agency Executive's counter-plan. By the end of 1936 territorial holdings had been accumulated in the valley under the ownership of the JNF, but Jewish settlements had not yet been established. The land purchases of the JNF in the Beisan Valley had been consummated since 1929 with a view to creating territorial contiguity between Jewish settlement in the Jezreel Valley and the Jordan Valley. Because the valley was divided among many Arab owners, the plots that were purchased were small and scattered, without creating contiguous blocs that would afford the creation of new settlements. By 1935, 23,000 dunams had been purchased by the JNF, while other Jewish bodies had purchased an additional 2,000 dunams. All these lands were retained by Arab leaseholders. In 1935, the JNF began taking measures to insure that the retention of the land should be performed by Jewish bodies. However, genuine Jewish settlement on the lands that were purchased was thwarted by the outbreak of the disturbances in spring 1936. Only during the latter part of 1936 did the first kibbutz, Tel Amal, settle in the western part of the valley. In the first week of 1937, another kibbutz, Sde Nahum, settled in the western part of the valley, while at the beginning of April the moshav Beit Yosef settled in the northern tip of the valley.[3]

The Beisan Valley was almost devoid of Jewish settlements when, during the first months of 1937, the tendencies of the Royal Commission were disclosed, and it subsequently emerged that the Royal Commission had officially excluded the valley from the areas of the Jewish State. This necessitated a Zionist settlement effort in order to augment the prospects for including the valley within the areas of the Jewish State when the British made their final determination regarding the partition boundary.[4] In the context of settlement activities in the Beisan Valley, Joseph Weitz, who, as mentioned, headed the Lands Department of JNF, contended the following in 1937:

> the political hour threatens us with the amputation of parts of our country and their removal from our possession. If they are to cast lots to partition the country it is evident that the Beisan Valley will be removed from our possession because no Jewish settlements exist there. In such a case we will forfeit one of the most important areas for our agricultural settlement. The creation of a network of Jewish settlements which will embrace the valley from one end to the other will foil this scheme of severing it from us. The conditions for purchasing land in this valley produced a situation in which land would be purchased in various parcels in all directions of the valley. This factor which at the beginning was a negative one from the standpoint of settlement plans in normal times, now becomes an advantage. Thanks to it we have the opportunity to establish settlements that will serve as a chain around the valley and to a certain extent they will exert control over the entire valley which is sparse in population, rich in territory and commands the Jordan ...

Weitz called upon the Zionist leadership to embark immediately upon the establishment of settlements at the periphery of the valley (see Map 10) to pave roads and to continue land purchases but without taking account of the financial expenses required for such settlement.[5]

Acting on Weitz's principles, the Settlement Department of the Jewish Agency and the JNF jointly formulated a plan for settling the Beisan Valley. According to this plan, the settlements would be established precisely at the edges (in the circumference) of the valley, with a view towards ensuring the inclusion of the entire valley in the final boundaries of the Jewish State. At a much later stage, settlements would be established in the heart of the valley. As one can definitely discern from Map 11, the kibbutzim Tirat Zvi, Maoz Haim, Kfar Ruppin, Neve Eitan and Messilot, which were founded in the Beisan Valley in the course of the years 1937–38 against the backdrop of the partition plan, were established at the edges of the valley. Kibbutzim were established in the center of the valley only at a later stage (see Map 12).

At the beginning of June 1937, the Jewish Agency Executive, under Shertok's pressure, adopted a decision to move a kibbutz to the southern edge of the Beisan Valley. This decision was made despite the fact that settlement there was isolated and very dangerous from a security stand-

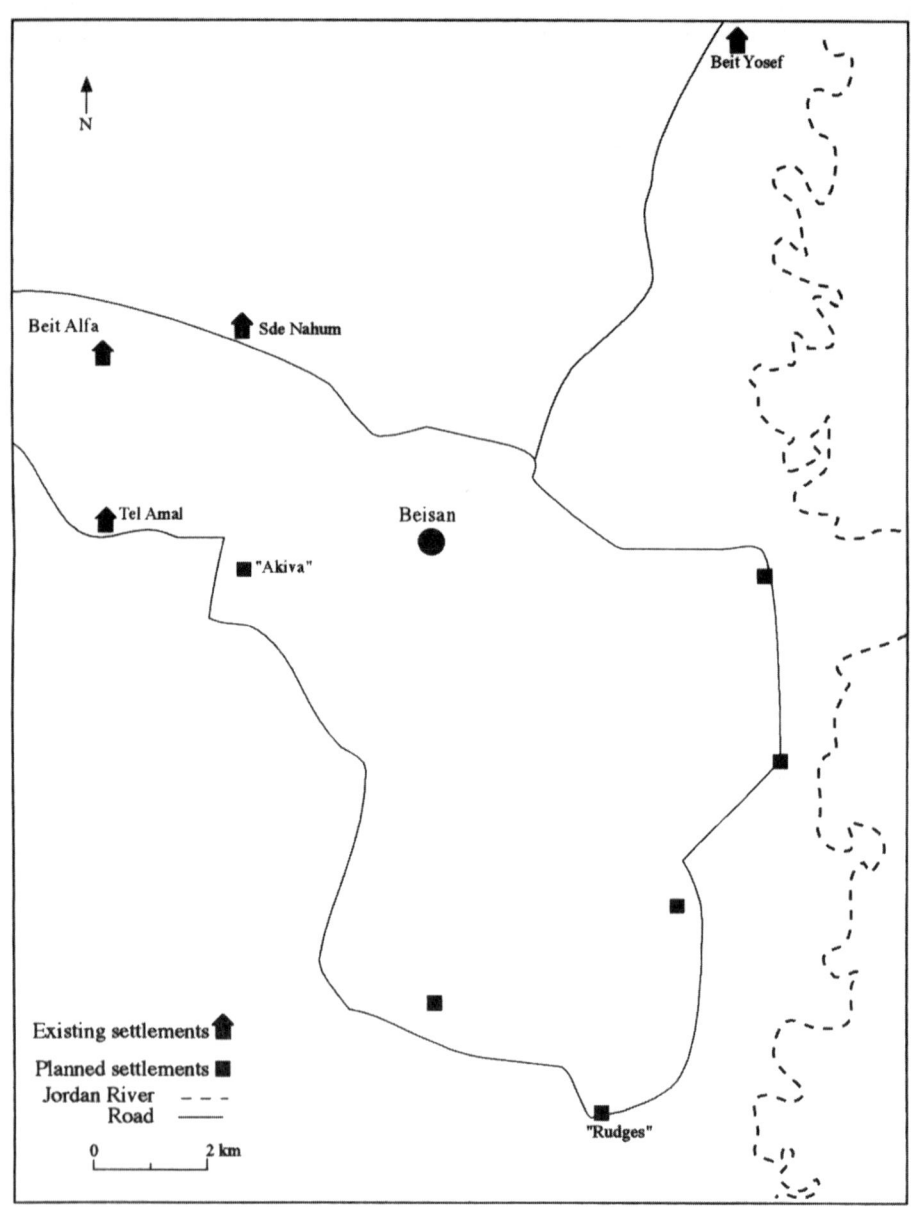

Map 10: Joseph Weitz's Plan for Settling the Beisan Valley, 1937

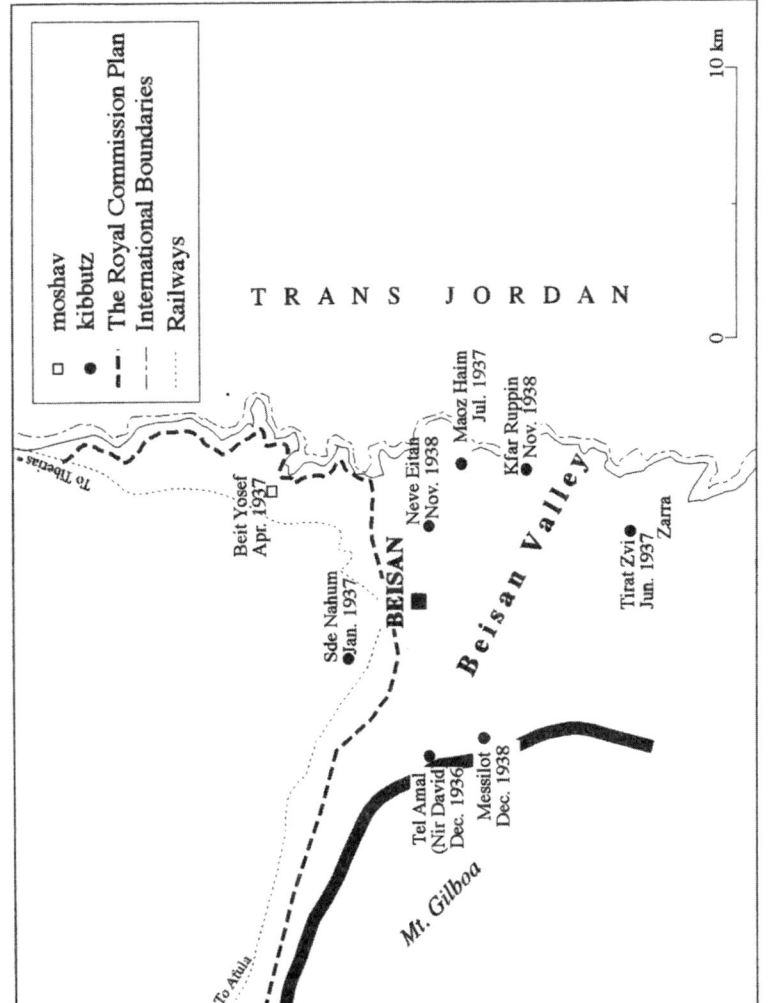

Map 11: Jewish Settlements in the Beisan Valley, 1936–38

Legend:
- □ moshav
- ● kibbutz
- – – The Royal Commission Plan
- – · – International Boundaries
- ···· Railways

TRANS JORDAN

To Tiberias

Beit Yosef
Apr. 1937

Sde Nahum
Jan. 1937

BEISAN

Neve Eitan
Nov. 1938

Maoz Haim
Jul. 1937

Kfar Ruppin
Nov. 1938

Beisan Valley

Tirat Zvi
Jun. 1937

Zarra

Tel Amal
(Nir David)
Dec. 1936

Messilot
Dec. 1938

Mt. Gilboa

To Afula

10 km

0

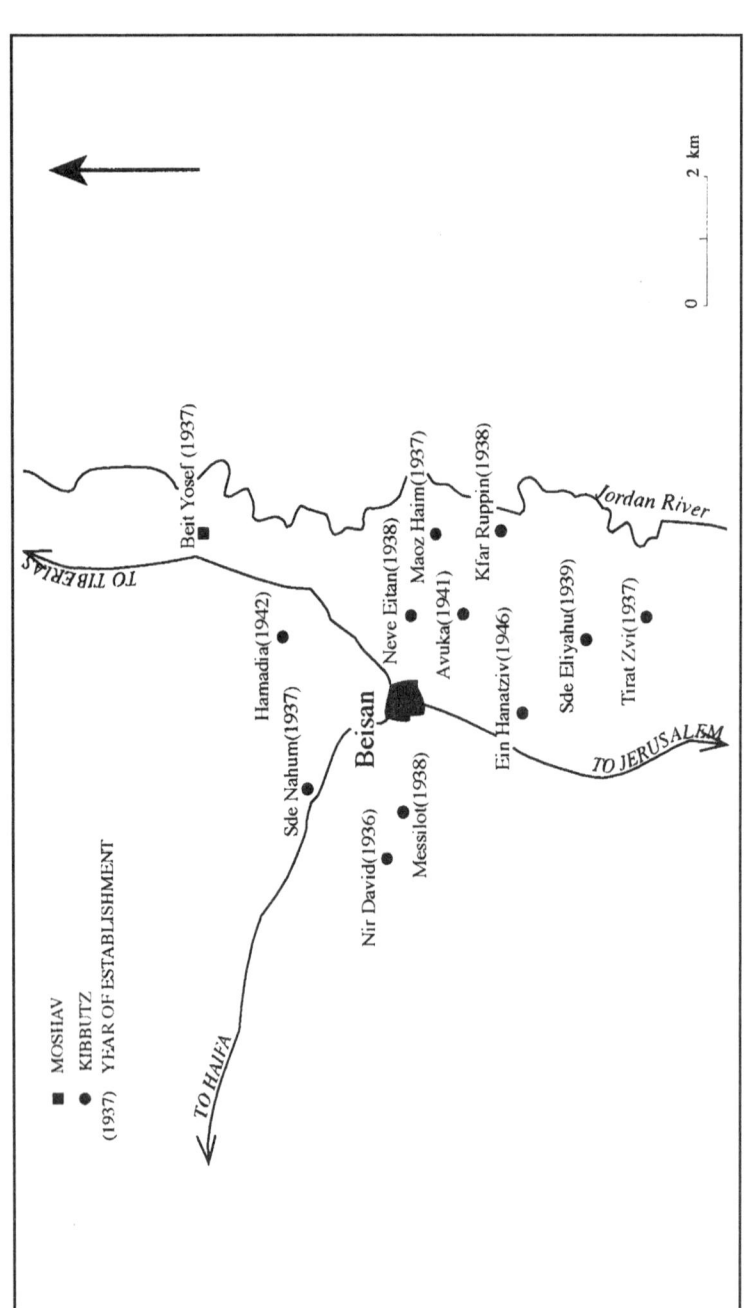

MOSHAV
KIBBUTZ
(1937) YEAR OF ESTABLISHMENT

TO HAIFA

Nir David(1936)

Messilot(1938)

Sde Nahum(1937)

Hamadia(1942)

Beisan

Ein Hanatziv(1946)

TO JERUSALEM

Sde Eliyahu(1939)

Tirat Zvi(1937)

Avuka(1941)

Kfar Ruppin(1938)

Maoz Haim(1937)

Neve Eitan(1938)

Beit Yosef (1937)

TO TIBERIAS

Jordan River

0   2 km

Map 12: Jewish Settlements in the Beisan Valley up to 1948

point, irrespective of the appreciable budgetary difficulties attendant to settlement in that location.[6] This was the intended beginning of the implementation of the plan to settle the Beisan Valley as described above. In a discussion that preceded the decision, Shertok (apparently also under the influence of Weitz and other settlement leaders such as Avraham Hartzfeld, who headed the agricultural center of the General Workers Confederation), dwelt on the supreme political importance inherent in settling the south of the valley, which obligated immediate settlement:

> It was his opinion that the most southern point was to be conquered. He doesn't know what will be the fate of the Beisan Valley when the country was partitioned into regions if such a partition would take place. Our position in the Beisan Valley is murky. We dispose of territorial capital there but it is dispersed and it has also been overrun to a certain extent by Arabs. However, if our southern point will be Zarra [the location where kibbutz Tirat Zvi settled and which had previously been purchased by the JNF – see Map 11] there is hope that we could salvage Jewish territory also in other points. He could not promise that even if we will do everything to settle the area it will be incorporated into the Jewish region, but we must make it as difficult as possible for the British Government to steal this area from us ... The [Zionist] institutions must determine that we should speed up as much as possible our entry into this location. If this proves impossible due to fiscal consideration, this would be most tragic. One thing or another – either we abandon this location or we take hold of it via people who will be ready to settle this area over time with all the dangers implicit in such settlement ...[7]

Indeed, Shertok's words had their effect and decisively influenced the adoption of the decision to position the kibbutz on the southern edge of the Beisan Valley; at the end of June, kibbutz Tirat Zvi settled on this site.[8] A few days later, at the beginning of July, kibbutz Maoz Haim settled at the eastern end of the Beisan Valley.[9] In the following months and during the course of 1938, the settlement strategy for conquering the Beisan Valley, which sprang from the political considerations of incorporating the valley into the final boundaries of the Jewish State, were completed (see Map 11). In subsequent years (1939–46), Jewish settlement activity concentrated on the center of the Beisan Valley (see Map 12). Indeed, the reinforcement of settlement in the Beisan Valley continued apace, to a large extent for political reasons, but these were not directly connected to the partition plan of the years 1937–38.[10]

In addition to settlement in the Beisan Valley, which enjoyed priority, by the end of 1937 two additional kibbutzim had settled beyond the

boundaries allotted to the Jewish State according to the Royal Commission's plan. These were kibbutz Ein Gev, east of Lake Tiberias, and
kibbutz Kfar Menahem, on the south-eastern border of the Jewish State,
according to the partition plan of the Royal Commission. These settlements, together with Tirat Zvi and Maoz Haim, constituted 40 per cent
of the settlements that were founded at the initiative of the settlement
institutions of the World Zionist Organization from June 1937 until the
conclusion of that year (see Map 13).[11]

*Intensified settlement efforts from the beginning of 1938 with the
Galilee enjoying priority*

At the close of 1937, and the start of 1938, the Jewish Agency Executive
and JNF decided to intensify the joint effort to purchase lands and settle
them immediately in the Galilee and in regions that were included in the
boundaries of the Jewish State according to the Executive's partition plan
but were not incorporated in the boundaries of the Jewish State according
to the Royal Commission's partition plan. The particular importance that
the Jewish Agency Executive and the JNF attached to intensified activity
as a tool for achieving political goals is attested to by, among other things,
the joint decision of the two bodies to raise the fabulous sum of £2 million
in the Jewish world for settlement purposes (and by the personal involvement of Weizmann, who was not normally involved in settlement matters),
in the joint deliberations of the Executive and the JNF). As a result of the
deliberations, and given the agricultural lands offered for sale, it was
decided to implement land purchases with a view towards settling them
as rapidly as possible in accordance with the following geographical
priority: the Galilee and especially the Western Upper Galilee ('so there
should be Jewish land alongside the boundary of Lebanon';[12] 'we must do
our utmost to make it difficult for them to remove the Galilee from our
possession');[13] the Beisan Valley; the north-west boundary of Samaria
and the Wadi Ara region;[14] the region of kibbutz Kiryat 'Anavim, west of
Jerusalem, which, as may be recalled, was included under the Executive's
Plan within the boundaries of the Jewish State but which the Royal
Commission incorporated in the mandatory enclave. The possibility of
purchasing land south of the southern boundary of the Jewish State as
drawn by the Royal Commission was also considered. A short while later,
the JNF reached an internal decision to limit land purchases within the
Jewish State according to the Royal Commission's proposal (save for the
Galilee) to the bare minimum to avoid drawing on the resources needed
for implementing the political purchases. It would appear that by assigning
a low priority to the Kiryat 'Anavim region, the JNF had accepted Ben-

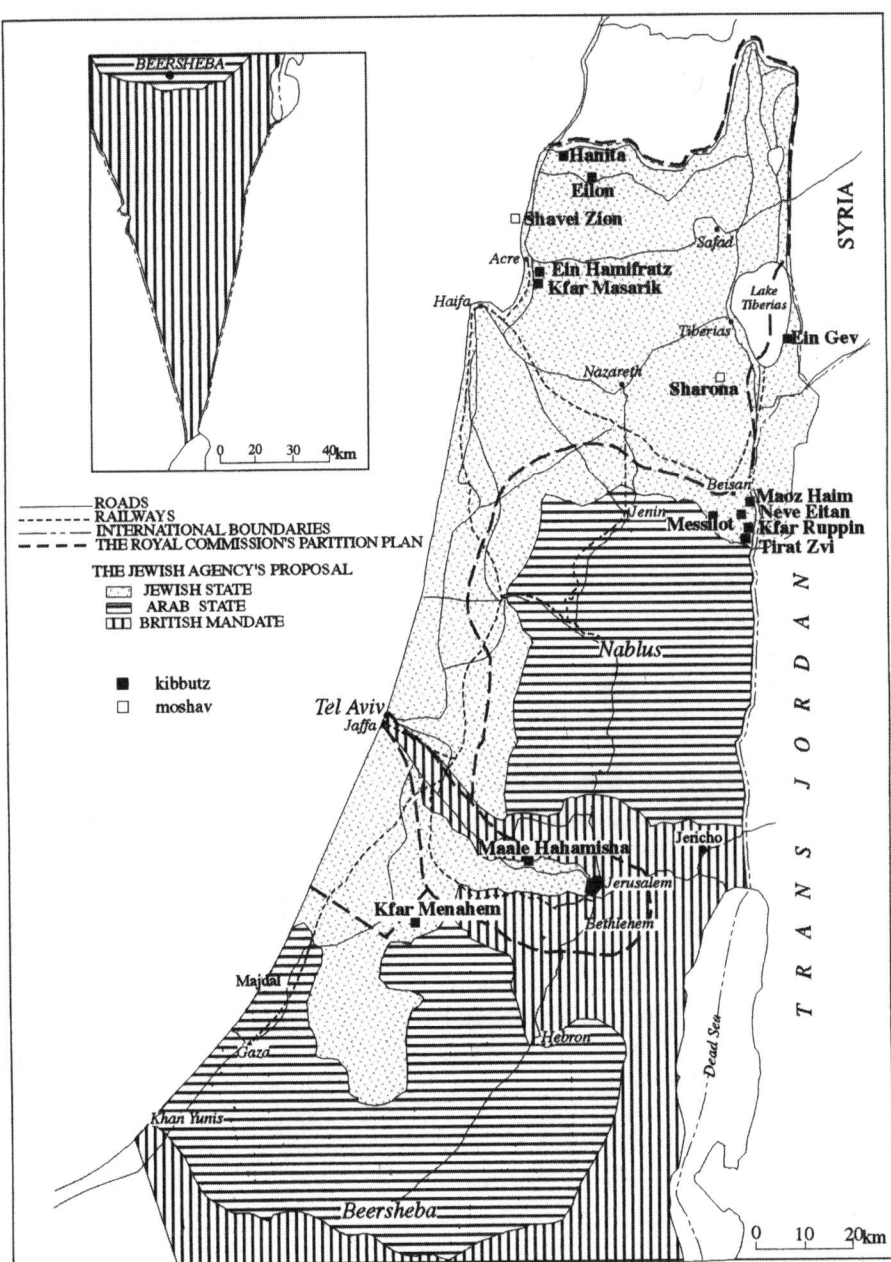

Map 13: Jewish Settlements in the Galilee and Outside the Perimeter of the Jewish State
Set by the Royal Commission, May 1937–December 1938

Gurion's assessment that no settlement limitations would be imposed in the region contemplated for the British enclave by the Royal Commission's plan.[15]

The Galilee therefore obtained supreme priority and, in the words of Ussishkin, Chairman of the JNF, who summarized one of the JNF's deliberations that took place in 1938: 'In the event that a proposal for purchasing a tract of land in the north of the country arrives, which would lead to reinforcing the Jewish Community's position from a territorial–settlement and strategic–political perspective, then this proposal takes priority over all other proposals'.[16] The importance of 'conquering' the Galilee also led the JNF to agree to share part of the expenses for site preparation that were entailed in settling the mountainous Galilee area.[17]

The joint decisions of the Jewish Agency and the JNF from the start of 1938 paved the way for the JNF's entry into negotiations on the purchase of 57,500 dunams in various portions of the Upper Galilee; about 5,000 dunams in the Beisan Valley; 6,000 dunams on the north-west border of Samaria; and 4,000 dunams in the vicinity of Kiryat 'Anavim on the main highway between Jerusalem and Tel Aviv. Likewise, negotiations were conducted regarding the purchase of 7,000 dunams south of the southern boundary of the Jewish State following the Royal Commission's proposal. From the beginning of 1938 until the publication of the Report of the British Partition Commission at the close of that year, the purchase of 18,500 dunams in the Upper Galilee, about 5,000 dunams in the Beisan Valley, and 1,600 dunams on the boundary of Samaria and Wadi Ara had been realized. Likewise, the purchase of an additional 8,300 dunams on the boundary of Samaria, which had been decided before the start of 1938, was completed. Let it be emphasized that a breakdown of the lands that the JNF decided to purchase at the start of 1938 reveals that of those lands that it actually purchased in that same year, about 80 per cent fell in regions that were included in the Executive's partition boundaries but excluded from the Royal Commission's boundaries.[18]

From the beginning of 1938 and until the close of that year, the settlement bodies of the World Zionist Organization established 15 new settlements in Palestine. Two-thirds of these were in the Galilee and in areas that were included in the boundaries of Jewish State according to the plan of the Executive, rather than in the partition boundaries of the Royal Commission. In the Galilee, the kibbutzim Hanita, Eilon, Kfar Masarik, and Ein Hamifratz as well as the moshavim Sharona and Shavei Zion; in the Beisan Valley, the kibbutzim Kfar Ruppin, Neve Eitan and Messilot; on the Jerusalem–Tel Aviv road, kibbutz Maale Hahamisha (see Map 13). Let us note that the lands of part of these settlements already had been purchased prior to 1938 and that in the years following 1938 additional settlements were established on the lands that had been purchased previously, under the impetus of the partition plan.[19]

URBAN SETTLEMENT: JERUSALEM AND HAIFA

The activity of the JNF in the sphere of land purchases in Jerusalem also reflects the partition map of the Jewish Agency Executive, which divided Jerusalem and incorporated New Jerusalem into the areas of the Jewish State. The JNF already had decided by the start of 1937 on a number of extensive purchases: on Mount Scopus for the development and expansion of the Hebrew University and the Hadassah Hospital; in the western part of Jerusalem for urban housing developments and the creation of an urban Jewish contiguity in the western part of the city between the neighborhoods of Beit Hakerem and Rehavia (see Map 7). These purchases, which were already being processed, received added importance once the Royal Commission's plan regarding Jerusalem was disclosed, and the Executive immediately countered with a demand to incorporate New Jerusalem into the areas of the Jewish State.[20] Given the Royal Commission's recommendations, the JNF decided to pursue its efforts to purchase land in Jerusalem and, in the words of Ussishkin, 'The Jewish National Fund will have to concentrate all its forces on behalf of Jerusalem'.[21] Priority on purchases would be accorded first and foremost to Mount Scopus, which Ussishkin contended '[it] will be the cultural center of the Jewish people with thousands of students and hundreds of professors'.[22]

In a captivating discussion that arose in the JNF directorate at the end of 1937 on the question of 'The Old City or Mt Scopus', Ussishkin (who opposed the partition of Jerusalem)[23] rejected a proposal to accord preference to the Old City. Indeed, Ussishkin contended that he would have preferred to redeem the Old City and forgo Mount Scopus if there were tangible offers for purchase in the Old City. However, after he was pushed to the wall by concrete proposals for JNF projects in the Old City, which Rabbi Berlin (another member of the directorate) raised, Ussishkin disclosed his opinion regarding the Old City: 'We have no guarantee that we can implement anything tangible in the Old City. If we expend the money or most of it for purchasing land in the Old City, a situation can arise where we will have invested the money and purchased the land and despite this, the Jewish Old City will be abandoned'. Ussishkin therefore made peace with the partition of Jerusalem in line with the opinion of the Jewish Agency Executive and demanded that the bulk of JNF efforts be channeled to strengthen the Jewish hold on Mount Scopus. As may be recalled, this was a location that had no real Jewish demographic presence. Given its symbolic nature, the Jewish Agency Executive demanded its incorporation into the areas of the Jewish State.[24]

It would appear that, with regards to Haifa too, the Executive felt the need to rely on settlement, especially an urban one. As we saw earlier, the Jewish Agency Executive attached extreme importance to having the Jewish State exert total control over this city and did not agree to the imposition of a temporary mandatory regime. During the course of 1938, we observe Ben-Gurion's call to do everything to allocate the urban immigration arriving in Palestine to Haifa, rather than Tel Aviv, and to ensure that urban settlement in Haifa would prosper: 'We must do everything to direct the new immigration to Haifa in order to increase the number of Jews in Haifa and create a large Jewish majority there and so endow its port with a Jewish character ... The addition of 20,000 residents to Tel Aviv won't add and won't detract. The increment of 20,000 Jews in Haifa assures our control and future in Haifa'.[25] Indeed, whereas in 1937 the Jewish population in Haifa numbered 50,000 people, in 1940 it totaled 62,000 (56 per cent of the city's total population), with the bulk of the Jewish population increase having occurred in the years 1938–39. The settlement of the kibbutzim Kfar Masarik and Ein Hamifratz during the latter half of 1938, in the area north of Haifa Bay, strengthened the Jewish hold in the vicinity of Haifa and fastened Jewish positions in the vicinity of Acre.[26]

NOTES

1. Orren (1978), pp. 22–37; Avneri (1980), p. 168; Dothan (1993), p. 221; CZA, file KKL10 Protocol of the JNF Directorate's meetings on 6 December 1937 and 25 April 1938; CZA, file S25/2956, letter from Ben-Gurion to the JNF, 27 December 1937; Weitz (1965), Vol. 1, p. 191; CZA, file S25/3786, Ben-Gurion's comments on the Ormsby-Gore letter, undated (but it is clear that they are from the beginning of 1938); Sharett (1937), p. 220; CZA, Protocol of the Inner Zionist General Council's meeting on 3 November 1937 – Shertok's statement; CZA, Protocol of the Inner Zionist General Council's meeting on 21 June 1937; CZA, Protocol of the Zionist General Council meeting, Session 7, 23 April 1937. See also Ben-Gurion (1937), p. 463, who contended, *inter alia*, in December 1937 that 'if the state is established we are still unsure about the Upper Galilee ... despite the commission's decision, the area North of Acre and West of Safad is in danger because no Jewish settlements exist there (except for Naharia), while Arab settlement there is dense'. See also ibid., p. 465; CZA, Protocol of the Jewish Agency Executive's meeting on 4 July 1937, Shertok's statement; CZA, file KKL10 Protocol of the JNF Directorate's meeting on 6 December 1937; CZA, Protocol of the Inner Zionist General Council's meeting on 11 January 1938.
2. The newspaper *Davar*, 19 November 1937.

3. Weitz (1947), pp. 76–7; Gvati (1982), pp. 298–9; CZA, file KKL10, Protocol of the JNF Directorate's meetings on 4 January 1937 and 3 March 1937; Katz (1994b); Gavish (1991), pp. 124–31.
4. Sharett (1937), pp. 100–4, 144.
5. CZA, file KKL/8318, letter from Weitz to Ussishkin on 19 April 1937 – the citations are from there; CZA, Protocol of the Zionist General Council meeting, Session 7, 23 April 1937 – statement by Weitz; ibid. – Ussishkin statement; ibid., Session 8, 25 April 1937 – statement by Avraham Hartzfeld; Land and Settlement (1937).
6. Regarding the manifold dangers and the difficulties of settling in the Beisan Valley, see, for example, CZA, Protocol of the Jewish Agency Executive's meeting, on 31 January 1937 – Shertok's statement.
7. CZA, Protocol of the Jewish Agency Executive's meeting on 6 June 1937. See also CZA, Protocol of the Inner Zionist General Council's meeting on 21 June 1937; Orren (1978), pp. 26–7
8. Report of the Executive Committee of Hapoel Hamizrahi (1942), p. 125.
9. Bein (1982), p. 269.
10. See in detail Orren (1978), pp. 22–37, and Katz (1994b); see also Maps 11 and 12.
11. Orren (1978), pp. 24–37; Bein (1982), pp. 268–9. See also Map 13.
12. CZA, file KKL10, Protocol of the JNF Directorate's meeting on 6 December 1937 – statement by Ben-Gurion.
13. Ben-Gurion (1937), p. 463.
14. As may be recalled, the Jewish Agency attached great importance to control over the Wadi Ara artery, which connected the coastal plain with the Jezreel Valley and the Galilee, and, as opposed to the recommendation of the Royal Commission, included the artery in its entirety within the boundaries of the Jewish State.
15. CZA, file KKL10, Protocol of the JNF Directorate's meeting on 6 December 1937; CZA, Protocol of the Jewish Agency Executive's meeting on 21 January 1938; CZA, Protocol of the Inner Zionist General Council's meeting on 11 January 1938 – statements by Ben-Gurion and Ussishkin; CZA, Protocol of the Jewish Agency Executive's meeting on 1 May 1938; Ben-Gurion (1937), pp. 462–5; Ben-Gurion (1938), pp. 10–19; Sharett (1938), p. 79; Orren (1978), pp. 39–40.
16. CZA, Protocol of the JNF Directorate's meeting on 25 April 1938.
17. Orren (1978), p. 42.
18. CZA, Protocol of the Jewish Agency's meeting on 13 February 1938; CZA, file KKL10, Protocols of the JNF Directorate's meetings on 6 December 1937, 8 February 1938, 25 April 1938, 6 July 1938, 7 October 1938 and 14 December 1938.
19. CZA, file KKL10, Protocol of the JNF Directorate's meeting on 25 April 1938. See the conclusions in the following sources: Bein (1982), pp. 268–9; Orren (1978), pp. 38–49; Jewish Villages in Israel (1949). The settlement in 1938 at Hanita in the Western Upper Galilee, very close to the Lebanese border, and the continued acquisition of land in the vicinity symbolized the 'conquest' of the Galilee and to a large extent the unique Zionist settlement praxis that was carried out during the course of 1938. On this, see Hinberger (1978); Orren (1978), pp. 43–9; Sharett (1938), p. 89. See also Map 13, p. 171.
20. CZA, file KKL10, Protocol of the JNF Directorate's meeting on 4 January 1937; CZA, Protocol of the Inner Zionist General Council's meeting on 21 June 1937; CZA, file KKL 5/8432, discussion in the JNF regarding the medical school and workers' apartments on Mount Scopus on 6 April 1937; ibid., file KKL 5/10077, letter from the JNF to S. Schwartz on 1 January 1939.
21. CZA, Protocol of the Inner Zionist General Council's meeting on 21 June 1937.
22. CZA, file KKL10, Protocol of the JNF Directorate's meeting on 6 December 1937 – the citation is from there; ibid., Protocol of the JNF Directorate's meetings on 8 August 1938 and 13 August 1937.
23. See, for example, CZA, Protocol of the Inner Zionist General Council's meeting on 20 June 1938.

24. CZA, file KKL10, Protocol of the JNF Directorate's meeting on 6 December 1937 – the citation is from there. See also CZA, Protocol of the JNF Directorate's meeting on 8 August 1938. See also CZA, file KKL5/10073, letters from Weitz to Hassidoff on 8 May 1938 and 27 June 1938, when the JNF turned down a proposal to purchase plots in Jerusalem's Old City as well as CZA, file KKL5/10075, letter from the JNF to Binyamin Yehuda on 2 January 1939 and CZA, file KKL5/8431, letter from the JNF to the Jewish Community Committee of Jerusalem on 14 July 1937 – letters in which Ussishkin turns down the request that he and the JNF should take tangible initiatives in the Old City.
25. Ben-Gurion (1938), p. 224 – the citation is from there. See also ibid., pp. 120, 223, 348, 404.
26. Orren (1978), p. 64.

Postscript or Prelude?
The Jewish Agency's Partition Plan –
an Episode or a Portent?

At the close of 1938, the option for solving the Palestine problem via partition was laid, at least temporarily, to rest. By the end of 1937, in response to pressures from the Foreign Office, the British government had begun to backtrack from the partition policy that it had adopted only a few months previously. This was primarily due to the vehement Arab stance in Palestine and throughout the Arab world against partition, and the apprehension that British interests would be severely damaged as a result – especially in the event of an imminent European conflagration (which was already in the air). In such a case, the Arab world would be arrayed alongside Britain's foes, if Britain chose to implement partition in Palestine. The Colonial Office and its head, who supported the partition plan, found it difficult to contend with the position of the Foreign Office. Accompanying the terms of reference given to the Partition Commission, requesting that the Commission recommend boundaries for two homogeneous countries and their population to the maximum extent possible without any forcible transfer, was a secret letter that the government sent to the Commission's chairman. In this letter, the government also allowed the Commission to recommend that 'no scheme of partition that they could devise was likely to prove practicable'. A joint reading of the terms of reference and the secret letter may shed light on the finding that the government expected the Commission to arrive at. Even before the Commission departed for Palestine, the Foreign Office believed that the partition plan would be imminently rescinded and was confident that the Commission would rule that the plan was impracticable. Clarifications in this vein were also provided to the Arab capitals.[1]

The Partition Commission truly 'did not prove a disappointment' and, in particular, it did not disappoint the Foreign Office. It came to the unanimous conclusion that, within the purview of its authority, it could not recommend partition boundaries that would offer a feasible possibility for establishing a Jewish State and an Arab State where each would be self-sufficient. An analysis of the Partition Commission's report and its findings should be undertaken in the scope of another study. Let us note here that in the context of its findings, the Commission to a large extent rejected the Jewish Agency Executive's boundary proposal because it could lead to the inclusion of a large Arab population in the areas assigned to the Jewish State, which stood in contradiction to the Commission's terms of reference. The Jewish Agency Executive's demand to include the Galilee in its entirety within the Jewish State was rejected by the Partition Commission, and in specific places the boundary line as proposed by the Executive was also turned down. Thus in responding to the Executive's demands for expanding the Jewish State in the Beisan Valley and in the adjacent area east of the Jordan, the Commission noted that it would not be desirable if the city of Beisan, which was entirely Arab, were to be included in the Jewish State. The valley itself, in its opinion, should be earmarked for creating farms for those Arabs who might want to transfer from the Jewish to the Arab State. With regards to the area east of Jordan there was no guarantee that the Trans-Jordanian government would agree to transfer areas from Trans-Jordan to the areas of the Jewish State. The Partition Commission also disputed the security considerations that had guided the Jewish Agency Executive when it determined the boundary lines. It did not accept the Agency Executive's demand to incorporate West Jerusalem into the area of the Jewish State because this seemed impractical both for administrative reasons and, primarily, because it would arouse vigorous Arab opposition.[2]

Simultaneous with the publication of the Partition Commission's report in October 1938, the British government announced that, as a result of the report, it had been apprised that the political, administrative and financial difficulties attendant upon implementing partition were so great as to make implementation unrealizable. Instead, the government announced that it intended to carry on with its responsibility for ruling the entire country and would attempt to solve the Palestine problem through Jewish–Arab agreement. For this purpose, it intended to invite representatives of the Palestinian Arabs, representatives of the neighboring countries, and representatives of the Jewish Agency to London for discussions 'regarding future policy, including the question of immigration to Palestine'.[3] This was the *coup de grâce* to the partition plan and the Jewish Agency Executive's involvement on the issue. However, the burial of the partition plan as a method for solving the Palestine problem proved only temporary. During the course of the 1940s, the proposal would return to the various international and Zionist negotiating tables and appeared to be on the threshold of implementation with the United Nation's (UN) decision of 1947 to solve the Palestine problem within the framework of partition.[4]

The Jewish Agency Executive and its leaders – Weizmann, Ben-Gurion and Shertok – were not totally oblivious to the fissures in the British government's partition policy from the end of 1937 and during the course of 1938.[5] However, it is clear that until the end of 1938, they did not know what they would realize later, and what is evident today to an historian, namely, the extent of the British retreat from the partition proposal.[6] The Executive strove at home and abroad to persuade people of the merits of solving the Palestine problem via partition. It continued during the latter half of 1937 and in the course of 1938 with preparations towards partition within the context of plans and positions that it had formulated with the assistance of its experts on the various partition issues. These actions along with the Agency's policy and activity in the settlement sphere serve to inform us that, from the Agency's perspective, a partition process was in the offing. It would appear that the Experts Committee's deliberations on the issue of partition, the experts' memoranda, the deliberations in the Executive, the testimony of Executive members before the Partition Commission, and the tens of documents and memoranda that the Executive dispatched to the Partition Commission would have had a much lower profile and a much narrower scope if it had been clear to the Executive that Britain was not intent upon partition. About a month before the Partition Commission's report, Ussishkin contended that 'It is undoubtedly premature to recite the prayer for the dead, not only the extended prayer but even the abbreviated version over the partition proposal. It is clear that the Partition Commission will bring forth some sort of proposal for partitioning the country, and not a different proposal.'[7] Ben-Gurion became aware of the 'crude and blatant fraud' perpetrated by the British government, by the very content of the terms of reference that it bestowed on the Partition Commission (to include a minimum of Arabs in the Jewish State) and the way this was interpreted by the Commission, *only* after publication of the Commission's report, together with the government's announcement that partition could not be realized.[8] Even at this juncture, the British Colonial Secretary clarified: 'Partition is now being jettisoned but it is possible that it will again reappear after a short while.'[9]

* * *

The publication of the Partition Commission's report and the government's announcement led, as aforesaid, to the removal of the partition issue from the Jewish Agency Executive's agenda, at least temporarily. This naturally raises the question of whether the partition plan that the Jewish Agency formulated in 1937–38 was no more than an episode – important in its time, but lacking importance for the future – or was a portent for the future. In retrospect, we favor the latter possibility. Below we will try to clarify this contention and point to a connection between the variables analyzed in detail in the preceding chapters and the variables that we can observe 8–10 years later in a similar context on the eve of the State of Israel's formation and in the initial measures adopted by the new state. This connection existed, despite the dramatic events that had occurred in the interim, and first and foremost the Second World War and the Holocaust. It is important to emphasize that in general the central figures in Jewish Agency Executive on the eve of the State of Israel's formation, and when it took its first steps, were the very same people whom we encountered during the 1930s.

1. *A partition policy*: Partition as the most realistic way of obtaining a Jewish State in Palestine and a hoped-for solution to the Jewish–Arab dispute, won widespread support in the Jewish Agency Executive, i.e. the Jewish government-in-the-making, during the later 1940s and even became its explicit policy from 1946 onwards. Even beforehand, during the early 1940s, when Zionist policy spoke of creating a Jewish Commonwealth in the land of Israel (the Biltmore Program of 1942), some members of the Executive never abandoned the partition idea. Even in the Biltmore Program itself, no explicit opposition was expressed to the partition scheme. In 1944, other members of the Executive returned to the partition scheme, and in 1946 partition in practice became the Executive's policy. This policy did not merely signal a preparedness to discuss partition if the idea were proposed by the international bodies, but took the form of an active effort to influence the international bodies, and first and foremost the United States, to implement partition. The UN decision regarding partition that took shape first as the majority proposal of the United Nations Special Committee on Palestine (UNSCOP), and subsequently in the UN General Assembly resolution at the end of 1947, dovetailed with the Executive's policy.[10]

2. *The partition map*: The Executive's position during 1946 and until the publication of the majority decision in UNSCOP at the beginning of September 1947 was that one should obtain a preferable form of partition in a formula that was defined as 'Peel plus the Negev' plus West Jerusalem (to cite Ben-Gurion in May 1947, regarding Jerusalem: 'one should partition Jerusalem and add the Jewish portion to the Jewish State'). The mountain ridge of Judea and Samaria was to remain outside the boundaries of the Jewish State.[11]

In the year 1946, the Executive drew a partition map[12] as it had done in 1938, and it seems that it expressed the Agency's policy also in 1947. We contend that there exists a similarity, and in certain portions an identity, between the Executive's map of 1938 and the Executive's map of 1946–47. Firstly, no one disputes the identity on the Galilee issue between the two maps. Let us emphasize that even after the publication of the majority's proposal in UNSCOP (which awarded part of the Galilee to the Arab State), the Jewish Agency continued to demand the entire Galilee.[13] Thus, it is virtually certain that when it spoke of Jewish Jerusalem during the years 1946–47 the Executive was actually referring to the maps that it had drawn less than 10 years previously.[14]

Although during preparations on the map in 1938 voices in the Executive had called for its inclusion in the boundaries of the Jewish State, the Negev was excluded from the boundaries of the Arab State but incorporated within the boundaries of the British mandatory state. This was done primarily on account of the desire to secure the Galilee. The Executive demanded that Jewish settlement be permitted in the Negev, and it assumed that in the future it would pass under the control of the Jewish State. According to the Executive's concept, the Negev was therefore included in the mandatory state only for a transitional period. Now, during the years 1946–47, the need to expand the areas belonging to the Jewish State became more and more apparent in order to serve as destinations for absorbing mass immigration and to furnish a foundation for a development policy. When it became equally apparent that the British had no intention to remain in Palestine for a long time – in other words, there was no further room for a tripartite partition such as that proposed by the Executive in 1938 – the demand to include the Negev within the areas Jewish State is self-explanatory. Additional Zionist interests, to which we cannot devote attention here, and British tendencies from the early 1940s to incorporate the Negev within the boundaries of the Jewish State under the framework of partition,[15] also contributed to the Negev's inclusion within the Jewish State in the years 1946–47. The Jewish settlement reality that was created in the Negev during the 1940s reinforced the Jewish demand still further.

When, during the years 1946–47, it spoke of 'Peel' (in the context of 'Peel plus the Negev' with the addition of Jewish Jerusalem) the Executive did not mean this literally, i.e. the exact map proposed by the Royal Commission, but it really meant the amended Peel map in the spirit of the Executive's map of 1938 (save for the matter of Jerusalem and the Negev, to which we have already referred). Firstly, the principles that guided the Executive in drawing the boundary lines for the Jewish State, which it transmitted to the British Partition Commission, had not lost their saliency. Some, in the light of contemporary events, had even assumed greater potency. Secondly, the British partition plan from the early 1940s already incorporated on their maps some of the Executive's demands from 1938 for amendments in the Royal Commission's map (in the region of the Lake Tiberias, the Jordan Valley, the Beisan Valley and the mandatory corridor).[16] Ben-Gurion's 1946 plan for establishing the States of 'Judea' and 'Abdullia' and the Agency's partition map of 1946, had already given expression to these amendments.[17] Given this background, it is clear that the Executive did not intend to backtrack to the original Peel. Thirdly, in the period between the publication of the UNSCOP report, at the beginning of September, and the General Assembly resolution at the end of November 1947, the Executive attempted to exert influence to secure the inclusion of the area east of Jerusalem until the northern part of the Dead Sea, at least within the boundaries of Jerusalem's internationalized zone.[18] This fact recalls the Executive's demand of 1938, to include this zone in the boundaries of the mandatory state.

In determining the final partition map that was authorized by the United Nations in November 1947, Zionists' interests were presented in a clear-cut fashion by Shertok and Zalman Lifshitz (Lifshitz would subsequently have a role in determining the armistice-line boundaries). These two people played a central role in defining the Executive's partition map in 1938. Lifshitz, as may be recalled, was a central figure in the Boundaries Committee that the Political Department had established in 1937, and it was he who edited the Jewish Agency's partition map.[19] It is hard not to detect in the Report of the Subcommittee (Subcommittee # 1), which the United Nations appointed following the discussion of the UNSCOP Report, Zionist fingerprints recalling the principles that determined the Agency Partition Map of 1938. The UN Year Book sums up the report of the sub-committee, which included representatives from the United States and the Soviet Union and was submitted to the Assembly only a few days before the final decision on partition: 'As for boundaries, the sub-committee accepting the recommendations of UNSCOP in principle, proposed certain changes with a view to reducing, as far as reasonably possible, the size of the Arab minority in the Jewish State and to taking into account considerations of security, communications, irrigation and possibilities of future development.' The pragmatic–political approach that characterized the positions of the Agency Executive in 1947, and the readiness in the final outcome to make territorial concessions and accept less than the majority report of

UNSCOP in recompense for obtaining the coveted sovereignty, is quite familiar to us from the principles that shaped the Executive's partition map at the close of the 1930s.[20]

3. *Jerusalem*: From the time in 1946 that the Executive adopted a clear partition proposal and until the publication of the UNSCOP report, it believed that one should partition Jerusalem and include its western portion within the areas of the Jewish State. This was a clear continuation of its policy from the years 1937–38. Nonetheless, when it became clear that the majority in UNSCOP had recommended the internationalization of Jerusalem, the Executive did not reject this but it did not accept it either. Opinions here were equally divided. Some returned to the demand to partition Jerusalem for reasons similar to those that were expressed during the years 1937–38. Others, headed by Ben-Gurion, gave up the struggle and agreed to internationalize the entire city. Together with his fervent desire to obtain a Jewish State as quickly as possible – even at the cost of conceding Jerusalem (whereas a struggle could hold up or even sabotage the attainment of a state) – Ben-Gurion preferred the total internationalization of Jerusalem to the possibility of its being partitioned between the Arabs, the Jews and an international body that would assume control over the Old City. He believed (as opposed to the situation in the 1930s) that in the end result the Jews of Jerusalem would be citizens of a Jewish State[21] and the symbolic Jewish dimensions of the city would not be harmed as a result of its internationalization. In Ben-Gurion's own words: 'there is no need to be concerned for Jerusalem; Jerusalem is a Jewish City. The Jewish Agency will remain here as well as the university'.[22]

As the Executive found it difficult to decide the problem, the decision was shunted to the Zionist delegation at the UN deliberations, which was headed by Shertok.[23] The latter did attempt to exert influence, so that the wording of the final decision to be presented for ratification by the UN General Assembly would speak of partitioning the city and transferring its western portion to the areas of the Jewish State.[24] However, the bulk of Zionist efforts were devoted to guarantee the following issues in the framework of an internationalized city: extensive autonomies for the city's national units; the citizens of Jerusalem would also be citizens of the Jewish State; the period of internationalization would be limited to ten years, at the close of which a plebiscite would be held among the city's residents regarding its future political status. The Zionists intended to exploit the Jewish majority in Jerusalem.[25]

In any event, in contrast to the 1930s and the position that the Executive had adopted prior to the publication of the UNSCOP report in autumn

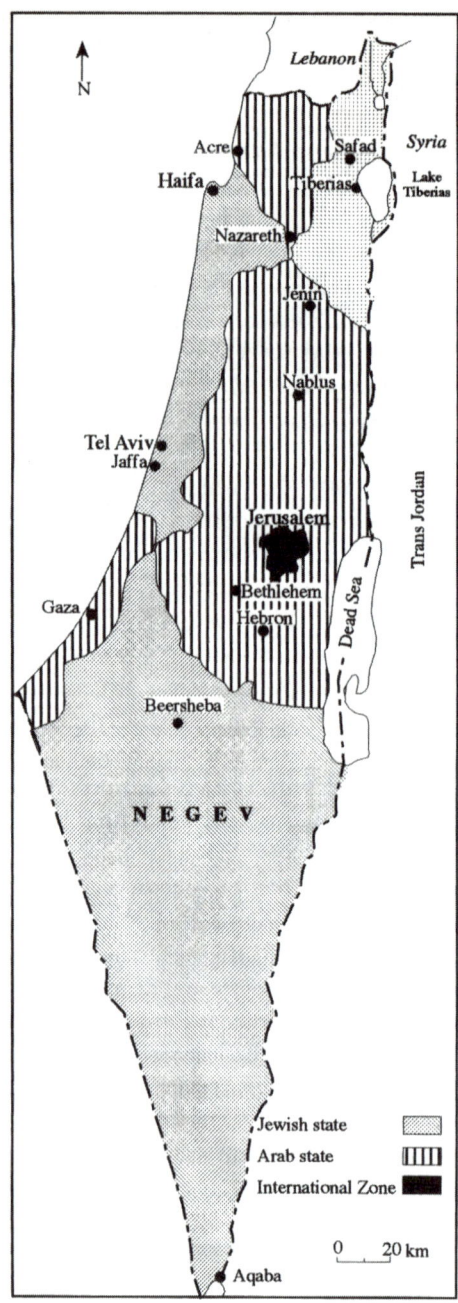

Map 14: UNSCOP Majority Proposal for the Partition of Palestine, August 1947

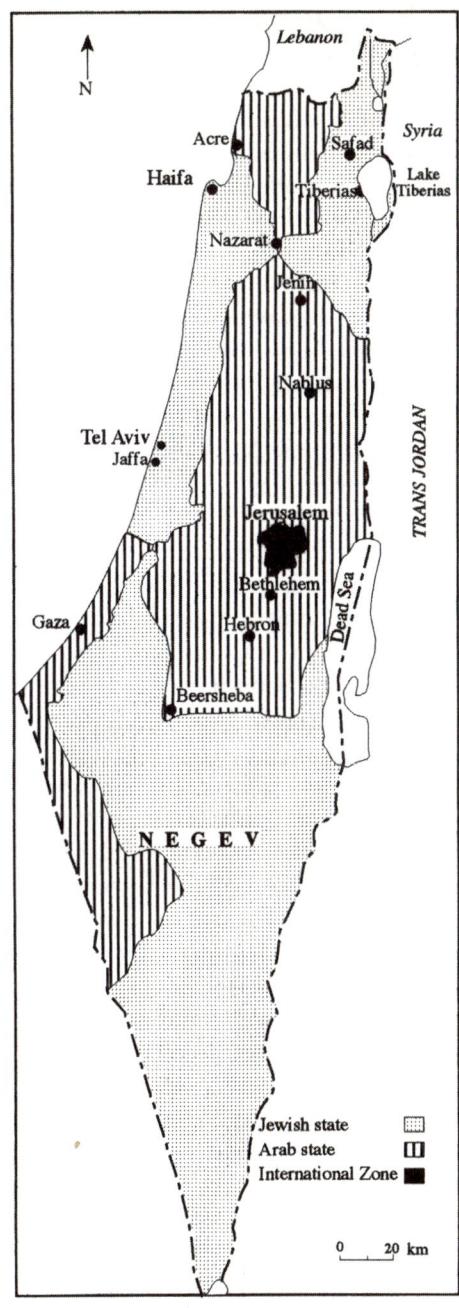

Map 15: UN Map for the Partition of Palestine, November 1947

1947, the Executive in fact conceded West Jerusalem as well. However, this concession was not of long duration. During the 1948 war, Israel backtracked from its agreement to internationalize Jerusalem. Furthermore, an analysis of Israeli strategy in this war in the Jerusalem theater restores us to the concept expressed in the Jewish Agency Executive's map of 1938: efforts were concentrated on controlling West Jerusalem and the corridor connecting it with the coastal plain while effectively conceding the Old City. It is not by chance that the armistice agreement signed by Israel and Jordan in 1948 established that West Jerusalem as well as Mount Scopus would be under Jewish sovereignty, whereas East Jerusalem and the Old City would be under the sovereignty of the Hashemite Monarchy.[26] From here it was but a short step to Israel's rejection of the renewed UN proposal of autumn 1949 to internationalize Jerusalem and to Israel's announcement at the close of that year that 'Jerusalem is an inseparable part of the State of Israel and its eternal capital'.[27]

4. *The roots of Israeli strategy in the 1948 war*: An analysis of Israeli strategy in the 1948 war, not only in the context of Jerusalem, and the position that it adopted in the talks that led to the armistice agreements, attests to a great affinity to the partition map prepared by the Jewish Agency Executive in 1938 and its underlying conceptions. The results of the war and the armistice agreements placed Israel in control of boundaries much more extensive than those which it had received from the UN decision of 1947 and which bore a greater resemblance (once we take into consideration our previous statements regarding the Negev) to the Executive's map of 1938. We have expanded elsewhere on the link between Israel's 1949 boundaries and the map produced by the Jewish Agency Executive in 1938.[28] Let us content ourselves here with the examples of the effort made to include Wadi Ara in its entirety within the territory of the Jewish State; the efforts to secure Jewish footholds in north-west Samaria and Mount Gilboa; the efforts to safeguard a corridor between Jerusalem and the coastal plain, and to attain the entire Galilee. On the other hand, again following the contours of the 1938 map, the Palestinian mountain ridge remained under Arab control.[29]

5. *Transfer of the Arab population*: The question of whether a forced transfer of Arabs in the course of the 1948 War did or did not occur has currently sparked controversy among scholars.[30] We cannot therefore establish a direct connection between the transfer as envisioned by the Jewish Agency Executive in the wake of the Partition Plan of the 1930s, and the Arab exodus during the 1948 War.

It is interesting to note that in a joint session of the Jewish Agency Executive and the Political Committee of the Inner Zionist General Council that took place in June 1938 and discussed the various issues of partition, Berl Katznelson (a member of the Political Committee) argued that the frontier areas deserved special preference when a transfer was implemented and Jewish settlements had to be established on the vacated frontier areas:

> I consider the question of who shall sit on the frontier to be one of the cardinal strategic and security questions confronting the Jewish State. If Arab settlements remain on the frontier, then no sentries will be of avail and no army will be of service if we do not settle the northern frontier. And if the transfer issue arises, then it will first be necessary to liberate the frontier in order to create Jewish villages there. These are delicate matters and perhaps it's awkward to mention them and they are subject to unfavorable interpretations, but Jewish settlements on the frontier comprise one of the country's strategic conditions. If there is any logic to transfer, then on the frontier there is more room for it than in any other place in the country. There is no need for me to explain the dangers if this matter won't be resolved ...[31]

According to Morris's study covering the years 1947–49, one can see that Katznelson's statement of 1938 was put into practice in the course of transfer activities implemented by the Israeli Army in the frontier regions during the months of November 1948 to July 1949. Concomitantly, the Jewish settlement bodies began planning the settlement of vacated frontier regions with new Jewish settlements. A short while later, a series of Jewish agricultural settlements were strung out along the frontiers.[32]

There are testimonies regarding plans for a voluntary transfer of Arabs during the 1950s to attain the very same objectives discussed during the 1930s (political–security objectives and vacating lands for Jewish settlement). In his book Joseph Weitz divulges details about 'Operation Yohanan' – a plan for transferring the Arabs of Jish to South America.[33] An additional testimony speaks of voluntary transfers which were actually effected at that time. Zalman Lifshitz, who served as an adviser in the Prime Minister's Office as well as in the Foreign Ministry and the Treasury,[34] wrote the following to M. Asaf during the summer of 1950:

> As far as I know, not only do they not prevent such Arabs from leaving but they encourage them to do so with all the means at our disposal ... negotiations are being conducted with those very same people whom you mention in your letter regarding the liquidation of their assets and their departure from the country. And if this has not yet materialized with regards to those whom you

mention, the fault lies not with the government's policy but with the special circumstances involved in matters such as these ... We will do whatever can be done in order to promote their emigration from the country under conditions that will not encumber the treasury and the country's economy and I hope that this activity will bear fruit ... If you could keep this top secret, I will reveal to you that hundreds of families have left the country in recent months under special arrangements that were undertaken for this purpose, once their assets were purchased from them and they were paid generously for them. In this manner we have solved severe problems that were pending regarding these Arabs ... It is obvious that not in every case the interested parties obtained satisfaction, however, one should not lambast the government for inaction or for an inflexible policy ...[35]

Weitz and Lifshitz, as may be recalled, served on the experts committee which had been set up by the Political Department of the Jewish Agency in 1937, a committee which discussed the transfer of the Arab population.

6. *The status of the Arab minority*: The Zionist Executive continued in the 1940s to enunciate the basic principles that it had formulated in 1938 with regards to the status and rights of the Arab minority in a future Jewish State. Thus, for example, in a 1946 memorandum, which the Jewish Agency Executive submitted to the Anglo-American Commission, the Executive cited the decisions taken by the Zionist Executive a year earlier, which determined that

the Jewish State will be based upon full equality of rights of all inhabitants without distinction of religion or race, in the political, civic, religious and national domains and without domination or subjection. All settlements will enjoy full autonomy in the administration of their religious, educational, cultural and social institutions. The Arabic language and Arab schools will enjoy full State rights and municipal self-government will be developed in all towns and villages. The State will exert all efforts to raise and equalize the standard of living of all the inhabitants of Palestine ...

As had been the case in the 1930s, it was similarly emphasized in the 1940s – when addressing the status of the Arab minority – that the Jewish State would not compromise in anything concerning Jewish immigration and the creation of an infrastructure for its absorption.[36] It would appear that the option of expropriating lands, which the Jewish Agency Memorandum of 1938 had not totally excluded, recurs in Ben-Gurion's opposition to an article in the majority report of UNSCOP, which prohibited expropriation.[37] Similar to the 1938 memorandum, the Jewish Agency Executive embraced at the beginning of December 1947 the US proposal, which postulated that minorities in the Jewish State or the Arab State who would not assume the citizenship of the state in which they resided would be compelled to leave it.[38]

7. *The demand for full sovereignty*: The Jewish Agency Executive's demand that the Jewish State be awarded full sovereignty returns at the close of 1947. This time it appears in the context of conditions that the Jewish Agency stipulated regarding the plan for economic union between the Jewish and Arab States – a plan that constituted a central component of the UNSCOP majority's partition plan and that, in principle, was acceptable to the Jewish Agency. The Agency summed up the issue as follows: 'A Jewish State must have in its own hands those instruments of financing and economic control necessary to carry out large-scale Jewish immigration and the related economic development, and it must have independent access to those world sources of capital and raw materials indispensable for the accomplishment of these purposes'.[39]

8. *Fundamental principles for establishing a Jewish State*: It would appear superfluous to dwell on the fact that during the 1940s and towards the establishment of the State, those core elements that were fundamental to the establishment of the Jewish State and that the Jewish Agency had proclaimed during 1937 and 1938 recurred: a democratic state, whose central goals during the initial years would be immigration and absorption. Likewise, the issue of security, which also takes center stage in the 1940s in the context future Jewish State, had already assumed a central role in the Jewish Agency Executive in 1937 and 1938. As may be recalled, security arrangements were pivotal in determining the map of the Jewish Agency's partition boundaries and the character of these frontiers (closed boundaries), and the defense budget headed the list of expenditure items in the future Jewish State's budget. It would appear that the roots of Ben-Gurion's 1947 approach of maintaining the Jewish Agency and the National Funds even within the framework of a Jewish State, already hark back to P. Naphtali's memorandum of 1937, which apportioned to the Jewish people the continued burden of financing land acquisitions and settlement even after the Jewish State had been formed.[40]

Just as it had replied to the Royal Commission's Report, the Executive felt in 1947 that the Jewish Agency, during the transition stage prior to the formation of the Jewish State, must command authority in the areas of immigration and absorption. A demand to shorten the transition period also recurs in 1947. Nonetheless, the special circumstances of 1947

induced the Jewish Agency to demand of the UN that the transition period
should be as brief as possible, and in any event less than the two-year period
recommended by the majority in UNSCOP.[41]

Given the Second World War and its results, the rising status of the
United States and the Soviet Union in the international arena during the
1940s, and the deterioration of relations between the Jewish Agency and
the British during those same years, it would appear difficult to expect a
similarity between the Executive's position in the late 1930s regarding the
fundamental foreign policy of a future Jewish State and the way it viewed
these matters in the 1940s and upon the establishment of the State.
Nonetheless, an important premise that we encountered in the 1930s
recurs in the 1940s: the aspiration for co-operation and beyond with the
neighboring Arab peoples.[42]

The Executive attitudes on the issue of religion in the future Jewish
State, again resurfaced in the latter half of the 1940s, when partition-based
solution could be anticipated. This time as well, the Executive expressed
its attitude on the religious issue to a large extent because of the demands
of Agudath Israel, and the Executive's negotiation tactics with this body
recall those of the 1930s. Two fundamental positions that the Executive
had expressed in the 1930s were enunciated: (a) in the Jewish State freedom
of conscience and religion will be guaranteed and the State would not
infringe on the religious outlook of its inhabitants; (b) The Jewish State's
constitution, which would be formulated upon the establishment of the
Jewish State, would be the source for determining the status of religion
and its interests in a Jewish State. Nonetheless, aside from decreeing the
Jewish Sabbath as the official day of rest in the Jewish State, to which the
Executive had already consented to in 1938, and awarding autonomy to
the various educational streams, which was the pre-existing situation, the
Executive met Agudath Israel's demands regarding ritual slaughter and
marital status which Agudath Israel sought to extend to the entire Jewish
State.[43]

9. *Settlement as a political tool*: In the 1940s the Jewish Agency and the
JNF again employed land purchases and settlement for the purpose of
attaining political goals, and with even greater vigor than they had
displayed in promoting the Jewish Agency Executive's partition plan in
the late 1930s. At the end of 1943 Ben-Gurion emphasized: 'We are living
in a period of decision which can determine our future for generations.
Facts and deeds will carry great weight. In today's situation nothing can
exert greater weight than Jewish settlements. All land purchases which
are important to us from a political standpoint must be consummated and

we should take hold of the land'.[44] The need for brevity constrains us from detailing in the framework of this work the Zionist settlement praxis and its role in obtaining political goals during the 1940s, and first and foremost their influence on the boundaries of the future Jewish State. This issue has already been awarded attention in scholarly research.[45] Let it suffice to give just two examples: (a) the settlement activity in the Negev in order to secure the Negev's ultimate inclusion within the boundaries of the Jewish State, and (b) the plans to establish outposts in various frontier locations – some of which were implemented – and which took place after the UNSCOP report became known, 'in order to do something at this last moment to extend our boundaries'.[46]

* * *

It is therefore clear that the Jewish Agency Executive's partition plan prior to the Second World War and its preparations to establish a Jewish State did not constitute a mere episode but a portent. It would appear that the plan received its future authority at the time it was crafted when the major processes of Jewish nation-building in Palestine had already been completed.[47] Just as the Royal Commission's partition plan marked a turnabout in the modern history of Palestine, and was a theoretical forerunner of the UN's plan in 1947,[48] the Jewish Agency's partition plan similarly marked a turning point from which there was no retreat regarding the Jewish Agency's attitude to partitioning the country, determining its frontiers and shaping the character and foundations of the future Jewish State in its early years. The Executive's experience in confronting the partition issue in the late 1930s was of great importance in the late 1940s. History will record whether the peace agreements that are currently taking shape between the government of Israel and the Palestinians will really lead to what the 'government in the making' had already accepted before it obtained a state.

NOTES

1. Katzburg (1974) pp. 35–44, 55–6; Fraser (1988) and especially p. 672 – the source of the quotation that Fraser cites from the cabinet meeting on 8 December 1937 in PRO, file CAB 23/90; Klieman (1983), pp. 82–113; Geva (1980), pp. 192, 203, 211; Eliash (1971), pp. 148–54; Dothan (1993), pp. 247–50; Cohen, M. (1978), pp. 38–72; the twenty-first Zionist Congress, stenographic report, 1939, pp. 35–8; Sharret (1938), p. 308. See Katzburg's comments (1984), pp. 88–94, where he contests the assumption that the very appointment of a Partition Commission revealed the British government's intention to challenge the partition policy and that the appointment was intended to camouflage the

government's true intentions. In his opinion, although the government had already displayed a discernible tendency to detach itself from partition in December 1937, it had not totally foreclosed this policy. The government did not want to abandon partition totally at that time, but preferred to leave the matter pending for a period of about one year. In the interim the Commission could perhaps delineate a partition plan that would prove acceptable to all parties. The developments during the course of 1938, especially in the international sphere, decisively tilted matters against partition.

2. See in detail PPCR (1938); Klieman (1983), pp. 106–8; Great Britain and Palestine 1915–1939 (1939), pp. 94–5; Beeley (1938), pp. 425–40; Cohen, M. (1978), pp. 38–49.

3. CZA, Official Proclamation of the mandatory government #8/38 on 9 November 1938; Klieman (1983), pp. 108, 157–9.

4. See, for example, Fraser (1984), pp. 151–91.

5. See, for example, CZA, Protocol of the Jewish Agency Executive's meetings on 12 December 1937, 26 December 1937, 21 January 1938, 25 September 1938, 7 October 1938, 9 October 1938; CZA, Protocol of the Inner Zionist General Council's meeting on 11 October 1938; Political Report of the Jewish Agency Executive, 1939, pp. 8–10; the twenty-first Zionist Congress, stenographic report, 1939, pp. 4–5, 34–7; CZA, file S25/3786, statement by Ben-Gurion on the Ormsby-Gore letter, undated, but evidently from the beginning of 1938.

6. See Katzburg's estimates in note 1.

7. CZA, Protocol of the Inner Zionist General Council's meeting on 11 October 1938.

8. Ben-Gurion (1938), p. 391; see also Weizmann's statement in the twenty-first Zionist Congress, stenographic report, 1939, pp. 35–7. Compare with Ben-Gurion's statement in CZA, file S25/3786, in note 5, upon the publication at the start of 1938 of Ormsby-Gore's letter, including the terms of reference for the Partition Commission. Ben-Gurion did not *then* note that the terms of reference effectively buried the partition idea. On the contrary he cautioned that 'one should not overly exaggerate the subsidiary set of instructions that was provided the Commission to diminish to the extent possible the retention of Arabs in the Jewish area and the retention of Jews in the Arab area'. He summed up his attitude towards the letter by saying that 'one should not exaggerate the importance of the letter, both in terms of what is positive or negative about it.'

9. CZA, Protocol of the Jewish Agency Executive's meeting of 13 November 1938.

10. Dothan (1993), pp. 341–5, 398–407, 441, 460–1, 470, 514–28, 558–60, 589–90; Ben-Gurion (1993a), pp. 26–31, 49–50; Ben-Gurion (1993b), pp. 21, 23–4, 57, 116, 127, 211–13, 261, 364, 518–21; Fraser (1984), pp. 155–6, 162–4; Kimmerling (1976), p. 48 ff.; Galnoor (1991), pp. 400–1; Heller (1981).

11. Ben-Gurion (1993b), p. 117 – the citation is from there; Dothan (1993), pp. 514–28, 558–60; Fraser (1984), pp. 156–60.

12. Fraser (1984), p. 159; Political Survey 1946–1947 (1947). See the map in Heller (1981).

13. CZA, file J1/8863, comments by Golda Meyerson at the Vaad Leumi General Council's meeting on 27 October 1947. See also the demand of the Jewish Agency for the entire Galilee even after the publication of the UNSCOP majority report, in the Yearbook of the United Nations (1949), p. 234. See also Ben-Gurion (1938), pp. 518–21.

14. See CZA, file S25/5410, memorandum 'Jerusalem under Partition' of 18 August 1947 prepared in the Jewish Agency. The vast majority of this memorandum is identical to the memorandum bearing the same title, which the Jewish Agency Executive submitted to the Partition Commission on 16 August 1938, in CZA, file S25/9239. Compare CZA, file S25/5143, letter from Dr N. Gelberg to Shertok on 30 August 1938, proposing the use of material that was prepared by the Jewish Agency Executive in advance of the peace conference that had taken place 20 years previously.

15. Dothan (1993), pp. 384–95; Fraser (1984), p. 163.

16. Dothan (1993), pp. 388–9, 394–5. Compare the map of the Royal Commission's proposal with the Cabinet Committee Partition Proposal, 1944, in Cohen, M. (1978), p. 176 to the map in Dothan (1993), p. 390.

17. Dothan (1993), p. 517–19; Ben-Gurion (1993a), pp. 81, 83.

18. Ben-Gurion (1993b), pp. 426–9.
19. See also Zalman Lif (1953).
20. Yearbook of the United Nations (1949), p. 239 – the citation is from there. It is known that representatives of the Jewish Agency actually voiced their position before the sub-committee. On this, see ibid., p. 243; Zalman Lif (1953); Ben-Gurion (1993b), p. 346; Fraser (1984), pp. 177, 182. See also Horowitz (1951), p. 284, regarding Zionist demands for controlling Mount Gilboa during the UN deliberations on partition. Indeed, in the final result the partition decision included a number of outposts on the Gilboa crest within the boundaries of the Jewish State.
21. Ben-Gurion (1993b), p. 426. See also Brecher (1974), p. 15, who cites Abba Eban's contention regarding the connection between the Royal Commission's Plan and the UN decision on internationalizing Jerusalem.
22. Ben-Gurion (1993b), p. 478. See also ibid., pp. 246, 272, 368, 393, 400–1, 426–7, 429, 490.
23. A similar discussion regarding Jerusalem also took place in the Vaad Leumi General Council, and by a majority of 5 to 4 the Vaad Leumi General Council decided to forgo the demands for partition on Jerusalem. On this see CZA, file J1/8863, Protocol of the Vaad Leumi General Council's meeting on 27 October 1947. See also Ben-Gurion (1993b), p. 367.
24. Yearbook of the United Nations (1949), p. 234; Fraser (1984), p. 172.
25. Dothan (1993), pp. 567–9, and in detail see Golani (1990), pp. 299–311.
26. Katz and Sandler (1995), pp, 160–3; Katz (1993), pp. 52–3; Golani (1989, 1990); Dothan (1993), pp. 595–6, 613–14; Pa'il (1981); Lorch (1989), pp. 377–403 and especially p. 386.
27. Golani (1990), p. 309.
28. Katz and Sandler (1995).
29. Ibid.; Dothan (1993), pp. 613–14; Ben-Gurion (1993b), p. 396. See also Shlaim (1988). Instructive testimony is provided by David Horowitz of the Jewish Agency, who took part in presenting the Zionist position during the deliberations that produced the UN decision of 1947. He relates that at a meeting that included Shertok, Ben-Gurion and himself with representatives of the British government in September 1947: 'Ben-Gurion drew with a broad gesture of his finger our concept regarding a possible plan for partitioning Palestine and his plan was vastly similar to the map that was realized after the War of Independence and the armistice agreement in 1949'. On this, see Horowitz (1951), pp. 172–3 as well as Ben-Gurion (1993a), pp. 353, 367.
30. Flapan (1987); Morris (1986, 1987, 1990); Karsh (1997), pp. 37–68.
31. CZA, Protocol of the Jewish Agency Executive's meeting with the Political Department of the Inner Zionist General Council on 12 June 1938. Let us add that Ben-Gurion had already previously noted (in response to a question posed by the Partition Commission, 'What will we do if an Arab revolt would erupt in the Galilee') that the Jewish Agency would erect a series of settlements along the border. On this see CZA, Protocol of the Jewish Agency Executive's meeting on 29 May 1938.
32. Morris (1987), pp. 237–53, 293; Golan (1993).
33. Weitz (1965, Vol. 4), pp. 358–65.
34. See Zalman Lif (1953).
35. CZA, file A402/187, letter from Z. Lif (Lifshitz), to M. Assaf on 9 August 1950.
36. The Jewish Case before the Anglo-American Committee (1947), pp. 301–3 (citation from there); Ben-Gurion (1993b), pp. 273, 438, 453; Declaration of Independence of the State of Israel.
37. Ben-Gurion (1993b), p. 365.
38. Ibid., p. 459. It would appear that the manifold dilemmas that typified the deliberations of the Jewish Agency Executive in 1938 in connection with the Arab minority, and the circumvention of difficulties in the memorandum submitted to the Partition Commission find expression to this date in the way that the State of Israel grapples with some components of this nettlesome issue.
39. Yearbook of the United Nations (1949), p. 235. See also Ben-Gurion (1993b), p. 415.

40. See, for example, Ben-Gurion (1993b), pp. 395–6, 452. On page 452 Ben-Gurion's words from November 1947 are cited: 'I am convinced that after the state is established ... there will remain a need for the Jewish Agency i.e. a World Zionist Organization, a JNF and Keren HaYesod, since the issue of immigration and the issue of settlement, will be on a much higher scale than presently ... The 600,000 Jews in Palestine will not be able to assume the burden of bringing over and settling one million Jews. This will also be the affair of the Jewish people ...'. Compare with P. Naphtali's memorandum in CZA, file S25/10050 of July 1937, which we referred to above on pp. 149–50.
41. Yearbook of the United Nations, in note 13, p. 235; Ben-Gurion (1993b), pp. 50–1, 264–5, 424, 426. In the end, there was no transition period preceding the establishment of the State of Israel.
42. The Jewish Case before the Anglo-American Committee (1947), pp. 302–3; Ben-Gurion (1993b), p. 495.
43. See in detail Ben-Gurion (1993b), pp. 24–5, 217–18, 227–8, 460–1; Friedman (1990).
44. CZA, file KKL10, Protocol of the JNF Directorate's meeting on 9 November 1943, see also Dothan (1993), pp. 377–8.
45. See, for example, Katz (1992a); Orren (1978); Weitz (1947).
46. Weitz (1965, Vol. 3), pp. 178–9 This was written on 2 September 1947.
47. Compare with Kimmerling (1976), p. 55. The settlement activity did bear fruit. Thus, for example, a contention was raised during the UN's discussions on determining the partition boundaries that the Beisan Valley should be included within the boundaries of the Arab State as the Royal Commission had decided. In response, the Zionist representatives presented the map of Jewish settlement in that area, which decided the issue in favour of the Zionist position. On this, see Horowitz (1951), p. 284.
48. See, for example, Shlaim (1988), p. 62; Katzburg (1984), pp. 93–4; Fraser (1984), pp. 130, 134, 165; Fraser (1988), pp. 677–8.

Sources

ARCHIVES

Central Zionist Archives, Jerusalem, (CZA)
Public Record Office, London (PRO)
Maps Archive of the Jewish National Fund (JNF), the Geography
Department of the Hebrew University, Jerusalem

NEWSPAPERS

Davar, Ha'Olam

PUBLISHED REPORTS, MEMORANDA, BOOKS, ARTICLES AND
RESEARCH STUDIES

Agudath Israel, Memorandum to the Royal Commission, Jerusalem, (23
    November 1936) (in Hebrew).
Andrews, G. E., *The Theory of Partition* (Reading, MA, Addison-Wesley, 1976).
Antonius, G., *The Arab Awakening* (Philadelphia, PA, J. B. Lippincott, 1938).
Avidar, Y., 'Security and Military Aspects Relating to the Partition Plan
    of 1937', in M. Avizohar and J. Friedman (eds), *Studies in the Palestine
    Partition Plans 1937–1947* (Sede Boqer, The Ben-Gurion Research
    Center, Ben-Gurion University of the Negev, 1984), pp. 172–8 (in
    Hebrew).
Avizohar, M. and Friedman, I. (eds.), *Studies in the Palestine Partition Plans
    1937–1947* (Sede Boqer, The Ben-Gurion Research Center, Ben-
    Gurion University of the Negev, 1984) (in Hebrew).
Avneri, A. L., *The Jewish Land Settlement and the Arab Claim of
    Dispossession 1878–1948* (Tel Aviv, Yad Tabenkin and Hakibbutz
    Hameuhad, 1980) (in Hebrew).

Beeley, H., 'The Administration of the British Mandate for Palestine 1937', in A. J. Toynbee, (ed.), *Survey of International Affairs*, Vol. 1 (1937; London, Oxford University Press, 1938), pp. 543–89.

Beeley, H., 'The Administration of the British Mandate for Palestine 1938–1939', in A. J. Toynbee (ed.), *Survey of International Affairs*, Vol. 1 (1938; London, Oxford University Press, 1949), pp. 414–92.

Bein, A., *Immigration and Settlement in the State of Israel* (Tel Aviv, Am Oved, 1982) (in Hebrew).

Ben-Gurion, D., *Memoirs*, Vol. 1 (1886–1993; Tel Aviv, Am Oved, 1971) (in Hebrew).

Ben-Gurion, D., *Memoirs*, Vol. 2 (1934–35; Tel Aviv, Am Oved, 1973) (in Hebrew).

Ben-Gurion, D., *Memoirs*, Vol. 3 (1936; Tel Aviv, Am Oved, 1973) (in Hebrew).

Ben-Gurion, D., *Memoirs*, Vol. 4 (1937; Tel Aviv, Am Oved, 1974) (in Hebrew).

Ben-Gurion, D., *Memoirs*, Vol. 5 (1938; Tel Aviv, Am Oved, 1982) (in Hebrew).

Ben-Gurion, D., *Towards the End of the Mandate – Memoirs, June 1946– March 1947* (Tel Aviv, Am Oved, 1993a) (in Hebrew).

Ben-Gurion, D., *Chimes of Independence – Memoirs, March–November 1947* (Tel Aviv, Am Oved, 1993b) (in Hebrew).

Bethell, N., *The Palestine Triangle* (London, André Deutsch, 1979).

Blanchard, R., 'The Exchange of Population Between Greece and Turkey', *Geographical Review* 15, 2, (1925) p. 449.

Brawer, M., *Israel's Boundaries* (Tel Aviv, Yavneh, 1988) (in Hebrew).

Brecher, M., *Decisions in Israel's Foreign Policy* (London, Oxford University Press, 1974).

Cohen, G., 'Mussolini, Italian Policy and Palestine, 1933–1935 (A Chapter in the History of the Idea of Partition)', *Zionism*, Vol. 3 (1973), pp. 346–417 (in Hebrew).

Cohen, M., *Palestine: Retreat from the Mandate – The Making of British Policy 1936–1945* (London, Elek, 1978).

Coupland, R., *The Empire in These Days* (London, Macmillan, 1935).

Coupland, R., *Report on the Constitutional Problem in India*, 3 parts (London, Oxford University Press, 1942–43).

Davis, H. H., *An International Community on the St Croix* (Maine, 1974).

Dothan, S., *Partition of Eretz Israel in Mandatory Period – The Jewish Controversy* (Jerusalem, Yad Yitzhak Ben Zvi, 1979) (in Hebrew).

Dothan, S,. *A Land in the Balance: The Struggle for Palestine 1918–1948* (Tel Aviv, Ministry of Defense Books, 1993).

Eddy, C. B., *Greece and Greek Refugees* (London, G. Allen & Unwin, 1931).

Elath, E., *Zionism and the Arabs* (Tel Aviv, Devir, 1954) (in Hebrew).

Elath, E., *The Struggle for Statehood*, Vol. 2 (Tel Aviv, Am Oved, 1982) (in Hebrew).

Elazari-Volcani, Y., *The Writings of Yizhak Elazari-Volcani*, (Vilkansky), Vol. 4 (Tel Aviv, N. Twersky, 1955) (in Hebrew).

Eliash, S., 'The Jewish Community in Palestine and the Peel Report of July 1937', submitted in partial fulfillment of the requirements for the Master's Degree in the Department of History, Bar-Ilan University, Ramat Gan, 1971 (in Hebrew).

Eliash, S., 'The Religious Zionist and Anti-Zionist Attitudes Regarding the Partition Plans 1937–1947', *Studies in the Palestine Partition Plans* (Sede Boqer, The Ben-Gurion Research Center, Ben-Gurion University of the Negev, 1984), pp. 55–74 (in Hebrew).

Ettinger, A. Y., 'Population Exchanges in Greece', *Davar* (3 December 1937a), p. 10.

Ettinger, A. Y., 'Land Problems in Greek Settlement', *Davar* (10 December 1937b), p. 10.

Ettinger, A. Y., 'The Requirements of Greek Settlement', *Davar* (17 December 1937c), p. 14.

Ettinger, A. Y., 'The Truth about the Inexpensiveness of Greek Settlement', *Davar* (31 December 1937d), p. 10.

Ettinger, A. Y., 'Population Exchanges in Greece and Greek Resettlement', *Davar* (14 January 1938), p. 4.

Ettinger, S., *History of the Jewish People* (Tel Aviv, Devir, 1969) (in Hebrew).

Feinberg, N., *Palestine under the Mandate and the State of Israel – Problems in International Law* (Jerusalem, Magnes Press, 1963) (in Hebrew).

Flapan, S., *The Birth of Israel* (New York, Pantheon, 1987).

Fraser, T. G., 'A Crisis of Leadership: Weizmann and the Zionist Reactions to the Peel Commission's Proposals 1937–8', *Journal of Contemporary History*, 23, 4 (1988), pp. 657–80.

Fraser, T. G., *Partition in Ireland, India and Palestine* (London, St Martin's Press, 1984).

Friedman, M., 'The Chronicle of the Status-Quo: Religion and State in Israel', in Varda Pilowsky (ed.), *Transition from Yishuv to State 1947–1940 – Continuity and Change* (Haifa, University of Haifa, Herzl Institute for Studies in Zionism, 1990), pp. 47–80 (in Hebrew).

Galnoor, I., 'Territorial Partition of Palestine: The 1937 Decision', *Political Geography Quarterly*, 10, 4 (October 1991), pp. 382–404.

Galnoor, I., *Territorial Partition* (Albany, State University of New York Press, 1995).

Gavish, D., *Land and Map* (Jerusalem, Yad Yitzhak Ben Zvi, 1991) (in Hebrew).

Gelber, N. M., 'The Issue of Palestine's Boundaries at the Peace Conference of 1919–1920', in Asher Weizer and B. Z. Luria (eds) *Karl Jubilee Volume*, Vol. 10 (Jerusalem, Kiryat Sefer and Israel Bible Research Society, 1960), pp. 288–352 (in Hebrew).

Geva, A., 'The Political Struggle in the Yishuv Following the Partition Plans of the Royal Commission', doctoral thesis, The Hebrew University, Jerusalem, 1980 (in Hebrew).

Glassner, M. I., *Political Geography* (New York, Wiley, 1992).

Golan, A., 'The New Settlement Map of the Area Abandoned by the Arab Population within the State of Israel, During Israel's War of Independence and After (1948–1950)', thesis submitted for the degree of Doctor of Philosophy, The Hebrew University, Jerusalem, 1993.

Golani, M., 'The Leadership of the Yishuv and the Question of Jerusalem during the War of Independence', *Cathedra*, 54 (1989), pp. 156–72 (in Hebrew).

Golani, M., 'Jerusalem from International Status to Incorporation in the State of Israel', in Varda Pilowsky, (ed.), *Transition from 'Yishuv' to State 1947–1949: Continuity and Change* (Haifa, University of Haifa, Herzl Institute for Studies in Zionism, 1990), pp. 299–312 (in Hebrew).

Gottmann, J., 'The Pioneer Fringe of Palestine: Settlement Possibilities South and East of the Holy Land', *The Geographical Review*, 27, 4 (1937), pp. 550–65.

Granot, A., *A People Settles In* (Jerusalem, Devir and Jewish National Fund, 1951) (in Hebrew).

Great Britain and Palestine 1915–1939 (London, Royal Institute for International Affairs, 1939).

Grenville, J. A. S., *The Major International Treaties 1914–1945 – A History and Guide* (London/New York, Methuen, 1987).

Gvati, C., *A Century of Settlement*, Vol. 1 (Tel Aviv, Hakibbutz Hameuhad, 1982) (in Hebrew).

Gwynn, D., *The History of Partition 1912–1925* (Dublin, Brown and Nolan, 1950).

Heller, J., 'Zionist Policy After the Second World', in Joseph Hacker (ed.), *Shalem* (Jerusalem, Yad Izhak Ben-Zvi, 1981), pp. 213–293 (in Hebrew).

Heller, J., *The Struggle for the Jewish State* (Jerusalem, Zalman Shazar Center, 1984) (in Hebrew).

Hinberger, Y., *Hanita – 'Wall and Tower' – Type of Settlement* (Haifa, Sulam Tzur and Gaaton, 1978) (in Hebrew).

Hope-Simpson, J., *Report on Immigration, Land Settlement and Development* (London, HMSO, 1930).

Hope-Simpson, J., *The Refugee Problem* (Oxford, Oxford University Press, 1939).

Horowitz, D., *On a Mission for State and Homeland* (Jerusalem, Shocken, 1951) (in Hebrew).

Jeffries, J. M. N., *Palestine: The Reality* (London, Longman's Green, 1939).

Jerusalem in Zionist Vision and Realization (ed. Hagit Lavsky) (Jerusalem, Zalman Shazar Center, 1989) (in Hebrew).

Jewish Villages in Israel (Jerusalem, Jewish National Fund, 1949).

Johnstone, W. C., *The Shanghai Problem* (Stanford, CA, Stanford University Press, 1937).

Karsh, E., *Fabricating Israeli History* (London, Frank Cass Publishers, 1997).

Katz, Y., 'Purchases of JNF Lands in Gush Etzion and South of Bethlehem (1940–1947)', *Cathedra*, 56 (1990), pp. 109–35 (in Hebrew).

Katz, Y., 'The Formulation of the Jewish Agency's Proposal for the Boundaries of the Partition 1937–1938', *Zion – A Quarterly for Research in Jewish History*, 56, 4 (1991), pp. 401–39 (in Hebrew).

Katz, Y., *Jewish Settlement in the Hebron Mountains and the Etzion Bloc* (Ramat-Gan, Bar Ilan University Press, 1992a) (in Hebrew).

Katz, Y., 'Transfer of Population as a Solution to International Disputes', *Political Geography*, 11, 1 (1992b), pp. 55–72.

Katz, Y., 'The Political Status of Jerusalem in Historical Context: Zionist Plans for the Partition of Jerusalem in the Years 1937–1938', *Shofar*, 11, 3 (1993), pp. 41–52.

Katz, Y., 'The Palestinian Mountain Region and Zionist Settlement Policy, 1882–1948', *Middle Eastern Studies*, 30, 2 (1994a), pp. 304–29.

Katz, Y., 'The Partition Plan of Palestine and Zionist Proposals for the Beisan Valley', *The Jewish Journal of Sociology*, 36, 2 (December 1994b), pp. 1–20.

Katz, Y., 'The Re-emergence of Jerusalem: New Zionist Approaches in Attaining Political Goals Prior to the First World War', *Political Geography*, 14, 3 (1995), pp. 279–93.

Katz, Y., 'Status and Rights of the Arab Minority in the Nascent Jewish State', *Middle Eastern Studies*, 33, 3 (1997), pp. 535–69.

Katz, Y. and Sandler, S., 'The Origins of the Conception of Israel's State Borders and its Impact on the Strategy of War in 1948–1949', *The Journal of Strategic Studies*, 18, 2 (1995), pp. 149–71.

Katzburg, N., *From Partition to White Paper – British Policy in Palestine 1936–1940* (Jerusalem, Yad Yitzhak Ben Zvi, 1974) (in Hebrew).

Katzburg, N., 'Retreat from Partition, 1937–1938', in *Studies in the Palestine Partition Plan 1937–1947* (Sede Boqer, the Ben-Gurion Research Center, Ben-Gurion University of the Negev, 1984), pp. 88–94 (in Hebrew).

Kimmerling, B., 'The Conduct of the Jewish–Arab Conflict and Nation Building During the Mandatory Period', *State, Government and International Relations*, 9 (1976), pp. 35–66 (in Hebrew).

Kimmerling, B., *Zionism and Territory – The Socio-territorial Dimensions of Zionist Politics* (Berkeley, CA, University of California Press, 1983).

Klieman, A. S., 'The Resolution of Conflicts through Territorial Partition: The Palestine Experience', *Comparative Studies in Society and History*, 42, 2 (1980a), pp. 281–300.

Klieman, A. S., 'In the Public Domain: The Controversy Over Partition for Palestine', *Jewish Social Studies*, 42, 2 (1980b), pp. 147–64.

Klieman, A. S., *Divide or Rule – Britain, Partition and Palestine 1936–1939* (Jerusalem, Yad Yitzhak Ben Zvi, 1983) (in Hebrew).

Klieman, A. S. (ed.), *The Partition Controversy, 1937* (New York and London, Garland, 1987).

Ladas, S. P., *The Exchange of Minorities: Bulgaria, Greece and Turkey* (New York, Macmillan, 1932).

Land and Settlement at the Meeting of the Zionist General Council, (Jerusalem, Executive of the World Zionist Organisation, April 1937) (in Hebrew).

League of Nations, *Protection of Linguistic, Racial and Religious Minorities by the League of Nations, Provisions Contained in the Various International Instruments at Present in France* (Geneva, League of Nations, 1927).

League of Nations, Permanent Mandates Commission, *Minutes of the 19th Session*, Geneva, 4–19 November 1930.

League of Nations, Permanent Mandates Commission *Minutes of the 20th Session*, Geneva, 9–27 June 1931.

League of Nations, *Official Journal*, 'Minutes of the 67 Sessions of the Council', Geneva, 9–15 May 1932.

League of Nations, *Official Journal*, 'Records of the 18 Ordinary Sessions of the Assembly', Geneva, 1937a.

League of Nations, Permanent Mandates Commission, *Minutes of the 32nd Session*, Geneva, 30 July–18 August 1937b.

Lorch, N., 'Ben-Gurion and Jerusalem as Israel's Capital', in H. Lavsky (ed.), *Jerusalem in Zionist Vision and Realization* (Jerusalem, Zalman Shazar Center, 1989), pp. 377–403 (in Hebrew).

Masalha, N., *Expulsion of the Palestinians* (Washington, DC, Institute for Palestine Studies, 1993).

Mendelsohn, K., *The Balance of Resettlement* (Leiden, A. W. Sijthoff, 1939).

Morgenthau, H., *I Was Sent to Athens* (New York, Doubleday, Doran & Co., 1929).

Morris, B., 'Joseph Weitz and the Transfer Committees 1948–1949', *Middle Eastern Studies*, 22, 4 (1986), pp. 522–61.

Morris, B., *The Birth of the Palestinian Refugee Problem 1947–1949* (Cambridge, Cambridge University Press, 1987).

Morris, B., *1948 and After – Israel and the Palestinians* (Oxford, Clarendon Press, 1990).

Nedava, J., 'Population Exchange Plans for Solving the Palestine Problem', *Gesher*, 24, 1–2 (1978), pp. 153–67 (in Hebrew).

Ofer, P., 'The Galilee in the Partition Plan of the Peel Commission', in A. Shmueli, A. Sofer and N. Kliot (eds), *The Lands of Galilee*, Vol. 1, (Haifa, University of Haifa and Ministry of Defense, 1983), pp. 461–8 (in Hebrew).

Orren, E., *Settlement Amid Struggles* (Jerusalem, Yad Yitzhak Ben Zvi, 1978) (in Hebrew).

Pa'il, M., 'Israeli–Zionist Strategy Regarding Jerusalem During the War of Independence', *Jerusalem in the Modern Period* (Jerusalem, Yad Yitzhak Ben Zvi and Ministry of Defense, 1981) (in Hebrew).

Palestine – A Study of Jewish, Arab and British Policies, Vol. 2. (New Haven, CT, Esco Foundation for Palestine, Inc., 1980).

Palestine Partition Commission Report (PPCR), presented by the Secretary of State for the Colonies to Parliament by Command of His Majesty (London, HMSO), October 1938.

Palestine Royal Commission Report (PRCR), presented by the Secretary of State for the Colonies to Parliament by Command of His Majesty (London, HMSO), July 1937.

Paz, Y., 'A Zionist Partition Plan for Jerusalem', *Cathedra*, 72 (1994) pp. 113–34 (in Hebrew).

Peel, R., 'The Report of the Palestine Commission', *International Affairs*, 16, 5 (1937), pp. 761–79.

Pentzopoulos, D., *The Balkan Exchange of Minorities and its Impact upon Greece* (Paris, Mouton, 1962).

Political Report of the Executive of the Jewish Agency Submitted to the Twenty First Zionist Congress at Geneva, August 1939 (Jerusalem, the Jewish Agency for Palestine, 1939) (in Hebrew).

Political Survey 1946–1947 – Memorandum submitted to the United Nations

Special Committee on Palestine (Jerusalem, the Jewish Agency for Palestine, July 1947).

Porat, C., 'Zionist Policy on Land Settlement in the Negev, 1929–1946', thesis submitted for the degree of Doctor of Philosophy, the Hebrew University, Jerusalem, 1989 (in Hebrew).

Prescott, J. R. V., *Political Frontiers and Boundaries* (London, Hutchinson University Press, 1987).

Reches, E., 'The Underlying Principles of the Policy towards the Arabs in Israel', in Varda Pilowsky (ed.), *Transition from 'Yishuv' to State 1947–1949: Continuity and Change* (Haifa, University of Haifa, Herzl Institute for Studies in Zionism, 1990), pp. 291–8 (in Hebrew).

Reichman, S., *From Foothold to Settled Territory, 1918–1948* (Jerusalem, Yad Yitzhak Ben Zvi, 1979) (in Hebrew).

Reichman, S., Katz, Y. and Paz, Y., 'The Absorptive Capacity of Palestine, 1882–1948', *Middle Eastern Studies*, 33, 2 (1997), pp. 338–61.

Report of the Executive of the Zionist Organization to the XII Zionist Congress, Political Report (London, World Zionist Organisation, 1921).

Report of the Executive of the Zionist Organization and of the Jewish Agency for Palestine Submitted to the XXI Zionist Congress, Geneva, August 1939 (Jerusalem, the Jewish Agency for Palestine, 1939) (in Hebrew).

Report of Executive Committee of Hapoel Hamizrahi Movement to the Eighth Conference (Tel Aviv, Hapoel Hamizrahi, 1942) (in Hebrew).

Rose, N., 'The Debate on Partition 1937–1938: The Anglo–Zionist Aspect, I, the Proposal', *Middle Eastern Studies*, 7, 1 (1970), pp. 297–318.

Rose N., 'The Debate on Partition 1937–1938: The Anglo–Zionist Aspect, II, the Withdrawal', *Middle Eastern Studies*, 7, 1 (1971), pp. 3–24.

Rubinstein, E., 'From Community to State: Parties and Institutions', in B. Eliav (ed.), *The Jewish National Home* (Jerusalem, Keter, 1976) (in Hebrew).

Sachar, H., *A History of Israel* (New York, Alfred A. Knopf, 1976).

Shapira, A., 'Time Perception as a Factor in the Partition Controversy 1937', *Studies in the Palestine Partition Plans 1937–1947* (Sede Boqer, Ben-Gurion Research Center, Ben-Gurion University of the Negev, 1984) (in Hebrew).

Sharett, M., *Making of Policy, The Diaries of Moshe Sharett*, Vol. 1 (1936; Tel Aviv, Am Oved, 1976) (in Hebrew).

Sharett, M., *Making of Policy, The Diaries of Moshe Sharett*, Vol. 2 (1937; Tel Aviv, Am Oved, 1971) (in Hebrew).

Sharett, M., *Making of Policy, The Diaries of Moshe Sharett*, Vol. 3 (1938; Tel Aviv, Am Oved, 1972) (in Hebrew).

Sharett, M., *Making of Policy, The Diaries of Moshe Sharett*, Vol. 4 (1939; Tel Aviv, Am Oved, 1974) (in Hebrew).

Sheffer, G., *Moshe Sharett, Biography of a Political Moderate* (Oxford, Oxford University Press, 1996).

Sherwood, R. E., *Roosevelt and Hopkins* (New York, Harper, 1948).

Shlaim, A., *Collusion Across the Jordan* (Oxford, Oxford University Press, 1988).

Sofer, A., 'Full Equality of Rights for Arabs: Is it Possible?', *Nativ*, 6, 2 (1993) pp. 50-3 (in Hebrew).

Stettinus, E. R., *Roosevelt and the Russians* (New York, Doubleday, 1949).

Strickland, C. F., *The Possibility of Introducing a System of Agricultural Cooperation in Palestine* (Jerusalem, government of Palestine, 1930).

'The British Viewpoint', *Seeds of Conflict*, Series 7, Palestine, The Twice Promised Land (KTO Press, 1978).

The Jewish Case before the Anglo-American Committee of Inquiry on Palestine as Presented by the Jewish Agency for Palestine, Statements and Memoranda (Jerusalem, the Jewish Agency for Palestine, 1947).

The Jewish Plan for Palestine – Memoranda and Statements presented by the Jewish Agency for Palestine to the United Nations Special Committee on Palestine (Jerusalem, the Jewish Agency for Palestine, 1947).

The Lausanne Conference on Near Eastern Affairs 1922–1923 (London, HMSO, 1923).

'The Problem of Palestine: A Note on the Report of the Royal Commission', *The Geographical Review*, 27, 4 (1937), pp. 566–73.

The Twentieth Zionist Congress, Zurich 3–21 August 1937, Stenographic Report (Jerusalem, Executive of the World Zionist Organisation and Jewish Agency for Palestine, 1937) (in Hebrew).

The Twenty First Zionist Congress, Geneva 16–25 August 1939, Stenographic Report (Jerusalem, Executive of the World Zionist Organisation, 1939) (in Hebrew).

Treaty of Peace between the United States of America, the British Empire, France, Italy and Japan and Poland, signed at Versailles, 28 June 1919 (London, HMSO, 1919).

United Nations General Assembly, Second Session, Lake Success (New York, UN, 1947).

Ussishkin Jubilee Volume (Jerusalem, Committee for Publishing the Ussishkin Jubilee Volume, 1933) (in Hebrew).

Waterman, S., 'Partitioned States', *Political Geography Quarterly*, 6, 2 (1987), pp. 151–70.

Weitz, J., *Our Settlement Activities in a Period of Storm and Stress 1936–1947* (Merhavia, Sifriat Poalim, 1947) (in Hebrew).

Weitz, J., *Creating a Land Legacy* (Tel Aviv, N. Twersky, 1951) (in Hebrew).

Weitz, J., *My Diary and Epistles to the Sons*, Vols. 1–5 (Tel Aviv, Massada, 1965) (in Hebrew).

Weizmann, C., *The Jewish People and Palestine*, statement made before the Palestine Royal Commission in Jerusalem, 25 November 1936 (London, World Zionist Organisation and Keren HaYesod, 1939).

Weizmann, C., *Trial and Error* (London, Hamish Hamilton, 1949).

Welles, S., *Where Are We Heading?* (New York, Harper, 1946).

Wilson, E. M., *Decision on Palestine* (Stanford, CA, Hoover Institute Press, Stanford University, 1979).

Year Book of the United Nations 1947–1948, Department of Public Information, United Nations, Lake Success (New York, UN, 1949).

'Zalman Lif – His Life and Work', *Eretz Israel*, Vol. 2 (Jerusalem, 1953), pp. 2–10 (in Hebrew).

Index